Cavendish
Publishing
Limited

KV-680-175

UNIVERSITY OF WOLVERHAMPTON
NOT FOR LOAN

EUROPEAN COMMUNITY LAW

UNIVERSITY OF WOLVERHAMPTON
NOT FOR LOAN

WITHDRAWN

Keep for Historical
Purposes
JB 16.1.16

WP 0873548 4

TITLES IN THE SERIES

Cavendish
Publishing
Limited

UNIVERSITY OF WOLVERHAMPTON
LIBRARY

Acc No. 873548   CLASS

CONTROL   34
                       R42 2
DATE 25. SEP. 1995 SITE GRO
                    AL

WITHDRAWN

EUROPEAN COMMUNITY LAW

Peter J Groves, LLB, MA, PhD,
MITMA, Solicitor
Visiting Lecturer in Law
London Guildhall University

First published in Great Britain 1995 by Cavendish Publishing Limited,
The Glass House, Wharton Street, London WC1X 9PX
Telephone: 0171-278 8000 Facsimile: 0171-278 8080

© Groves, P 1995

All rights reserved. No part of this publication may be reproduced,
stored in a retrieval system, or transmitted in any form or by any
means, electronic, mechanical, photocopying, recording or otherwise,
without the prior permission of the publisher and copyright owner.

The right of the author of this work has been asserted in accordance
with the Copyright, Designs and Patents Act 1988.

Any person who infringes the above in relation to this publication
may be liable to criminal prosecution and civil claims for damages.

British Library Cataloguing in Publication Data

Groves, Peter
European Community Law – (Lecture Notes Series)
I Title II Series
341.2422

ISBN 1-85941-043-X
Cover photograph by Jerome Yeats
Printed and bound in Great Britain

To my mother

Outline Table of Contents

Detailed Table of Contents

Table of Cases

Table of Statutes

Table of Treaties

Table of Directives

Table of Regulations

Chapter 1

The Foundations

There have been many attempts over the centuries to unite Europe. Mostly they have involved the use of force and have been short-lived or totally unsuccessful. The creation of the European Communities in the period since the second world war, and the subsequent transition to a European Union, has been the most successful. The fact that Europe has enjoyed the most prolonged period of peace in its history testifies to the scale of the achievement.

There are many accounts of the creation of the European Coal and Steel Community and the later Atomic Energy Community and Economic Community, and of their subsequent development. An understanding of the history of the Community is important to an understanding of the goals of the Treaties and the operation of the institutions they create, but here a brief account of the Treaties themselves will suffice.

The Second World War devastated Europe. Reconstruction was unavoidable and the war had created a desire to secure a peaceful future. The belief that integration offered the way forward was developed and nurtured by statesmen such as Konrad Adenauer in Germany, Robert Schuman and Jean Monnet in France, and Alcide de Gasperi in Italy.

The process of reconstruction was financed by the US through the Marshall Plan, but was rejected by the Soviet Union and the countries of Eastern Europe within its sphere of influence. Integration was obliged to proceed only in western Europe, and even then the UK kept its distance, preferring to pursue the goal of international co-operation by fully independent states.

The Organisation for European Economic Co-operation (now the Organisation for Economic Co-operation and Development) was set up to co-ordinate the economies of the countries receiving Marshall Aid funds through the European Recovery Programme. Negotiation and co-operation between European countries was also encouraged by the establishment in 1949 of the Council of Europe, a body which exists alongside the European Community structures.

The Council of Europe remains an intergovernmental organisation, proceeding only by unanimity of its members. This was not sufficient for those who thought that integration

1.1 The unification of Europe

1.1.1 Post-war Europe

was the way forward for Europe and that something more radical was required.

1.2   Treaty of Paris 1951

The Paris Treaty established the European Coal and Steel Community (ECSC), the first of the three European Communities to be set up. Based on the assumption that if the European powers, particularly Germany and France, placed under common control their strategic industries they would lose the ability to wage war on each other, the ECSC Treaty (Article 1) creates a common market for these goods.

It is important to note that the motives behind the ECSC were not wholly economic. Political integration was also on the agenda. The Preamble to the Treaty of Paris states that the signatories were:

'Resolved to substitute for age-old rivalries the merging of their essential interest; to create, by establishing an economic community, the basis for a broader and deeper community among peoples long divided by bloody conflicts ...'

The notion of pooling the strategic resources of France and Germany (with an invitation to other countries) was the idea of the French Foreign Minister, Robert Schuman. Belgium, the Netherlands, Italy and Luxembourg (collectively: 'the Six') decided to participate in the creation of the first of the European Communities.

The Treaty, which runs to 100 Articles divided into four Titles, sets out the objectives of the ECSC including; employment growth and increased standards of living. These are to be attained by preventing practices which hinder free competition and the Treaty creates institutions to effect such practices. The Treaty also contains detailed economic and social provisions to achieve its aims.

Article 3 of the Treaty sets out its goals:

- ensuring an orderly supply to the common market which it set up;

- ensuring that consumers enjoy equal access to sources of supply; and

- promoting international trade.

Article 4 ECSC lists matters which are regarded as incompatible with the common market. These include import and export duties or charges having equivalent effect, quantitative restrictions on the movement of goods (ie quotas), and state subsidies.

Title 4 of the Treaty creates four institutions. These are the High Authority, the Common Assembly, the Special Council

of Ministers and the Court of Justice. These have now merged
with their counterparts in the other Communities.

Economic and social provisions are contained in Title 3,
including Article 65 ECSC, which prohibits agreements
tending to distort competition (and has its counterpart in
Article 85 of the EEC Treaty).

Central to the Treaty of Paris was the establishment of new
institutions, independent of the Member States, which were
given power to supervise the coal and steel industries of the
states. This transfer of legislative and administrative power
was the essential step towards integration.

To create a European Defence Community was the next
intention, and this it may now be said to have borne fruit with
the inclusion of the Common Foreign and Security Policy in
the Maastricht Treaty (see below). In 1952, a Treaty to create a
supra-national community with common institutions,
common armed forces, and a common budget was signed by
'the Six' in Paris but never ratified by the French parliament.
Its place was taken in part by the Western European Union, in
which the UK did participate and which was set up in 1955.
Defence and security matters have also remained the preserve
of the North Atlantic Treaty Organisation (NATO) set up in
1949 which brought together the original members of the
ECSC without Germany (which at the time was unable to
participate) but with the UK, US, Canada and others.

1.3 The European Defence Community

There are in fact two Treaties of Rome. One established the
European Atomic Energy Community (Euratom), and is dealt
with below. The other established the European Economic
Community (EEC), which historically was the most important
of the three Communities. The EEC Treaty itself has now been
amended by the Single European Act (SEA) and by the Treaty
on European Union (TEU) concluded in Maastricht. The TEU
formally renamed the EEC the European Community (EC).

1.4 Treaty of Rome (25 March 1957)

Like the Paris Treaty, the two Rome Treaties created
autonomous institutions which would be responsible for
developing the new structure. From the start they were more
than mere intergovernmental arrangements.

The Treaty of Rome sets out in its Preamble that it was
designed to lay the foundations for 'an ever closer union'. It
was intended to ensure economic progress by removing
barriers, to improve living conditions, and to abolish
restrictions on international trade. The Preamble is a valuable
aid to the interpretation of the Treaty. Unlike the position in
the UK, where preambles are not considered part of the

operative section of a legal document, continental jurisdictions have always attached great importance to them.

The Treaty of Rome (as amended) comes in six parts:

- Articles 1 to 8C: general principles

  The common market is progressively established during the transitional period of 12 years (now expired). Article 3 deals with the establishment of the common market by:

  (a) eliminating customs duties and quantitative restrictions;

  (b) abolishing obstacles to free movement;

  (c) setting up the common agricultural and common transport policies;

  (d) avoiding the distortion of competition;

  (e) approximating the laws of the Member States.

  Article 4 originally provide for the establishment of four institutions to achieve these goals. These were the Council, the Commission, the European Assembly and the European Court of Justice (ECJ). The Assembly has since been renamed the European Parliament.

  The EEC Treaty also set up two further institutions: the Economic and Social Committee (ECOSOC) and the Court of Auditors. The Court of Auditors has now been added to the original list of four institutions. It also established the European Investment Bank, and, following the Maastricht amendments, the European Central Bank. These are dealt with in further detail in later chapters.

- Citizenship of the Union

  Part 2 of the Treaty, inserted at Maastricht, creates the concept of citizenship of the newly-created European Union.

- Policy of the Community

  The four Titles of Part 3 of the EEC Treaty are the basis of the common market:

  Title I. Articles 9 to 37 set out the principles of free movement of goods. The provisions include the all-important Articles 30 and 36. In fact, most of the others have by now expired and are no longer of interest.

  Title II deals with the Common Agricultural Policy.

  Title III covers four important freedoms: the free movement of workers (Article 48), the freedom of establishment (Articles 52-58), the freedom to provide services (Article 59) and the freedom of movement of capital (Article 67).

  Title IV covers the establishment of the Common Transport Policy.

Title V deals with common rules including the rules on competition covering agreements between undertakings, abuses of dominant positions, dumping and state aids. Other provisions found under Title V include tax provisions and the important Articles on the approximation (or harmonisation) of laws, central to the creation of the single market. Of the provisions on social policy, Article 117 promotes improved working conditions and Article 119 provides for equal pay for work of equal value. These are dealt with in greater detail later.

Title VI deals with economic and monetary policy, *Title VII* with the common commercial policy, *Title VIII* with social policy, *Title IX* with culture, *Title X* with public health, *Title XI* with consumer protection, *Title XII* with trans-European networks, *Title XIII* with industry, *Title XIV* with economic and social cohesion, *Title VI* with research and technological development, *Title XV* with environment, and *Title XVII* with development co-operation. Titles XIV, XV and XVI are recent additions by the SEA and Titles VII, IX, X, XI XII, XIII and XVII were added by the TEU.

- Association agreements

  Part Four of the Treaty permits the Community to enter into agreements with non-member countries.

- Institutions

  Title I contains provisions governing the institutions. Articles 137-192 deal with the powers, duties and composition of the European Parliament, the Council, the Commission, the ECJ and now also the Court of Auditors. Articles 194-198 deal with the Economic and Social Committee, the Committee of the Regions, and the European Investment Bank. This part of the Treaty also contains financial provisions.

  The Treaty of Rome can be compared to a constitution with secondary legislation made under the powers it confers.

  There are several protocols to the Treaty. For example, there is one covering the Statute for the ECJ, Title III of which contains the procedural rules of the Court.

1.5   Euratom (25 March 1957)

The European Atomic Energy Community, established by the Euratom Treaty, has the aim of contributing towards higher living standards in Member States. This is to be achieved by creating the conditions necessary for the establishment and growth of the nuclear industries. Its structure mirrors that of the Treaties of Paris and Rome. A nuclear common market is set up by Articles 92 to 106.

1.6	**Merger Treaty and Convention on Common Institutions**	The Convention, dated (like the two foregoing Treaties) 25 March 1953, merged the Assembly (now the Parliament), the Court of Justice and the Economic and Social Committee. The Treaty established a single Council and a single Commission for all three Communities. It was signed on 8 April 1965 in Brussels and came into effect on 1 July 1967.
1.7	**Accessions**	Membership of the Community was not limited to the original six. Article 237 EEC (now Article O TEU) provided for any European State to join the Community, and the Community has now undergone four enlargements.
1.7.1	First	The UK was determined after the war to remain one of the super powers and was reluctant to bind itself to discriminating against Commonwealth imports. However, it applied to join the Community in 1961, but France objected. The application was renewed in 1967 (with applications from Ireland and Denmark, and later Norway), and following President de Gaulle's retirement in 1969, negotiations were able to proceed.
		The first enlargement of the Community took place in 1973. The Accession Treaty was signed by Denmark, Ireland and the UK on 22 January 1972. (Norway had decided in a referendum not to proceed with its application.) The UK's membership of the Community was endorsed by a referendum in 1975.
		The Treaty made the provisions of the original Treaties and the acts of the institutions binding on new Member States. Article 227(4) EEC applies it to those European territories for whose external relations a Member State is responsible. Gibraltar is therefore part of the Community (though not for the purposes of the CAP or VAT), while UK sovereign bases on Cyprus are not. A Protocol to the Accession Treaty covers the Channel Islands and the Isle of Man, stating that only the rules on the free movement of goods apply there.
1.7.2	Second	The second enlargement occurred with the accession of the Hellenic Republic (Greece). It was signed in Athens in 28 May 1979 and came into effect on 1 January 1981. The Treaty notably contains transitional provisions concerning agriculture.
1.7.3	Third	The third enlargement was when Spain and Portugal joined the Community, in 1986. The Accession Treaty was signed in Lisbon and Madrid on 12 January 1985.
1.7.4	Fourth	Austria, Sweden and Finland became members on 1 January 1995. Norway again decided in a referendum to stay out. This stage of the Community's development is dealt with further below.

Signed in Luxembourg on 17 February 1986 and The Hague on 28 February 1986, the SEA amends the Community's basic legislation. Its philosophy was to transform relations between Member States into a Union. It expands the competence of the Community (see the section on the Treaty of Rome above) and adjusts the institutional structure.

Article 2 is important because it creates the European Council, a twice-yearly meeting of the heads of Government of the Member States. In fact, this merely formalised what was already happening, though it was significant that this was done. For more details on the European Council see below, Chapter 2.

Article 13 SEA inserted into the EEC Treaty a new provision, Article 8a, which includes a commitment to 'adopt measures with the aim of progressively establishing the internal market over a period expiring on 31 December 1992'.

The SEA also made amendments dealing with the machinery of the institutions. It established the co-operation procedure, which speeded up the legislative process to ensure the single market could be completed more rapidly and also gave enhanced legislative powers to the Parliament. It set up the Court of First Instance and introduced economic and social cohesion, research and technological development, and the environment into the Treaty for the first time.

1.8 Single European Act

The Treaty on European Union (TEU) was agreed in Maastricht on 11 December 1991. The texts were finally ratified after referendums in several Member States (including Denmark which originally rejected the Treaty and France, which narrowly approved it), contentious debates in the UK Parliament, and a ruling of the German Constitutional Court, and came into effect on 1 November 1993. The TEU extends Community action into new areas: notably economic and monetary union; justice, home affairs and immigration; and the common foreign and security policy. These last two are based on intergovernmental co-operation.

Most of the changes under the TEU are by amendments to the Treaty of Rome (EEC). Accordingly, it is now essential to read the Treaty of Rome subject to the amendments made at Maastricht, and in this book we shall deal throughout with the amended provisions except where it is necessary to consider the original wording.

The TEU makes some important institutional changes too. The powers of the Parliament are enhanced and steps are taken to tighten up the Community's financial controls. The express inclusion of the doctrine of subsidiarity ensures that

1.9 The Treaty on European Union

the powers of the Community are not used where there is nothing to be gained from action at Community level.

The TEU also creates the European Union which as seen, was an aim of the original Treaty, and provides for every person who is a citizen of a Member State to be a citizen of the Union. Citizenship confers the right to move freely and to reside within the territory of any Member State, and the right to vote and to stand as a candidate in municipal and European Parliament elections in the Member State of residence (Italy has always allowed non-nationals to stand for the European Parliament: David Steel as he then was featured on the Italian Liberal list in the 1984 election, which at that time seemed the best way for his party to get a member into the European Parliament). These principles require implementation by the Council acting unanimously on a proposal from the Commission and after obtaining the assent of Parliament. The rights to participate in elections do not extend to general elections.

The citizen also has the right to petition the European Parliament. The same right is extended to any natural or legal persons residing in a Member State or having their registered office there. The right to petition only covers matters within the competence of the Community and those which directly affect the petitioner.

The Maastricht Treaty also creates the Community Ombudsman, who is dealt with in greater detail in Chapter 2.

1.9.1   European Community and European Union

The European Union which the Maastricht Treaty creates consists of several elements, of which the European Community is one. In addition the Union embraces the European Coal and Steel Community and the European Atomic Energy Community; intergovernmental co-operation on a common foreign and security policy; and intergovernmental co-operation in the fields of justice and home affairs. Thus the three Communities make up one of three 'pillars' of the Union, whilst the two forms of intergovernmental co-operation form the remainder.

Legislation is made by the European Community, not the Union, and therefore we will continue to speak of the EC. However the Commission of the European Communities has changed its name, and is now called the European Commission – which was what many called it anyway.

1.10   European Economic Area

The European Economic Area (EEA) came into existence on 1 January 1994. It represents an amalgamation of the European

Community's common market with the European Free Trade Area (EFTA).

EFTA was established in 1959 as an association of seven West European states. The UK's relative economic strength was a problem for the organisation from the outset. It was designed to create an area in which there would be no tariff barriers or other restrictions on trade, and at the insistence of the UK, agricultural products were specifically excluded from the scope of the agreement so as not to jeopardise its relations with the Commonwealth.

The Agreement on the EEA was signed on 2 May 1992 in Oporto by the EC and its Member States, and the then seven members of EFTA; Austria, Finland, Iceland, Liechtenstein, Norway, Sweden and Switzerland (although Switzerland and Liechtenstein later decided not to ratify the Agreement). It came into operation at the beginning of 1994. However, the pending EC Membership of three of its large members left its future, and that of EFTA in doubt. Iceland and Liechtenstein were planning to forge bilateral links with Brussels, making the EFTA structures redundant: Norway's rejection of membership of the EC puts the future in a different light.

The EEA is the largest and most integrated economic entity in the world, with a population of 372 million people. The Agreement lays the foundations for an efficient and unified market based on the model of the EC's single market. It has common rules and conditions of competition backed up with administrative machinery and dispute resolution arrangements. It builds on the 1972 and 1973 free trade agreements between the Community and EFTA which were essentially concerned with the elimination of customs duties on industrial products. It guarantees the four freedoms set out in the Treaty of Rome, and the five participating EFTA countries will largely adopt EC legislation in these areas. There will also be co-operation between the Community and the EFTA states in other fields, ie:

- fields relating to economic activity which directly affect the four freedoms, the so-called 'horizontal policies' including social policy, consumer protection, the environment, statistics and company law;

- areas subject to Community policies outside the four freedoms: EFTA participation in Community programmes, projects and actions concerning R&D, the environment, social policy, information services, education, training and youth, small and medium-size enterprises, tourism, the audiovisual sector and civil protection.

EFTA countries will be informed and consulted throughout the gestation of Community legislative initiatives, so they will be more readily applicable in the EFTA countries. But the impression remained (in the words of Finnish President Martti Atishaari) that: 'we were silent partners', with little influence.

On the institutional side, the EEA has a council responsible for giving political impetus to the implementation of the Agreement. It also lays down guidelines for the Joint Committee, designed to ensure closer mutual understanding between the Community and the EFTA countries. Finally there is an EEA Consultative Committee, akin to the Economic and Social Committee of the Community: this brings together what are referred to as the 'social partners'.

1.11   Enlargement

The EFTA countries are also among a number of aspiring members of the Community. The prospect is one of considerable enlargement in the coming decades.

A group of EFTA countries had already formally applied for membership at the time of the EEA's creation. These were (with their year of application) Austria (1989), Sweden (1991), Finland, Switzerland, and Norway (1992). Austria, Sweden, and Finland became members on 1 January 1995. In addition several Mediterranean nations have also submitted applications; Turkey (1987), Cyprus and Malta (1990).

Other countries have indicated an intention to join: the remaining EFTA countries, Iceland and Liechtenstein (although in July 1993 there were no Icelandic political parties in favour of membership due largely to fisheries problems); Central and East European nations including the Czech and Slovak Republics, Poland and Hungary; the Baltic States (Latvia, Lithuania and Estonia); Bulgaria; Romania; and now Albania.

Applicants have to satisfy three conditions for membership:

- European identity;
- democratic status; and
- respect for human rights.

Applicants must also accept the Community system and be prepared to implement it. The obligations of membership presuppose a functioning and competitive market economy and an adequate legal and administrative framework in the public and private sectors.

Membership entails acceptance of the so-called *aquis communautaire*, or the existing body of EC law. This includes the Treaties and all legislation adopted to implement them, plus all adopted declarations and resolutions and all international agreements. Transitional arrangements will be set out in the accession Treaties, having been agreed in the accession negotiations. The possibility of aspiring members accepting some form of diluted membership remains open: countries could pick the parts of the Community they liked, such as the internal market, and pass for the time being on matters such as the social dimension or environmental policy, according to remarks made by Commission Vice-President Henning Christophersen in Prague in March 1994.

Some of the applicants are well-placed to become members in the foreseeable future, others may take time.

1.11.1   Outstanding applications

- Turkey is likely to have difficulties taking on the obligations of the Communities social and economic policies, according to the Commission's 1989 opinion on its application. The Commission called for the existing association agreement between the Community and Turkey to be more actively and effectively applied to speed up its rate of development.

- Cyprus could be integrated into the Community without great economic difficulties. However the partition of the island, and the lack of movement of persons, goods and services between the two entities, is a big problem. A solution must be sought through the United Nations, while the existing association agreement is applied to assist with economic integration.

- Malta's desire for membership poses no special problems. The Corfu Summit in June 1994 confirmed that the accession of Malta and Cyprus would constitute the next phase of enlargement, following the determination of then existing applications.

- Hungary officially applied for membership on 1 April 1994. The other Visegrad countries, Poland and the Czech and Slovak Republics, have no timetable for membership but they are aiming to request a start to formal negotiations by 1996, leading to membership by the end of the century. The Commission expect the Polish application to be received shortly.

  As preparatory steps, the Community has entered into so-called 'Europe Agreements' with the above countries, referred to by Commission Vice-President Christophersen as 'training camps' for full membership. These are designed to consolidate democratic structures and to accelerate the development of market economies.

- Europe Agreements have also been signed by Bulgaria and Romania, and agreements on trade and co-operation have been signed with the Baltic states and with Albania.

- In its opinion on Austria's membership, the Commission stated that the whole Community would benefit from accession. Austria's membership would assist economic and monetary union, and it is strategically located in the centre of the new Europe. However, a problem is Austria's neutral status, which would have to be maintained.

  Along with Sweden, Finland and Norway, Austria signed its accession treaty at the Corfu summit in June 1994. Austria voted heavily in favour of membership of the Community in a referendum held to coincide with the 1994 European Parliament elections, on 12 June. Some 66.4% voted for joining the Community.

- The Commission believes that, for the most part, Sweden's membership would be beneficial, but there are problem areas such as agriculture (farmers in the north of the country need special support), state monopolies (including alcohol), competition policy and regional policy. The common defence policy would also pose difficulties, since Sweden is another neutral power. Sweden held a referendum on 13 November 1994, following a general election in September. There was significant opposition to membership; but a 52.2% majority for membership was finally secured.

- According to the Commission similar problems to those facing the Swedish accession face Finland. The Finns voted in favour of membership by 53% on 16 October.

- Norway would strengthen the Community and the European Union in a number of ways, the Commission believes. Its macro-economic policy has successfully achieved inflation rates well in line with future EMU requirements whilst possessing a comprehensive environmental policy which would complement that of the Community. It was a founder member of NATO and an associated member of the WEU and therefore contribute to a common foreign and security policy. Agriculture, regional policy, fisheries, state aids, state monopolies and competition policy in general may however cause setbacks. The Norwegian referendum on 28 November, however, reflected membership: opposition centred on the desire to retain control over fish stocks, and the fact that due to its oil reserves Norway is economically relatively independent.

To illustrate how byzantine the workings of the Community can be, the admission of the new members was at one stage threatened by the Italian government's demands for a retroactive condoning of Italy's cheating on milk quotas. Italy would not agree to a budget increase: Spain had said it would not ratify the new members unless the decision to increase the revenue ceiling, reached at the Edinburgh summit in 1992, was made legally secure. Spain is a prime beneficiary of structural aid and so-called 'cohesion' spending.

The Commission reported in June 1992 on the challenge of enlargement. It emphasised that 'widening' and 'deepening' must proceed together.

1.11.2   The future

Enlargement will have a major impact on decision-making in the Community. The numbers of Commissioners and MEPs, the working practices of the institutions, the number of votes each Member State has in Council and the number required for a qualified majority (which as we shall see caused difficulty in the context of the latest enlargement), the number of official languages, and other issues will all have to be resolved. With 20 or even 30 members, these could create serious problems.

The principle of subsidiarity set out in the Maastricht Treaty will assist, but the Community should not attempt to undertake any task better left to Member States.

For applicant countries, the benefits of the internal market are now available via the EEA, but they want to be involved in the decision-making process. For Central and Eastern European would-be members, improved security is also on the agenda. Germany championed the eastward enlargement of the Community during its presidency of the Community in the second half of 1994, despite apparent French suspicion and reluctance. No timetable is likely to be set for enlargement eastward until 1996, with new members joining perhaps at the turn of the century: for the time being, the Commission is working on a 'shopping list' of measures required of aspirant members, and the talk is of a two-speed Europe, or 'variable geometry'.

The appearance of a two-speed Community was created partly by the UK's opt-out on social policy matters at Maastricht. It now provides a convenient device to enable routes to be mapped out for the countries of eastern Europe to join, without having to address all the ramifications that would have for the Common Agricultural Policy.

The idea of proceeding at different speeds achieved greater notoriety in September 1994 when Germany's ruling CDU published a report suggesting that there should be a 'hard core' of five Member States (the original six excluding Italy). Those left out of this premier division were distinctly unhappy about German dominance: nevertheless, in many ways variable geometry is already a reality.

1.12	**The Brussels Convention 1968**	The Convention on Jurisdiction and Enforcement of Judgments in Civil and Commercial Matters was signed on 27 September 1968 in Brussels. The first three new Member States signed an Accession Convention on 9 September 1978, and Greece, Spain and Portugal adhered later. Interpretation of the Convention is a matter reserved to the ECJ. It is implemented in the UK in the Civil Jurisdiction and Judgments Act 1982.

The Convention provides a complete code on how and when legal action can be taken and judgments enforced in the courts of other Member States. 'Forum shopping', seeking to bring an action where it will be most beneficial, is possible under the Convention. Persons domiciled in a Member State may be sued in its courts, regardless of their nationality. The fact that a writ is served in the jurisdiction does not of itself result in the courts having jurisdiction to hear the matter.

The Convention applies to civil and commercial matters only. It has no application to revenue matters, nor to customs, administrative law, matrimonial property, bankruptcy, or social security. But it does cover maintenance – the creditor can sue where domiciled.

The Foundations

The European Community consists in fact of three Communities: the European Coal and Steel Community (ECSC), the European Economic Community (EEC), and the European Atomic Energy Community (EAEC). The European Economic Community is the most important, and is the main subject of this book.

The Treaty of Rome, signed in 1957, set up the EEC. It has been amended by the Single European Act (SEA) of 1985 and the Treaty on European Union (TEU) signed in Maastricht in 1991.

The TEU also creates a European Union, of which the (three-part) Community is one pillar. The others are intergovernmental cooperation in common foreign and security policy, and intergovernmental cooperation in the fields of justice and home affairs.

The Communities, the Union and the Treaties

The EEC originally consisted of six members. It has grown since by four enlargements: the UK joined in 1973, and most recently Sweden, Finland and Austria joined in 1995.

The Community will continue to grow with the addition of smaller Mediterranean countries and, later, former eastern bloc nations. Turkey also seeks membership.

This widening of the Community will continue in parallel with a deepening of the relationships between Member States. However, pursuing the two simultaneously will not be easy, and not all Member States will be able to proceed at the same speed. The likelihood is that a two-speed Europe (or 'variable geometry') will emerge, raising new constitutional problems.

Membership

Chapter 2

Institutions

Essential to an understanding of the work of the Community is a grasp of the roles of the different institutions which it comprises. These consist of:

- the European Parliament;
- the Council;
- the European Commission;
- the European Court of Justice;
- and several other bodies.

Their respective roles are dealt with below in greater detail.

The Treaty contains important provisions about the functions of the various institutions, and their rights to participate in the processes of the Community. The Treaty establishes a series of checks and balances, like the written constitution of a sovereign state, to control the exercise of power. These procedures are dealt with in the following chapters on the institutions or in the chapters which deal with Community legislation.

The European Parliament, of all the institutions of the Community, has changed most since the earliest times. Initially known as the Common Assembly of the Coal and Steel Community, it called itself a Parliament from 1962. However, it was not until the SEA that it officially received this designation.

2.2   The European Parliament

Originally, Parliament consisted of ministers of the Member States' national Parliaments, who attended meetings as delegates. The Common Assembly of the ECSC had 78 members; in 1958, the Assembly for all three communities came into being with 142 members.

2.2.1   Composition

The founding Treaties envisaged that the Assembly would propose a system for its own election (Article 138 EEC, Article 21 ECSC and Article 108 Euratom). The Council would then unanimously lay down the provision needed for Member States to approve as their respective constitutions required. In the UK, this entailed passing the European Assembly Elections Act 1978.

Proposals to hold direct elections were first made in 1960, but it was not until the Paris Summit of December 1974 that Member States agreed they would take place. The Parliament made new proposals in 1975, and the Council then took a year to make its decision. The agreement was signed in Brussels (along with the Act on Direct Elections) on 20 September 1976 but was not ratified until 1978 (due in part to the time the UK took to pass its legislation). Direct elections were first held in June 1979.

2.2.2   Systems of election

Neither the Council Decision, nor the Act on Direct Elections, specify a common electoral procedure. The Council may agree a common procedure on a proposal from the Parliament (Article 138(3) EEC), and following the Maastricht amendments to the Treaty, the Council must act unanimously on the Parliament's proposals once obtaining Parliament's assent. This must be given by an overall majority of Members of the European Parliament (MEPs), not just those voting.

All Member States, except the UK, use some form of proportional representation for election to the Parliament (and in Northern Ireland a single transferable vote system is employed). The Parliament currently has 626 members: 99 from Germany; 87 from each of France, Italy and UK; 64 from Spain; 31 from the Netherlands; 25 from Belgium, Greece and Portugal; 22 from Sweden; 21 from Austria; 16 from Finland; 16 from Denmark; 15 from Ireland; and 6 from Luxembourg.

The Council Decision provides that the holders of certain offices are disqualified from becoming MEPs. Members of the Commission or the Court of Justice, and members of national governments may not become MEPs. Members of national Parliaments may be elected and several members have dual mandates. Before direct elections all MEPs were national MPs. In the first directly elected Parliament there was a much higher proportion than now. Even now, some well-known national politicians are elected to the Parliament, usually because they are placed at the head of their party's national list to give it extra credibility. For example, Italian Premier Silvio Burlesconi headed his party's list in all five electoral regions: and the leader of France's *Front National*, Jean-Marie le Pen, is also an MEP. Frequently such individuals resign shortly after being elected.

Elections take place every five years, from the Thursday morning to the Sunday evening of a week chosen unanimously by the Council after consulting the Parliament. Member States select the day on which their poll takes place: the UK always votes on a Thursday (so polling day was 9 June in the 1994 European Elections) whereas most Member States vote on Sundays.

The Council may vary the date of the elections by one month either way from the fifth anniversary date. The votes are only counted after polling has finished in all Member States.

MEPs sit in political, not national, groups. A minimum of 12 MEPs from three Member States may form a political group, or 18 MEPs from two Member States or 23 from one. In the present Parliament, there are nine groups. They range from the Left Unity group (former communists) to the neo-fascist European Right. The Socialist group is the largest (and its largest national contingent is the British Labour group): the second largest group is the (Christian Democrat and British Conservative) European People's Party.

The Parliament has a President whom it elects for a two and a half year term in a secret ballot. He or she chairs plenary meetings of the Parliament, and has administrative and ceremonial duties. These can be delegated to 14 Vice Presidents also elected by the Parliament. In addition, the President, Vice Presidents and five quaestors (additional members elected by the Parliament from among their number) constitute the Parliament's Bureau. The quaestors have no voting rights in the Bureau. This body has several administrative and financial functions, including responsibility for the Parliament's secretariat and the appointment of the Secretary-General and proposing the membership of the Parliament's Committees.

The Enlarged Bureau includes the Bureau *and* the leaders of the political groups. It takes decisions on internal organisational matters and on the Parliament's relations with non-Community institutions and organisations. It also has a consultative role: the President of the Council consults the Enlarged Bureau on the appointment of the President of the Commission. Finally, it sets the agenda for part-sessions (or plenary sessions) of the Parliament.

2.2.3   Structure

The Parliament meets in plenary session for 60 days a year, divided into 12 part-sessions, each of a week. No meeting is held in August. In practice it always meets in Strasbourg: in the Cases 258/85 and 51/86 *France v European Parliament* (1988) the ECJ observed that only exceptionally could the Parliament hold plenary sessions anywhere but Strasbourg while (paradoxically) upholding the Parliament's decision to build a chamber in Brussels.

The majority (over 70%) of Parliament's committee meetings are held in Brussels, the remainder taking place monthly in Strasbourg and sometimes Luxembourg.

2.2.4   The work of the Parliament

Committees can request to meet elsewhere, which the President or the bureau can authorise. In contrast Luxembourg is the base of the Parliament's Secretariat, an arrangement which has meant much transporting of paperwork and other items between there and Parliament's meeting places. In 1981 Parliament resolved to move most of the Secretariat to Brussels and Strasbourg, but in Case 108/83 *Grand Duchy of Luxembourg v European Parliament* (1984), the ECJ ruled that the Parliament's decision to implement that resolution was void since a Decision of 1965 on the provisional location of certain institutions provided for the Secretariat to remain in Luxembourg.

In Cases C-213/88 and C-39/89 *Luxembourg v European Parliament* (1991) the court allowed the Parliament to provide certain facilities in Brussels and Strasbourg and to transfer some staff to those cities. Such an internal re-organisation was within its powers.

Parliament has a number of committees dealing with a variety of different subjects. They have two roles; scrutinising proposed legislation, and producing non-legislative reports.

Legislative proposals that come to Parliament are assigned to one of the standing committees. If the subject matter falls within the remit of more than one, it will be assigned to the committee chosen by Parliament but others may be asked for their opinions. The committee considers the proposal and reports to a plenary session. It may put forward amendments and may recommend that Parliament accept or reject the proposal.

Committees prepare reports within their areas of competence, seeking to persuade Parliament to pass a resolution on the subject. They are entitled to set up fact-finding missions, hear evidence from experts, or create *ad hoc* working parties.

Committees may meet in public if they decide to do so. A senior commission official or commissioner frequently attends and occasionally the President of the Council is represented. In particular, the President attends the political affairs committee to discuss European political co-operation at least four times a year.

2.2.5   The rôle of the Parliament

Article 137 says that Parliament shall exercise the advisory and supervisory tasks given to it by the Treaty. These have since been expanded, and Parliament's role takes four forms: it supervises the other institutions, it is involved in making legislation, it has a power of veto over accession and association agreements, and it has an important role in the budgetary process.

The Parliament is given supervisory power over the other institutions in four ways.

- *Censure*. The Parliament exercises power over the Commission by having the ability to censure the Commission, which would oblige it to resign (Article 144). Two thirds of the MEPs present and voting would have to support such a motion, and those MEPs would have to constitute an overall majority of the Parliament. Such a motion would have to be tabled by a political group or by one-tenth of the MEPs. At least 24 hours must have elapsed before it can be debated, and another 48 hours before it is voted on. No motion of censure has ever been carried.

  Parliament gave the new members of the Santer Commission, whose terms began in 1995, a very hard time, and the performance of some of the new Commissioners was generally considered to be very poor. Several had little knowledge of Community policy.

- *Questions*. MEPs and the Parliament may question the Council and the Commission, and those two institutions have the right to be heard by Parliament. The Commission is required to reply to questions from Parliament; the Council is not, but in practice does. At each session there is a question time for oral and written questions. These are usually directed at the Commission.

  Parliament debates the annual legislative programme presented by the President of the Commission at the start of each year. It also discusses the Commission's annual general report, but this retrospective review of the Commission's activities is naturally less influential than the debate on what it proposes to introduce in the coming year. Parliament will also have the opportunity to debate the annual report of the President of the European Bank which will be required in Stage III of EMU.

  The Council is not obliged to report to Parliament, but the incoming Presidency presents the programme of the next six months and reports on what has been achieved at the end of the period. The President of the European Council also reports to Parliament every six months and makes a written report on progress towards European union. Article D TEU now makes these reports obligatory.

  Amendments made to the Treaty at Maastricht require that Parliament be informed of several additional matters within the Council's remit concerning economic convergence.

- *Committees of inquiry.* Parliament may establish committees of enquiry to investigate alleged contraventions of EC law or incidents of maladministration. Such committees have investigated a number of matters (including for example, the rise of racism and fascism in Europe) but may not *insist* on being able to cross-examine members of the Council. That, and the fact that the media pays little attention to their reports, makes this procedure relatively ineffective.

  A committee of inquiry is set up at the request of a quarter of MEPs. Once established, a committee must report within nine months.

- *Legal proceedings.* Parliament has always had *locus standi* under Article 175 to bring actions in the ECJ against the Council and the Commission for failure to act. It can also intervene in proceedings before the court in any case, but only to support the submissions of one party (Article 37 Statute of the Court of Justice).

  The Parliament has also claimed the right to bring actions for annulment of decisions of other institutions under Article 173. However its right to do so is not clear cut. In the *Comitology* case (Case 302/87 *European Parliament v EC Council* (1988)), the ECJ held that it could not. But in Case 70/88, *European Parliament v EC Council* (1990), it granted the Parliament limited *locus standi* providing Parliament is seeking only to safeguard its prerogatives and the action is founded only on submissions alleging infringements of those prerogatives. The Council had adopted a regulation under Article 31 which requires consultation with Parliament. But Parliament argued that it should have been adopted under Article 100a using the co-operation procedure. The court held that:

  'Parliament's prerogatives include participation in the drafting of legislative measures, in particular participation in the co-operation procedure laid down in the EEC Treaty.'

  See also Case C-295/90 *Re Student's Rights European Parliament v EC Council* (1992).

  This extension of Parliament's right to take action is difficult to reconcile with the wording of Article 173, which does not mention Parliament at all. The Commission mooted the possibility of giving Parliament *locus standi* at the intergovernmental conference prior to the SEA and the fact that no such change was made the Court found persuasive in *Comitology*. However after Maastricht, Article 173 has been amended to give Parliament power to bring an action to protect its own prerogatives.

The Parliament's supervisory powers can be initiated, *inter alia*, by a *petition* or by a complaint to the *Community Ombudsman*.

(a) *Petitioning the European Parliament*

Petitions can be addressed to Parliament by citizens or residents of, or legal persons whose registered office is in, a Member State (Article 138d). They must be on a matter which is within the field of activity of the Community, and directly affects the petitioner. Unless the matter relates to the internal workings of Parliament, it will be able to do nothing formal about it. However, it can use its influence with the other institutions and can help publicise the case.

Petitions are assigned to the relevant committee by the President of the European Parliament. If it considers the Petition admissible, the committee may conduct hearings and produce a report. Because the number of petitions has increased significantly in recent years, a Committee on Petitions was set up in January 1987. It handles complaints that Member States have failed to comply with Community law, by referring them to the Commission which may then take action under Article 169 EC.

(b) *The Community Ombudsman*

Maladministration by the Community institutions may also now give rise to a complaint to the Community Ombudsman created at Maastricht. Article 138e EEC empowers the Ombudsman to conduct 'own initiative' investigations, as well as responding to complaints. Complaints may be made either direct by the person affected or via an MEP.

The Ombudsman's jurisdiction does not apply if the matter is, or has been, the subject of legal proceedings.

If maladministration is found, the matter is referred to the institution concerned. It has three months to respond. After considering the response, the Ombudsman forwards a final report to Parliament and to the institution concerned, as well as informing the complainant of the outcome. The Ombudsman will also report annually to Parliament.

The Ombudsman is appointed by Parliament for its five-year term and can be re-appointed. The ECJ may, at Parliament's request, dismiss the Ombudsman if he or she no longer fulfils the conditions required for the performance of the duties of the office, or is guilty of serious misconduct. (Compare the conditions for the removal of a Commissioner.) The appointment is full-time and must be completely independent. Regulations and general conditions governing the performance of the Ombudsman's duties are laid down by Parliament after receiving an opinion from the Commission and with the approval of the Council.

| 2.2.7 | Parliament's legislative rôle |

Parliament becomes involved in the EC's law-making process in six ways:

- *Consultation* gives Parliament the chance to express its opinion on proposed legislation. It embodies the essential concept of democratic control and is a crucial element in the institutional balance created by the EEC Treaty. Consultation is required by the Treaty in certain situations. Parliament is also sometimes consulted about legislative proposals where there is no Treaty requirement. The application of the consultation procedure to legislation is dealt with below, Chapter 3.

  Parliament must also be consulted over certain non-legislative matters. The President of the Commission is nominated by the Member States after consulting the Parliament, which later gets to vote to approve the Commission as a whole. Article 109f(1) EC required consultation in the second stage of EMU on the appointment of the President of the EMU, while Article 109a(2) requires consultation on the appointment of officers of the ECB in the third stage.

  If Parliament is not consulted where it should be it is an infringement of an essential procedural requirement. The Court of Justice would be able to declare the measure void under Article 173: see, for example, Case 139/79 *Roquette Frères v Council* (1980).

- The *co-operation procedure* introduced by Article 100A (inserted by the SEA) gave Parliament a greater rôle. This is examined below, Chapter 3.

- The *co-decision procedure*, which is modelled on the co-operation procedure, is a more comprehensive system. It was introduced by the TEU: see Articles 189A-C EC. It means that virtually all legislature proposals must now be submitted to the Parliament. See Chapter 3.

- The Treaty now provides (since Maastricht) for a *conciliation procedure* to determine differences between the three institutions. In fact a conciliation procedure was, for limited purposes, first established by a Joint Declaration in 1975. The procedure uses a Conciliation Committee to seek an agreement between Parliament and Council. It consists of representatives of the two institutions with the participation of the Commission. The Commission's remit is to take all initiatives which may help the conciliation process. It is able at this stage to amend its proposal.

The original aim of the conciliation procedure under the Joint Declaration was to preserve Parliament's prerogative in budgetary matters. Under the Budgetary Treaties of the 1970s, it had the final say on non-compulsory expenditure, and it was logical that it should also have more of a say in measures which have a significant impact on that part of the budget. The procedure can be invoked provided the proposal is of general application, it has 'appreciable financial implications', and it relates to expenditure that is not required under measures already in existence.

Any of the three institutions may invoke the procedure if these criteria are met and the Council proposes to depart from Parliament's opinion. Once Parliament has given its opinion in the consultation procedure then a conciliation committee is set up to seek agreement between the Council and Parliament. Normally this must be done within three months. The conciliation process was used recently in the case of the proposed biotechnology patents directive.

- The SEA introduced the concept of requiring Parliament's *assent*, though only in very limited circumstances. Parliament must assent to the accession of new Member States and to association agreements with third countries. At Maastricht the Member States agreed to extend this requirement to other non-budgetary legislation. The list of such measures is still modest and in most cases the Council has to act unanimously as well, making it particularly difficult to pass such a measure.

- At Maastricht, Parliament was also given a limited power to *initiate* legislation. This is in fact the same power always enjoyed by the Council; to request the Commission to submit any appropriate proposals on matters where Parliament considered that a Community measure is required for the purpose of implementing the EEC Treaty.

Parliament had a consultative role in the budgetary process even before the Budgetary Treaties of 1970 and 1975 which amended the provisions of the Treaties relating to the budgets. With 'own resources' funding for the Community from 1970, whereby the Community derives its income from customs duties and levies on agricultural imports rather than from contributions from the Member States, it was given more control over the budget. This was the first major extension of

2.2.8   Budgetary role

the Parliament's powers. The Budgetary Treaties gave the Parliament greater powers over the 'non-compulsory' part of the budget – that part concerned with the functioning of the institutions.

Each year the Commission puts a preliminary draft budget to the Council before 1 September. The Council must agree a draft budget (by qualified majority) and submit it to Parliament on or before 5 October. Then Parliament has 45 days in which to act. It may either:

- Amend the non-compulsory expenditure parts of the budget by an absolute majority;

- Propose modifications to the compulsory expenditure parts (ie, that portion of the budget arising unavoidably from the application of the rules of the Community – especially the CAP) by a simple majority of MEPs voting; or

- Fail to do anything, in which case the budget is deemed to be finally adopted.

The Council has 15 days in which to act on amendments or proposed modifications. By qualified majority it can modify Parliament's amendments to the non-compulsory part of the budget, but reductions in compulsory expenditure proposed by the Parliament will stand unless rejected by a qualified majority of the Council. Likewise, proposed reductions will be dropped unless the Council adopts them by a qualified majority.

The budget is deemed to be finally accepted if the Council proposes no modifications to Parliament's amendments on non-compulsory expenditure and accepts Parliament's proposals on compulsory expenditure. If it does not, the modified budget goes back to Parliament for a second reading. At this stage Parliament has no power to alter compulsory expenditure parts of the draft. It can amend or reject the Council's changes to its own first reading amendments on non-compulsory expenditure, but only by an *absolute* majority, ie a 3/5 majority of MEPs voting.

An absolute majority and two-thirds of those voting may also reject the draft budget altogether and ask for a new one to be submitted. If Parliament takes none of these actions within 15 days the budget is deemed to have been adopted.

Parliament cannot freely increase non-compulsory expenditure in the budget. The Commission is required to declare a maximum rate of increase by 1 May each year for the budget submitted on the following 1 September. If the Council proposes a rate of increase grater than half the maximum rate,

Parliament may add up to half the maximum rate. Council and Parliament are also permitted to agree to a rate higher than that set by the Commission.

In Case 34/86 *EC Council v European Parliament* (1986), the court upheld the Council's action for annulment of a budget adopted by the President of the European Parliament which contained increases in non-compulsory expenditure much greater than the maximum rates of increase set by the Commission. The correct procedure to secure agreement between Council and Parliament had not been followed.

Under the SEA, Parliament has a veto over the accession to the Community of new Member States and over new association agreements.

2.2.9 Accession and association agreements

Membership applications are dealt with by Article O TEU (previously known as Article 237 EEC) and, as seen, require the assent of Parliament. Applications are referred to the appropriate Parliamentary committee. The committee, a Parliamentary group or 23 individual MEPs, may propose that a debate be held before negotiations start, and Parliament may by simple majority request the Council and the Commission take part. A further debate will be held when the Council and the Commission have completed the negotiations and a vote will be taken on the requisite assent after Parliament receives the committee's report.

Before the SEA the Council had to consult Parliament on association agreements with non-Member States, with Unions of states, or with international organisations. The SEA amended the requirement that Parliament assent by an absolute majority; a simple majority of members actually voting now suffices. At Maastricht amendments were made which apply the same rules to further types of agreements.

Most legislative authority under the Treaties vests in the Council. It consists of members of the governments of Member States, the actual composition depending on the subject under discussion. For example, when the Common Agricultural Policy is under consideration the agriculture ministers of the Member States would make up the Agriculture Council. Likewise there are specialist transport, finance and other councils. The General Council consists of foreign ministers.

2.3 The Council

The onus of coordinating the work of the different councils, which may have divergent aims (eg agriculture ministers seeking to increase expenditure and finance ministers trying to restrict it), is placed on the Member State which holds the Presidency of the Council. This rotates every six months, passing between Member States in alphabetical order.

Germany held the Presidency for the second half of 1994: France (which comes after Deutschland alphabetically) took over at the beginning of 1995.

Six months is a short time for the Presidency to make much impression and the permanent General Secretariat of the Council, under its Secretary General, performs an important function.

Meetings of the Council, which are not held in public unless it unanimously decides so, are convened by the Presidency or at the request of a member or of the Commission. The Council is now operating an 'openness' policy under a code on public access to information, to introduce a greater degree of what is usually referred to in Community circles as 'transparency', but paradoxically claims that information about progress on this is covered by secrecy rules. However, a register of how ministers vote in Council is being introduced: but the Dutch government and the Parliament have mounted a legal challenge against the council's refusal to divulge information.

The Commission attends Council meetings of right. The Council may, however, decide by simple majority to meet without them. Which particular Commissioners attend will depend on the subject under discussion.

2.3.1	Voting

The Council votes in three ways:

(a) *Simple majority*

By Article 148(1) EEC the Council acts by a simple majority unless the Treaty provides otherwise. It usually does so provide. Since the issue is closely bound up with the degree to which Member States retain their sovereignty – simple majority voting entails the maximum loss of sovereignty and unanimity the minimum – the question of whether the Treaty gives powers for the Council to adopt a particular measure in this way is often very significant.

For example: in Case 56/88 *UK v EC Council* (1989) the UK government challenged Council Decision 87/569, concerning an action programme for the vocational training of young people. It argued that Article 128 EEC, which empowers the Council to lay down general principles for implementing a common vocational training policy, did not cover the establishment of continuing programmes involving substantial expenditure. Article 235, which requires unanimity in a situation where action is necessary to attain the objectives of the Community but where the Treaty has not specifically provided for it, should have been used. The ECJ rejected the UK's argument, on the grounds that if the Treaty gave the

Council the power to adopt a common vocational training policy it must also have given it the means to carry it out. The provisions on vocational training were changed in TEU: the cooperation procedure now applies.

A simple majority suffices for:

- adoption of the Council's rules of procedure. Other procedural decisions are also taken on the same basis, but sometimes the Treaty requires common accord between the institutions;

- requesting the Commission to undertake studies under Article 152 for the attainment of the common objectives of the Treaty;

- an opinion convening an intergovernmental conference to consider amendments to the Treaty. (Once such a conference is convened, of course, it must proceed by unanimity.)

The Council could formerly conclude international agreements by a simple majority (Article 228): but this provision was changed by the TEU to provide for qualified majority voting or unanimity.

(b) Qualified majority

Article 148(2) sets out the qualified majority voting procedure. Prior to the 1995 enlargement a total of 76 votes was allocated to the 12 Member States, according to their respective sizes. The distribution of the votes is not entirely proportionate, and the smaller states are given more voting power than population alone would dictate.

The qualified majority required to pass a measure under this provision was 54. This total could be achieved by seven Member States voting together; likewise, a blocking minority of 23 votes could be achieved by three Member States.

The size of the vote needed to block a proposal was a contentious issue in the latest round of enlargement talks. The accession of Sweden, Finland, and Austria will result in an increase in the total number of votes in the Council to 90, and if the blocking minority were to remain at the same proportion, it would then become 27 votes. But Britain and Spain held out for the retention of 23 as the blocking minority; the UK government was not prepared to agree to a change requiring it to assemble more votes, which would entail finding another ally, before it could stop a proposal with which it disagreed.

Compromise was finally reached; the figure for a blocking minority was set at 27, but where there were 23 to 26 votes against, the decision would be postponed and there will be a 'reasonable delay' to allow the Council to do 'all in its power' to resolve the differences. Following Norway's non-accession, the relevant figures were revised. The total number of Council votes is 87: the qualified majority is 62: the block minority is 26. The size of the blocking minority will again be examined at the 1996 Intergovernmental Conference, to allow for the enlarged Union of up to 20 states.

This illustrates how closely tied the voting procedures are to the issue of national sovereignty. The Treaty originally envisaged that qualified majority voting would be the usual way of doing business after the transitional phase of building the Community was completed in 1966. But at the time Member States were guarding their sovereignty, and de Gaulle's 'Empty Chair' policy had effectively prevented any progress on the basis of unanimity for several months. The problem was resolved by the Luxembourg Compromise of January 1966, which amounted to an extension of the unanimity requirement.

Throughout the 1980s Member States became more prepared to concede the principle of qualified majority voting. The Single European Act provided for more decisions to be taken this way. Nevertheless, the Luxembourg Compromise remains in place permitting (in theory) a Member State to exercise a veto where its vital national interests are at stake. In fact, the UK's right to exercise a veto was rejected in 1982 when the government sought to prevent the Agriculture Council setting prices before the General Council had agreed the British contribution to the Community budget. However, rejection of the right to veto was based on the fact that this particular matter was not of 'very important interest'. Germany successfully blocked a reduction in support prices for cereals and colza in 1985, and both Ireland (in 1986) and Greece (in 1988) have used the Compromise to get a better deal for their farmers.

In essence, there are still enough Member States who support the concept of a veto to ensure that it remains. For as long as a blocking minority refrains from voting against a Member State which has invoked the Compromise, it stays. But the TEU extends the use of qualified majority voting, and the fact that all the Member States recently assented to this may make it difficult for one of them to claim the right to exercise a veto.

(c) *Unanimity*

The Council is often required by the Treaty to act unanimously. Abstentions do not count against. Therefore, a single Member State voting in favour can pass a proposal provided all the others abstain.

Many matters of constitutional importance (including for example, changes in the numbers of judges and Advocates General in the ECJ, or the number of Commissioners) require unanimity. So too do some politically sensitive issues (such as the harmonisation of indirect taxes and the authorisation of State aids in exceptional circumstances). Some matters relating to the Council's procedure also require unanimity.

Finally, unanimity is required for the Council to amend a Commission proposal or to pass, under the cooperation procedure, a measure which Parliament has rejected. This requirement is crucial to maintaining the balance between the EC institutions.

COREPER is responsible for preparing the work of the Council and for carrying out the tasks assigned to it by the Council (Article 4, Merger Treaty). It existed prior to the Merger Treaty, but that was its first formal recognition.

There are two COREPERS:

- COREPER 1 consists of the deputy Permanent Representatives of the Member States to the EC;

- COREPER 2 consists of the Permanent Representatives (Ambassadors) themselves.

The two are equal but COREPER 2 deals with major institutional and political questions.

The Chair of COREPER rotates with the Presidency of the Council. Each Member State maintains a permanent representation in Brussels. The civil servants working in them have highly developed expertise in the workings of the Community, so as well as representing their national governments in discussions about council business they relay information back to their governments.

Proposals from the Commission are discussed in working parties set up by COREPER, and then in the full COREPER (1 or 2 as appropriate) in the presence of a Commission representative. COREPER highlights the items which the Council needs to discuss with care. If the Working Party is in agreement, the proposal is put into Part I of the agenda of the COREPER: if there is no dissent it will then go on to the Council agenda as an 'A' item. Unless a Member State raises an objection in Council, it will be formally passed by the Council. If there is an objection it goes back to COREPER for further discussion.

2.3.2   Committee of Permanent Representatives (COREPER)

If the Working Party does not agree, the matter is placed in Part II of COREPER's agenda. COREPER may be able to resolve the differences and put it on the Council agenda as an 'A' item: if it cannot, it will appear as a 'B' item, meaning that further discussion is needed. Contentious points will be highlighted.

2.4   European Council

Not to be confused with the Council of Ministers or the Council of Europe, the European Council is the name given to regular meetings of the heads of government of the Member States. It has its origin in the 'summit' of the (then) nine heads of government, plus the President of the Commission, in Paris in December 1974. The idea was that such meetings would have a remit for progressing the work of the EC, and political co-operation (then in its infancy). It would meet three times a year. Article 2 SEA now confirms the existence of the European Council as a distinct institution.

Three civil servants from the Member State which is the President for the time being of the Council attend the European Council Meetings, as do three members of the Council Secretariat and the Secretary General of the Commission. In 1986, the Member States agreed to limit the number of European Council Meetings to two a year. They feared that otherwise it would be called upon to act as a referee in disputes between specialist Councils. However, the Member State holding the Presidency may be tempted to hold 'emergency' European Council meetings. This happened four times between July 1989 and June 1991. The UK hosted two during its 1992 presidency, in Birmingham in October and in Edinburgh in December.

The European Council's role and powers have evolved organically, although the SEA and the TEU have gone some way to setting these out; Article D TEU states that the European Council 'shall provide the Union with the necessary impetus for its development, and shall define the necessary general political guidelines'.

The European Council has no direct law making powers, though its members could legally (excluding the President of the Commission) have constituted themselves the Council of Ministers and legislated. However, the EC Treaty (as amended at Maastricht) requires Council decisions to be taken at this level relating to the start of the third stage of economic and monetary union (the single currency).

Nor does the European Council displace the Commission's monopoly over initiating legislative proposals – at least in theory, but it can and does in practice launch political initiatives. It has set up *ad hoc* committees on different aspects of the development of the Community. It can set the agenda for reforms of the Treaty. The Commission still has to *prepare* the proposals, but it has not *initiated* them.

The Commission's powers of initiative have, however, been limited simply by the fact that it could not be sure of a favourable reception for its proposals. Now that the European Council brings the President of the Commission into contact with the heads of government, this problem has been reduced.

The Commission is often referred to as the EC's civil service. The comparison is of some value but should not be taken too far, as the administration of the Community is based on the French rather than the British system. The EC Treaties confer legislative and judicial functions on the Commission.	**2.5 The Commission**
The Commission is a collegiate body which now comprises 20 Commissioners, of whom one is designated the President. The number of Commissioners may be varied by unanimous decision of the Council. They are appointed by common accord of the governments of the Member States. The Commission must contain a national of each Member State. In practice, the five larger Member States nominate two each (the maximum), and the others one. The term of appointment of a Commissioner is five years (increased from four by the TEU). The term is renewable, although relatively few Commissioners serve more than one term. Sir Leon Brittan is an exception to the general rule.	2.5.1 Membership

Article 157 of the Treaty requires that Commissioners have only a 'general competence' but that their independence must be 'beyond doubt'. Therefore, although they are nominated by their governments, Commissioners are neither delegates nor representatives. Independence is, however, difficult to achieve; Commissioners who do not follow the line of their national governments may well find they are not reappointed. This is what happened when Lord Cockfield was replaced by Sir Leon Brittan in 1986. Despite having enjoyed a very successful term of office, which culminated in the publication of the White Paper on Completing the Internal Market (the cornerstone of the 1992 reforms), Lord Cockfield was thought by the UK government to have 'gone native'.

Before the Maastricht amendments, Article 14 of the Merger Treaty merely stated that there would be a president and six vice presidents of the Commission. They would be appointed by common accord for renewable two-year terms.	2.5.2 President

The vice presidents were created largely to recognise the seniority of some members of the Commissions. The President, on the other hand, has become a very significant appointment. Jacques Delors used the position to push the development of the Community forward in ways he wished to see, and as his term of office (already renewed for 10 years) reached its end (in January 1995) the succession was a contentious matter. It was the turn of a small Member State to 'have' the Presidency, and Belgian Premier Jean-Luc Dehaene was favourite for the position with French and German support, but his candidature was vetoed by the UK. The Luxembourg Prime Minister Jacques Santer emerged as a compromise candidate and promptly espoused (to the European Parliament which had to approve him) exactly those views which had made Mr Dehaene unacceptable to the UK.

| 2.5.3 | Method of appointment |

The TEU has established a new procedure (Article 158 EC) for appointing the President and other members of the Commission. The governments of Member States will nominate by common accord the person they intend to appoint as the President, on which they will consult Parliament (in practice they already do). The nominee will then be consulted by the governments before they nominate the intended Commissioners.

The entire Commission (President included) will then be voted on as a body by Parliament. If Parliament approves them (presumably by a simple majority) they will be appointed by common accord of the Member States.

The TEU removes the requirement to have six vice-presidents. Instead the Commission will have a discretion to appoint one or two from among its members. In December 1993, Commissioners Mañuel Marin and Henning Christophersen were appointed vice-presidents.

| 2.5.4 | Function of the President |

The President:

- chairs meetings of the Commission;

- proposes the allocation of portfolios among the Commissioners after informal preliminary discussions (the final decision is collective);

- represents the Community in the annual meetings of the Group of Seven (G7) industrial nations and sits on the European Council; and

- presents the Commission's annual programme to the European Parliament and replies to the debate on it.

Individual members of the Commission may only be dismissed during their term of office by the Court of Justice on application by the Council or the Commission. It will only do so if the Commissioner no longer fulfils the conditions required for the performance of their duties, or has been guilty of serious misconduct.

The whole Commission can be dismissed by Parliament. A motion of censure would have to be carried by a two-thirds majority of the votes cast, and that must be a majority of the members of Parliament. The power has never been used, partly because it is indiscriminate (it gets rid of good and bad Commissioners alike) and partly because Parliament would (pre-TEU) have had no formal say in the membership of the replacement Commission.

2.5.5 Dismissal

The Commission meets in private and usually reaches its decisions by a majority vote. In practice it tries to operate by consensus, which is desirable since the collegiate nature of the institution means that members must support its decisions in public even if they opposed them during voting

2.5.6 Decision-making

The Commission was given power by the Merger Treaty to adopt certain rules of procedure (see Article 162(2) EEC). Joined Cases T-79/89, T-84-6/89, T-89/89, T-91-2/89, T-96/89, T-98/89, T-102/89 and T-104/89, *BASF AG and others v Commission* (1992) (on appeal case C-137/92P, 15 June 1994) illustrate the importance of following these rules; Commission Decision 89/190 did not follow the requirements of Article 12 of the Rules of Procedure, requiring the original text of the Commission Decision to be annexed to the minutes which record their adoption. The Court of First Instance declared that the Decision did not exist, and overturned the fines imposed by the Commission on the members of a cartel of 14 PVC manufacturers because of discrepancies between the texts in German, English and French, and because President Jacques Delors had only signed the original decision in three of the five relevant language versions (French, German and English) leaving the competition Commissioner, Peter Sutherland, to sign the Italian and Dutch texts. On appeal, the Court said:

'Acts tainted by an irregularity whose gravity is so obvious that it cannot be tolerated by the Community legal order must be treated as having no legal effect.

The formal requirement has an important purpose:

Far from being, as the Commission claims, a mere formality for archival purposes, the authentication of the acts is intended to guarantee legal certainty by ensuring that the text ... becomes fixed in the languages which are binding.'

The Commission must deal with a large volume of business. Each Commissioner has a Cabinet, or personal staff, to assist them with preparing for the weekly Commission meetings.

Decision-taking is also facilitated by two short-cuts for non-controversial decisions; a written procedure, under which each Commissioner is sent a written proposal which will be adopted if none of them objects, and the delegation of routine decisions to the Commissioner responsible for that area (eg agriculture).

The Commission's provisional rules of procedure also authorise decision-making to be delegated to officials, the civil servants who comprise the services of the Commission. This can only ever apply to everyday decisions; the court emphasised the principle of collective responsibility in Case 5/85 *AKZO Chemie v Commission* (1986), although it accepts that this cannot apply to all decisions otherwise the Commission would be paralysed.

| 2.5.7 | The services of the Commission |

The civil servants who work for the Commission are not the vast bureaucracy some seem to believe. In 1991, they numbered 17,175: in contrast the UK had 553,863 civil servants on 1 April 1991, of which the Lord Chancellor's Department employed 11,223, which gives some indication of the size of the Commission's Services.

The services are organised into 26 Directorates General (DG): DG II deals with external relations, DG III with industry, DG IV with competition, and so on. Each Directorate General forms part of the portfolio of a Commissioner: some (for example, the transport or competition commissioners) will have only one DG to deal with, while others may have two or three.

| 2.5.8 | The legal service |

The Commission also has a separate legal service (though each DG has a number of lawyers working within it). The legal service is responsible for ensuring that Commission proposals comply with Community law, and that all the DG's follow a coherent legal policy. There are also jurist-linguists in the legal service who are responsible for producing 10 equally valid different language-versions of each piece of Commission legislation and for making sure that draft legislation is accurate in all the Community languages.

The Director General of the legal service attends meetings of the Commission to give legal advice.

Sometimes the responsible Director General will consult a Committee of National Experts on draft legislation. Some are permanent (eg the Scientific and Technical Research Committee and the Advisory Committee on Monopolies and Restrictive Practices), others are *ad hoc*, comprising representatives of interest groups.

2.5.9 Committees of National Experts

The Commission is nearly always required by the Treaty to initiate legislation. Although the ECJ can ask the Council to change the jurisdiction of the CFI, Parliament can draw up proposals for its elections for the Council to adopt, and the ECB may make recommendations on certain legislation under the TEU, most legislation still starts with the Commission. Furthermore while the Commission initiates the legislation, the major political initiatives in the Community frequently come from the European Council (on which, see above). In particular, progress towards economic and monetary union, which needed changes to the Treaty and was therefore beyond the Commission's powers, was made by an *ad hoc* group under the President of the Commission set up by the European Council at its Hanover meeting in 1988.

2.5.10 The Commission's legislative rôle

The Council is the body which passes the legislation, but where the power to propose is conferred on the Commission it participates in the Council meeting. The Council may only amend a Commission proposal unanimously, and if deadlock occurs in the Council the Commission is able to resolve it by amending its proposal.

The Commission adopted 7,335 instruments – directives, regulations, decisions, recommendations and opinions – in 1993. It has power to legislate itself in very limited circumstances under the Treaty, and by delegation from the Council:

- Treaty power

  The Commission had wider legislative powers during the early stages of the establishment of the Common Market, but these have mostly expired. Its remaining powers are under Article 48(3)(d) to make regulations placing conditions on the right of a worker who is a national of one Member State to remain in the territory of another after having been employed there; see Commission Regulation 1251/70 (OJ Spec Ed 1970, L142/24, p402): and under Article 90(3), to address Directives to Member States relating to the application of competition rules to public undertakings and certain other bodies, and to make decisions that particular state measures contravene the Treaty.

- Delegated powers

  The Commission passes much detailed legislation to do with the Common Agricultural Policy, under powers delegated by the Council under Article 43. And in the field of competition law, Regulations 19/65 2821/71 and others empowered the Commission to adopt legislation exempting groups of restrictive agreements from the competition rules under Article 85(3).

2.5.11   Control of Commission legislation

The Council has not given the Commission a completely free hand to pass delegated legislation. Often it will be required to act under the supervision of a committee of representatives of Member States. But Article 145 EC provides that the Commission shall have powers to implement general rules laid down by the Council. An overall framework for delegation is required by Article 145, rather than *ad hoc* arrangements.

The procedure to be followed if the Council intends to restrict the exercise of powers granted to the Commission is set out in the so-called *Comitology* decision Council Decision 87/373 (OJ 1987 L197/33). This also permits the Council to content itself by limiting the scope of the delegated powers. The Decision sets out three main procedures for the delegation of powers to the Commission: it also establishes special safeguard measures. Which of the procedures is followed is determined by the parent legislation.

- Procedure I

  This places no limit on the Commission's power to pass delegated legislation, but proposals must be submitted to an advisory committee consisting of representatives of the Member States and chaired by a Commission representative. The Commission must take the utmost account of the committee's opinion but is not bound by it.

- Procedure II

  This allows the Council to intervene if the Commission adopts measures which do not accord with the opinion of a committee constituted as in Procedure I. (The Commission's representative does not have a vote under this procedure.) This so-called 'management committee' votes according to the weighted voting procedure of the Council (Article 148(2)), and if it delivers an adverse opinion the Commission may defer application of the measures for a certain period. The Council may, during that time, take a different decision by qualified majority.

  The period during which the Council may take a different decision depends on which variation of this second procedure is used. It may be one month, or it may be specified in the legislation which delegates the power, up to a maximum of three months.

- Procedure III

  Here, a regulatory committee (constituted in the same way as a management committee in procedure II) must give a favourable opinion by a qualified majority. If it does not, the Commission must immediately submit a proposal to the Council. Depending again on the variant used, the Council may act by qualified majority during a period set out in the parent legislation (subject to a three month maximum). If it fails to do so, variant (a) allows the Commission to adopt its proposed measures. Under variant (b) the Commission may not adopt its measure if the Council has decided against it by a simple majority.

These arise under Article 100A, the provision inserted by the SEA to speed up the passage of harmonising legislation. The Council may delegate powers to the Commission to decide on such measures, but the Commission must consult Member States before taking a decision, *and* notify the Council and the Member States of any decision it takes.

2.5.12   Safeguard measures

A Member State may refer the Commission's decision to the Council, within a time limit specified in the parent legislation. Again, there are two variants, the second of which involves very little delegation to the Commission. Under variant (a) the Council may take a different decision by qualified majority, within the time limit, and under variant (b) (involving little delegation to the Commission) the Council may confirm, amend or revoke by qualified majority the Commission's decision, but if it does not do so within the time limit the Commission's decision is deemed to be revoked.

The variant (b) procedures, sometimes called the safety-net procedures, were protested by the Commission when they were set up. It thought there was a real danger that decisions simply would not be taken but it has not yet led to deadlock.

The EC Treaty gives the Commission executive powers in the following areas:

2.5.13   Commission as executive

- competition policy (Articles 85-93);

- safeguard measures (Article 115); and

- administering the European Social Fund (it also administers the other Community structural funds, namely the European Agricultural Guidance and Guarantee Fund, Guidance section, and the European Regional

Development Fund, under powers delegated by the Council).

The ECSC and Euratom treaties also give powers to the Commission.

| 2.5.14 | The Commission as guardian of Community law |

Article 155 EC (and similarly Article 8 ECSC and Article 125 Euratom) confers on the Commission the authority 'to see that the provisions for [the] Treaty and the measures pursuant to it taken by the institutions are carried out'.

Article 169 empowers the Commission to start infringement proceedings against a Member State that fails to comply with its Treaty obligations. These proceedings have three stages:

- a letter of formal notice. This tells the Member state that the Commission thinks the Member State is in breach, and invites a formal response;

- a reasoned opinion from the Commission, taking into account the Member State's response;

- reference to the ECJ for a ruling on whether the Member State has infringed.

These proceedings are dealt with in greater detail in Chapter 5, below.

In its role as guardian of the treaties, the Commission dealt with 2,097 cases of infringement in 1993. Of those, 588 were settled through dialogue with the national authorities concerned: only 184 cases were presented to the court.

2.6 The European Court of Justice

It is for the Court of Justice of the European Community (ECJ), which sits in Luxembourg, to ensure that the laws of the Community are properly followed. Article 164 EEC provides:

'The Court of Justice shall ensure that in the interpretation and application of this Treaty the law is observed.'

| 2.6.1 | Composition and procedure |

The court consists of 16 judges (three new ones having been appointed by the new Member States in 1995) and six advocates general. The advocates general have no equivalents in the English legal system. The Treaty sets out their role in Article 166 EEC:

'It shall be the duty of the Advocate-General, acting with complete impartiality and independence, to make, in open court, reasoned submissions on cases brought before the Court of Justice, in order to assist the Court in the performance of the task assigned to it by Article 164.'

The judges and the advocates general are appointed by common accord of the governments of each Member State for six years. While the appointment may be renewed, it is also possible for judges (and advocates general) to be removed from office if they no longer fulfil the requirements for appointment (although this has never happened). There is some confusion about whether the expression 'advocate general' should be hyphenated or not. The treaties use the hyphen, while the court has not done so since 1982 (see Brown, Brown and Jacobs' *The Court of Justice* (2nd edition, 1983) p 54).

Candidates for appointment to either position must be either qualified for appointment to a judicial position in their own country, or be *jurisconsults* of recognised standing, which includes academic lawyers. In practice, though the Treaty does not require it, Member States have each nominated a judge, a thirteenth (needed to ensure the court cannot be 'hung') being drawn from the five larger Member States in turn. The four larger Member States each nominate an advocate general too, and the seven smaller Member States and Spain take turns in filling the other two positions.

The judges select one of their number to be president for a term of three years. The presidency can be renewed. The president directs the judicial business and the administration of the court, presiding at hearings and over the court's deliberations and appointing one of the judges to be judge-rapporteur for each case. The president can order that a measure being contested before the court be suspended and may prescribe any necessary interim measures.

The court is allowed by the Treaty to form chambers of three or five judges to hear individual cases. Early on, the majority of decisions was still rendered by the plenary court (which could be as few as seven judges), but as its work load grew, more and more cases have been heard by chambers. The problem of the court's work load has also been addressed by creating the Court of First Instance (CFI)

The court makes all its decisions by a single judgment, so there is no way to tell whether the court was unanimous or who, if anyone, was in either the minority or majority. Contentious judgments may however sometimes be recognised by their style and brevity.

2.6.2   Working methods

The judges deliberate in private, in French, and the judge-rapporteur will write the judgment of the court. This will be carefully worded to command the support of the majority of the judges, hence the give-away features which serve to identify difficult decisions.

Procedure in the CFI is dealt with in part in Council Decision (ECSC, EEC, Euratom) 88/591 (OJ [1988] L319/1), the Decision which established the CFI.

2.6.3	Precedent

The highest courts in Member States are not bound by their own decisions, and neither is the ECJ. Thus it was able to change its decision in Case 302/87 (the *Comitology* case) in Case 70/88 *European Parliament v EC Council* (1990), to bring Parliament within the scope of Article 173 EEC.

Note, however, that in Case 283/81 *CIlFIT v Italian Ministry of Health* (1982), the court decided that a national court from which there was no appeal did not have to refer a question of Community law to the ECJ under Article 177:

'... where previous decisions of the Court have already dealt with the point of law in question, irrespective of the nature of the proceedings which led to those decisions, even though the questions at issue are not strictly identical.'

National courts may therefore follow a ECJ decision or refer it to Luxembourg under Article 177 for a preliminary decision, hoping that the court will decide not to follow its earlier decision.

Whether the CFI is bound by decisions of the ECJ, and whether a chamber is bound by a decision of the plenary court, are issues which are presently unresolved.

2.6.4	The Court as policy-maker

The ECJ has been criticised for going beyond its interpretative role and straying into the field of policy-making. According to Rasmussen in *On Law and Policy in the European Court of Justice* (1986), it makes policy choices in three circumstances; where the legal provision under consideration gives the judges wide discretion; where the Treaty is silent on important points of law; and where it reaches a decision which appears to depart from the requirements of the text. These situations will now be examined in greater detail.

(a) Wide discretion

The wording of the Treaty might leave it to the court to give a precise meaning to the provision. This is the case, for example, with Articles 12 and 30, which respectively deal with charges and measures having equivalent effects to customs duties and quantitative restrictions on imports respectively. What effect is 'equivalent' is a policy matter for the court to determine.

(b) Silence in the Treaty

If the Treaty is silent on an important point of Community law, there is no alternative but for the court to decide what the law should be. The Treaty may give indications in the text about what the answer should be as in Case 6/64 *Costa v ENEL* (1964) in which the doctrine of supremacy of Community law was not expressly stated in the Treaty but developed by the ECJ. Indeed, the Treaty may provide even less guidance. In Case 213/89 *R v Secretary of State for Transport, ex parte Factortame* (1990), the ECJ had to consider whether national law had to be disapplied pending the determination of another matter before the court, which could establish rights for the applicants in the later case. There the court controversially applied the policy argument that the effectiveness of Community law demanded that the national law be disapplied.

(c) Departure from the text

The court will very occasionally depart from a literal interpretation of the wording of the Treaty, taking advantage of some fundamental principle such as the rule of law to justify its action. This was the case in Case 294/83 *Les Verts v European Parliament* (1986), where on the face of Article 173 EEC the court had no jurisdiction to review the legality of acts of Parliament. (The provision has since been amended.) Since the Community is based on the rule of law, the ECJ decided that neither Member States nor the institutions can escape review of the conformity of their acts with the Treaty. Parliament has been given broader powers since the wording of the original Article 173 had been settled, and must now be within the court's jurisdiction.

See also Case 70/88 *European Parliament v EC Council* (1990), discussed above, para 2.2.

In early 1995, the UK Government suggested that the Council should be able to overrule the ECJ. This idea has not been well-received.

The court may review infringements of Community law by Member States, under Article 169 (which allows the Commission to take action) Article 170 (which allows Member States to commence proceedings), and other provisions (dealt with in Chapter 5).

2.6.5   Jurisdiction

The jurisdiction of the ECJ is dealt with in detail later, but briefly it undertakes judicial review and Article 177 references.

(a) Judicial review

Judicial review of the acts of the Council and the Commission is provided for in the Treaty in three ways:

- Article 173 empowered the court to review the legality of all acts of the Council and the Commission, except recommendations and opinions. This power has since been extended.

- Article 175 allows Member States and institutions of the Community to bring infringement actions before the court, where the Council or the Commission has failed to act.

- Article 184 allows the legality of Regulations to be challenged, in limited circumstances.

(b) Article 177 references

If Community law is not clear, a national court may refer the matter to the European Court of Justice, and in some circumstances must do so. The right to refer questions extends to tribunals such as industrial tribunals and immigration tribunals. The ECJ can give a preliminary ruling on the interpretation of the Treaty or of acts of the institutions. It can also rule on the validity of these acts. A reference must be made where there is no judicial remedy against the decision of the tribunal or court. Article 177 is dealt with in detail in Chapter 6.

2.7 **Court of First Instance**	The Court of First Instance (CFI) was created under the SEA. Article 168a EEC gave the Council the power to create it, and it began to hear cases in November 1989. The aim was to reduce the backlog of cases pending before the ECJ, but the general increase in the volume of cases and the right of appeal from the CFI (see below) have together meant that the backlog is no smaller than before the CFI came into existence. Additionally, the CFI has processed a disappointingly small number of cases.

The CFI has 12 members, and it sits in Luxembourg alongside the ECJ. It has no separate advocates general, though any member of the court can be called upon to act as one. This will always happen where the CFI sits in plenary session. Chambers of the CFI may request that an advocate general be appointed in complex cases, but the appointment must be by a plenary session.

2.7.1 Jurisdiction	The CFI normally operates with five chambers of three or five judges:

- The third, fourth and fifth chambers consist of three or four judges and hear staff cases: the Treaty provides that employment matters involving staff of the institutions be decided by the ECJ, and it was partly to remove these from the workload of the main court that the CFI was created. The first and second chambers have six judges each, and hear competition cases brought against a Community institution by a natural or legal person.

- Each judge is a member of two chambers, and hears both staff and competition cases. The Treaty requires that other types of actions be heard and determined by the ECJ, so there was no possibility of the CFI being given jurisdiction over them. Jurisdiction over some other matters relating to dumping and subsidies could have been transferred, but the Council decided not to do so.

Under the Maastricht amendments to the Treaty, Article 168a was changed to permit the Council to transfer any area of the ECJ's jurisdiction, except Article 177 references, to the CFI.

The court may sit in plenary session for particularly difficult cases. The quorum for such a sitting, as with the ECJ, is seven.

Judges of the CFI do not have to be as highly qualified as ECJ judges but must be independent and 'possess the ability required for appointment to judicial office'. The president is elected by the members of the court for a renewable three-year term and discharges a function similar to that of the President of the ECJ.

2.7.2   Composition

There is an automatic right of appeal against a decision of the CFI to the ECJ on a point of law only (Article 51 Statute of the CFI). Appeals must be lodged within two months and may be made by institutions of the Community even though they were not parties to the original case. The ECJ may quash the decision of the CFI, and either give judgment itself or refer the case back to the CFI.

2.7.3   Appeal

Article 4 EC provides that:

'The Council and the Commission shall be assisted by an Economic and Social Committee acting in an advisory capacity, and Article 193 EEC established the Economic and Social Committee. Its role is to provide opinions on legislative proposals, and Community legislation often recites the fact that the Committee has been consulted.'

2.8   **Economic and Social Committee**

Article 193 goes on to say:

'The Economic and Social Committee shall consist of the various categories of economic and social activity, in particular, representatives of producers, farmers, carriers, workers, dealers, craftsmen, professional occupations and representatives of the general public.'

This suggests that it is seeking to be a microcosm of society rather than a committee of experts.

The constitution of the Committee is governed by Article 194. The number of members of the Committee is set out, with the number of members from each Member State depending on the size of that country. The UK, along with France, Germany and Italy, has 24 members. The members are appointed from lists of nominees provided by the Member States, by the Council acting unanimously. Members of the Committee are appointed for four years.

The Member States are required by Article 195 to nominate twice as many people as they are permitted members, to give the Council a choice. The Council must consult the Commission, and may also seek the opinion of the European bodies which represent the various sectors to which the activities of the Committee are of interest.

Article 194 stresses that the members of the Committee are there in a personal capacity, and may not be bound by 'any mandatory instructions'. They have to act 'in the general interest of the Community' (words added to Article 194 by the TEU) like Commissioners.

The chairman and other officers of the Committee are elected for two years. The Chairman has the job of convening meetings: Article 196 provides that this is to be at the request of the Council or the Commission, and TEU has added a right for the Committee to convene on its own initiative.

The Committee is required by Article 197 to have specialised sections for the principle fields covered by the Treaty, in particular sections covering agriculture and transport. These operate within the terms of reference of the Committee, and may not be consulted in their own right.

The Committee is also empowered to set up sub-committees to prepare draft opinions on specialist subjects or in specialised areas. However, they may not produce their own opinions: the drafts they prepare have to be submitted to the full Economic and Social Committee.

Consultation of the Economic and Social Committee is mandatory if the relevant Treaty article so provides. Articles 100 and 100a both require that the Committee be consulted on legislation.

The Committee also has the power to issue opinions on its own initiative. This it had been doing since 1974 but the TEU has now formally granted the right, making the status of the Committee identical to that of the Parliament where the Parliament has only to be consulted.

Article 198 states that the Council or the Commission may set a time limit on the deliberations of the Committee. This may not be less than a month (extended by the TEU from 10 days) from the time the Chairman receives the notification of the time limit. If an opinion has not been given at the expiry of that period, its absence will not prevent further action: otherwise, the lack of an opinion from the Economic and Social Committee would be an infringement of an essential procedural requirement which would make the legislation void.

Other consultative bodies exist within the Community. One important example is the Advisory Committee on Restrictive Practices and Dominant Positions which has to be consulted on decisions in the field of competition policy. This Advisory Committee was set up under Regulation 17/62, which established the procedures for the enforcement and administration of competition policy.

2.9   Consultative bodies

The Advisory Committee comprises competent officials from the governments of the Member States. Each Member State appoints one official: the UK member is from the Department of Trade and Industry. Its opinions are not made public.

The Committee of the Regions is a new advisory body, of equal status to the Economic and Social Committee, established by the TEU (Articles 198a to 198c). It provides opinions on issues which might have particular effect on regions of the Community.

2.10   Committee of the Regions

It consists of representatives of local and regional bodies in the Member States: this is not necessarily limited to local and regional government. Precisely who is appointed to it is a matter for the Member States.

The Committee must contain a number of alternate members equal to its primary membership. It operates in much the same way as the Economic and Social Committee, except that it is not empowered to set up specialised sections or sub-committees.

It has the right to be consulted on matters within its competence and (where it considers that there are significant regional interests at stake) may give opinions on its own initiative. It also has the right to be informed when the Economic and Social Committee is consulted.

The TEU specifies that the Committee must be consulted in matters of:

- education, vocational training and youth (Article 126);
- culture (Article 128);
- public health (Article 129);
- trans-European networks (Article 129d); and

- economic and social cohesion (Articles 130b, 130d and 130e).

2.11   EIB

Article 129 provides for the establishment of a European Investment Bank. Its task is to contribute to the 'balanced and steady development of the common market in the interests of the Community' (Article 130).

It may apply its own resources and have recourse to the capital market, and may grant loans and give guarantees which facilitate the financing of certain projects in all sectors of the economy. The EIB's own resources come from the Member States, which subscribe capital according to their size. It may also raise loans from the Member States where it can show that it cannot borrow the money on the capital market.

The projects with which it may assist are:

- projects for developing less-developed regions;

- projects for modernising or converting undertakings or for developing fresh activities called for by the progressive establishment of the common market, where these projects are of such a size or nature that they cannot be entirely financed by the various means available in the individual Member States;

- projects of common interest to several Member States which are of such a size or nature that they cannot be entirely financed by the various means available in the individual Member States.

The Bank is run by:

- a Board of Governors, who are Ministers in the Member States' governments;

- a Board of Directors, appointed by the Board of Governors for five years and consisting of 22 directors and 12 alternates (pre-1995 enlargement membership) drawn from the Member States according to their size (the UK has three); and

- a Management Committee, consisting of a President and six Vice-Presidents appointed for six-year terms by the Board of Governors on a proposal from the Board of Directors.

2.12   Court of Auditors

The Court of Auditors, established originally by separate treaty in 1977 (the Treaty Amending Certain Financial Provisions of 1975), is now included in the list of institutions of the Community in Article 4 EC by virtue of an amendment made by the TEU. Before then, the ECJ had held in Case 257/83, *Williams v Court of Auditors* (1984) that it was not to be considered an institution, which limited its accountability. It deals with issues relating to the Community budget. Article 206a EC provides:

> 'The Court of Auditors shall examine whether all revenue has been received and all expenditure incurred in a lawful and regular manner and whether the financial management has been sound.'

Its members are appointed by the Council, which acts unanimously after consulting with the Parliament. They are drawn from 'among persons who belong or have belonged in their respective countries to external audit bodies or who are especially qualified for this office' and hold office for six years. They act by majority decision.

Despite its name, it is an administrative rather than a judicial body. Its members act like auditors in the private sector, visiting the bodies whose books they must examine and also Member States to monitor the implementation of Community policy.

Article 206b provides for the Parliament to give a discharge to the Commission relating to the implementation of the budget. The Parliament acts on the recommendation of the Council, and both institutions will first examine the accounts and financial statement drawn up by the Commission and the Court of Auditors' report.

In carrying out its functions, the Court of Auditors looks for 'irregularities' (or fraud). In recent years it has been particularly busy investigating abuses of payments under the Common Agricultural policy.

Summary of Chapter 2

Institutions

The EC Treaty establishes four main institutions:

- the European Parliament;
- the Council;
- the Commission;
- the Court of Justice (and the Court of First Instance).

It also creates several minor institutions.

The Parliament comprises elected representatives from the Member States. The method of election is left for each of the Member States to decide on. It operates through Plenary Sessions and a structure of Committees, which prepare reports on matters within their competence for Debate in Plenary.

The Parliament's role is fourfold:

- Supervisory. It may censure the Commission, question the Council and the Commissioners, set up Committees of Inquiry, and take legal proceedings under Article 175 (Failure of the Council or Commission to act) or (in limited circumstances) Article 173.

- Legislative. The Parliament must be consulted on some proposed legislation, co-operates in the making of some legislation, assents to some measures and has limited powers of initiation. Differences over some measures may be resolved by a conciliation procedure.

- Budgetary. The Parliament has considerable control over 'non-compulsory' areas of the Community budget, less over compulsory areas.

- Accession and Association agreements. The Parliament has a veto over these.

The Council passes most of the important legislation of the Community. It consists of Ministers from the Member States, and meetings are chaired by the Minister attending from the country which holds the revolving Presidency. It makes decisions sometimes by a simple majority, more often by a qualified majority (which requires 67 votes out of the 86 distributed between the Member States) and sometimes

The Parliament

The Council

unanimously. The Treaty article dictates the majority required. The Committee of Permanent Representatives – the Member States' ambassadors to the EC – do much preparatory work on Council business.

The Heads of Government of the Member States meet in a body called the European Council, recognised for the first time by TEU.

The Commission

The Commission is the EC's civil service. In fact, the Commission proper consists of 20 nominated individuals, appointed by the Council after scrutiny by the Parliament, who are supported by the civil service. This is organised into a number of Directorates-General.

The Commission has a President, whose identity (and political agenda) is very important. President Delors stamped his views firmly on the Commission. There are also two Vice-Presidents.

The Commission reaches decision by majority voting, but once a vote has been taken it becomes the view of the entire collegiate body. Some decisions may be taken using a written procedure.

The Commission initiates most EC legislation. It may legislate itself in limited circumstances, usually where the Council has delegated power to it, but even then the Council retains much control.

The Commission also fulfils a major executive rôle within the Community, especially in the field of competition policy.

The Commission is the guardian of Community law. Article 169 empowers it to bring enforcement actions against Member States which have not complied with their obligations under the Treaty.

The Court

The European Court of Justice ensures that EC laws are properly followed. Its decisions are published as a single decision, so individual judges' views are not discernable.

The Court of First Instance was created to relieve the ECJ of some of its caseload of competition and staff cases. Appeals lie from the CFI to the ECJ on points of law.

The ECJ undertakes judicial review under Articles 173, 175 and 184, and Article 177 references.

Economic and Social Committee

The Economic and Social Committee advises the Council and the Commission, providing opinions on legislative proposals. Article 100 and 100a both make it mandatory to consult the Economic and Social Committee.

Chapter 3

Legislation

The nature of Community legislation is explained in Article 189 EEC:

> 'In order to carry out their task, the Council and the Commission shall, in accordance with the provisions of this Treaty, make regulations, issue directives, take decisions, make recommendations or deliver opinions.
>
> A *regulation* shall have general application. It shall be *binding in its entirety* and *directly applicable in all Member States*.
>
> A *directive* shall be binding, as to the *result* to be achieved, upon each Member State to which it is addressed, but shall leave to the national authorities the choice of form and methods.
>
> A *decision* shall be binding in its entirety upon those to whom it is addressed.
>
> *Recommendations* and *opinions* shall have no binding force.'

The Official Journal of the European Communities (OJ) publishes these different types of legislation. Article 191 EEC requires that Regulations are published this way: directives and decisions have to be notified to the persons to whom they are addressed, but many are published in the OJ.

Regulations come into force on the date specified, or 20 days after publication if no date is specified.

The ECSC uses a different nomenclature for its legislation. Article 14 ECSC gives powers to make *decisions* and *recommendations*. These are broadly the same as EEC regulations (in the case of an ECSC general decision) and decisions (in the case of an ECSC individual decision) and directives (ECSC recommendations).

The fact that regulations are *directly applicable* enables litigants to rely on them in the English courts and tribunals. There are exceptions to this general rule which are dealt with below.

Directly applicable Community laws may be used in two ways:

- as a *defence*, as in *Application des Gaz SA v Falks Veritas* (1975), though in that case the court held that a general plea that the plaintiff was abusing a dominant position (see Chapter 13, para 13.3) was insufficient; and

- as a weapon, to claim damages or an injunction. In *Garden Cottage Foods Ltd v Milk Marketing Board* (1984) the plaintiff sought an injunction. In *Bourgoin v Minister of Agriculture, Fisheries and Food* (1986) damages were claimed. However, the right to claim damages, particularly in an administrative law context, is not settled.

3.3   Directives

Community law is usually intended to be absorbed indirectly into national legal systems. Hence directives are the most commonly-encountered (though not the most numerous) form of Community legislation.

In the UK, Community law is implemented occasionally by statute (see, for example, the Consumer Protection Act 1987, Part I of which implements the directive on liability for defective products, and the Trade Marks Act 1994) and more usually by statutory instrument. (Italy, by contrast, passes an annual EC directive implementing acts dealing with all its obligations at once.)

More commonly, directives are implemented by statutory instrument. The relevant ministers were given power by the European Communities Act 1972, s 2(2), to make regulations to implement a Community obligation. This includes any such provision as may be made by Act of Parliament: for example, the Equal Pay Act 1970 was amended by statutory instrument to implement a directive (see below, para 3.6.7).

3.3.1   Failure to comply

Failure to comply with a directive may give rise to Article 169 proceedings (see Chapter 5) – indeed, such a failure is the commonest reason for Article 169 actions. In Case 363/85, *Commission v Italy* (1987) the court stated:

> 'The transposition of a directive into domestic law does not necessarily require that its provisions be incorporated formally and verbatim in express, specific legislation; a general legal context may, depending on the content of the directive, be adequate for the purpose provided that it does indeed guarantee the full application of the directive in a sufficiently clear and precise manner so that, where the directive is intended to create rights for individuals, the persons concerned can ascertain the full extent of their rights and, where appropriate, rely on them before the national courts.'

There, although the Italian legislation did not follow the wording of the directives (on feedstuffs) the court did not find that this would jeopardise the attainment of the results to be achieved by the directives. The application was therefore dismissed. UK legislation now tends to follow the wording of the directive (see, for example, the Trade Marks Act 1994), which raises problems of interpretation.

The interpretation of legislation is invariably an important matter, and in Community legislation the common lawyer encounters an unfamiliar world. It appears at first sight to be vague and open.

3.4   Meaning

This is a result of the approach taken by the drafter. It proceeds from the general to the particular. The preamble to a piece of Community legislation will state that it has regard to the Treaty establishing the European Community, and will specify a particular Article. In the case of a harmonising directive, this might be Article 100a: in the case of a block exemption regulation, Article 85(3).

This general statement is an important aid to interpretation, since it means that if there are gaps in the legislation the court will look to the Treaty provisions to determine what the instrument was about initially. If the purpose was harmonisation, that goal will be kept in mind.

There will follow a series of paragraphs making up the preamble, which is a further guide to the purpose of the legislation. Indeed, if there is a conflict between the preamble and the wording of the instrument itself it is the preamble which will prevail.

One way to look at a legal text is to consider the natural and ordinary meaning of the words. However, in the Community this poses some special problems.

3.4.1   Literal and historical interpretation

First, there is the fact that the Treaty is valid in 12 languages and most instruments made under it in 11. (Irish is not included since most Irish speakers also understand English, and thus it is not considered necessary to produce all the secondary legislation in an Irish edition, though the Treaty and some other important documents are available in official Irish versions.)

Translations by their very nature cannot be absolutely faithful: nuances in meaning cause differences to creep in. In Regulation 123/85 – the motor vehicle distribution block exemption – for example, the meaning of Article 5(2) in the English version is far from clear, partly because of the use of the words 'in so far as' at the beginning of the paragraph where the French version uses 'lorsque' and the German, 'sofern'. Had the English text used the word 'when' it would have made a great deal more sense. (The problem is compounded by the fact that the English version then goes on to cross-refer to Article 5(1), while in French and German the reference is to Article 4(1), which works far better.)

Such problems have given rise to cases in the ECJ. In Case 29/69, *Stauder v Ulm* (1969) the court followed the more liberal French and Italian texts, so that Stauder did not have to reveal his name to get cheap butter, which is what he objected to: the German and Dutch texts seemed to require this.

Where there are discrepancies, it will not necessarily be that the court will follow the majority of language versions. In Case 150/80 *Elefanten Schuh v Jacqmain* (1981) the court ignored the word 'solely' in all but two language versions of Article 18 of the Jurisdiction and Judgments Convention. To give the word 'solely' meaning in the provision would not have been in keeping with the objectives and spirit of the Convention, according to the court.

The open texture of EC legislation also makes a literal approach to interpretation of limited use. Definitions of key terms are often lacking: so, for example, even now it is far from clear what 'worker' means in Article 48 of the Treaty. And in Article 36, the reference to 'industrial and commercial property' is difficult to reconcile with the concept of intellectual property, which it is taken to include. Whether to include copyright in this category has (as we shall see) been a contentious matter.

Having several different language versions also means that it may be possible to find a literal meaning to support whatever solution is wanted. In Case 283/81 *CILFIT v Italian Ministry of Health* (1982) the court used this as a reason to warn national courts of a last resort to take care before deciding not to refer a case to Luxembourg under Article 177 (see Chapter 6).

| 3.4.2 | Preparatory documents |

Although the court can, and does, rely on grammatical and textual analysis, this technique will usually yield alternative constructions and it frequently needs something more.

The court will sometimes turn to published *travaux préparatoires*, preparatory documents which chart the progress of the legislation. In Case 6/60, *Humblet v Belgium* (1960) the court looked at the opinions of the Member States' governments expressed in parliamentary debates leading up to the ECSC Treaty: but that case is exceptional.

More likely is that the court will consult such documents as the original Commission draft of a piece of legislation, which is published in the Official Journal. The views of the European Parliament and the Economic and Social Committee will also appear in the OJ, and will be referenced in the final version of the instrument.

The court generally favours adopting a teleological, or purposive, approach to interpretation. This looks at the broad purpose or object of the text, and given the way Community law is written this is an entirely appropriate approach.

3.4.3   Contextual and teleological interpretation

Allied to this is a contextual approach which has regard to the whole scheme of the Treaty rather than just a single provision. The preamble and Articles 2 and 3 of the Treaty set out the objectives of the Community and are important aids to interpretation.

In Case 6/64, *Costa v ENEL* (1964), a key case on the supremacy of Community law, the contextual method was employed to consider Article 53 as part of the chapter of the Treaty on the right of establishment. Viewed in this light, it was clear that it could have a direct effect between the individual and the state.

In interpreting the Treaty and other Community legislation, the court will often look to fundamental principles of Community law expressed in the Treaties (for example, the four freedoms set out in the Treaty of Rome) to enable it to fill in any gaps. It will also go further, looking for principles common to the laws of the Member States.

3.4.4   General principles

These principles include:

- Equality

  The notion of equality embraces the principle that similar cases must not be treated differently, and the burdens imposed by the law must be borne equally. In Case 152/81 *Ferrario v Commission* (1983) Commission staff working in Italy complained that parents entitled to an expatriate allowance also received a greater education allowance than others. The court held that the scheme was objectively justified: expatriates were paid more because they usually sent their children back home to be educated.

- Legal certainty and non-retroactivity

  Legal certainty requires that the effect of a provision be clear and predictable. Persons who have to ensure their conduct is within the law – for example, the rules on competition – need to be able to know in advance what those rules will require of them.

  For example, in Case 43/75 *Defrenne v SA Belge de Navigation Aérienne SABENA* (1976), the plaintiff, an air hostess, showed that she was entitled to pay parity with male cabin staff. She could claim back pay: but the court avoided opening the floodgates by providing that the judgment would not have retroactive effect for others.

- Legitimate expectation

  Legitimate expectation is a kind of estoppel: it is related to the concept of legal certainty. Where the conduct of an institution has led someone to believe that a particular course will be followed, they may rely on that expectation. In Case 120/86, *Mulder v Minister van Landbouw en Visserij* (1988) a dairy farmer gave up production for a year, encouraged by a Council regulation designed to achieve this end. When he came to restart production he found that milk quotas had been introduced and he could not get one. The court held that he could legitimately expect not to be subject to restrictions when he resumed production, and it held that the milk quota regulation did not apply to him.

- Proportionality

  The concept of proportionality involves the notion that the means used to achieve an end should be no more than is appropriate and necessary. Article 85(3) embraces the idea: restrictive agreements are permitted if they deliver benefits which would not be realised without the restrictions, but the restrictions must go no further than is necessary to secure those benefits. Motor vehicle dealer agreements are permitted even though they restrict competition (by allocating exclusive territories and restricting dealers to one make of car) because they ensure that owners can get spare parts and specialist servicing: but the agreements may contain only very limited restrictions on where dealers can buy spare parts.

- Natural justice

  Natural justice is a concept known to common law. It involves the right to a hearing, the right to examine evidence, and the right to be legally represented. In Case 17/74, *Transocean Marine Paint Association v Commission* (1974), the Commission imposed onerous conditions in a competition case. The Commission never mentioned in the lengthy correspondence leading up to the imposition of the conditions that it was minded to do so. There was a failure of natural justice because the company had never had the opportunity to express their point of view.

- Respect for fundamental human rights

  The principle of respect for fundamental human rights is closely associated with natural justice. They include (but are not limited to) sexual equality, freedom of religion and the right to a fair hearing.

Community legislation is made in different ways according to the type of instrument. Here we describe the process for making directives, which were originally adopted under the consultation procedure. Following the introduction of the Single European Act a co-operation procedure came into existence, giving the Parliament an enhanced role: and subsequently the Maastricht amendments have made further changes. These are explained in detail below, and a flow-chart showing the process will be found in the Appendix.

3.5   Making Community laws

The procedure originally used for passing directives gave the Parliament a purely consultative rôle.

3.5.1   The consultation procedure

• Compulsory consultation

The EEC Treaty originally required consultation with the parliament over legislation in a variety of areas. The SEA added to this list and further additions and changes were made at Maastricht.

Additionally, the Council cannot conclude international agreements without first consulting the Parliament, except for agreements concerning the Common Commercial Policy.

• Failure to consult

If Parliament is not consulted where it should be, that is an infringement of an essential procedural requirement. The Court of Justice would be able to declare the measure void under Article 173: see, for example, Case 139/79 *Roquette Frères v Council* (1980).

• Optional consultation

The Parliament's opinion is often given on legislative proposals from the Commission even where this is not required. This applies to measures passed under Articles 113 and 213 (relating to the Common Commercial Policy and the collection of information respectively). It also applies where the Commission adopts legislation under powers delegated by the Council: for example, block exemption regulations under Article 85(3) may be adopted by the Commission, since Council Regulation 19/65 delegates the power to do so: the EP has no right to be consulted on proposed regulations but will often express an opinion.

Failure to consult the EP where it was not compulsory would not automatically make the measure voidable. However, it is arguable that if a practice had developed of consulting the Parliament about measures of the same type, the ECJ might be prepared to declare it void.

- Reconsultation

  Where the Council or Commission substantially modifies a proposal, the EP may ask to be reconsulted. This will also apply where there has been a significant change in circumstances since Parliament gave its opinion.

  Unless the changes are as Parliament wanted, are purely technical, or leave the essential aspects of the most extensive provisions unaltered, the Council will be *obliged* to reconsult the EP. (See Case 41/69 ACF *Chemfarmie v Commission* (1970); Case 817/79, *Buyl v Commission* (1982); Case C-331/88, *R v Minister of Agriculture, Fisheries and Food and Secretary of State for Health, ex parte FEDESA and others* (1990)).

3.5.2   Co-operation

The co-operation procedure gives Parliament much greater say in the legislative process. It was introduced by SEA, in Article 149 EEC.

It applied to a number of provisions important for the single market, in particular the new Article 100a on legislation for the approximation of laws.

The Maastricht amendments moved the provision on cooperation procedure to Article 189c, and provided that in most of the cases where it applied under SEA, the new conciliation and veto provision would apply instead.

At the same time, more provisions which had formerly required consultation were changed to require co-operation. These included proposals for implementing the Common Transport Policy, implementing decisions relating to the European Social Fund, and Community action on environmental policy. Also, as we have already seen, measures on vocational training became subject to the cooperation procedure where formerly there had been no requirement even for the Council to consult the EP.

Some new areas of community competence introduced at Maastricht also employ the co-operation procedure.

- Procedure

  The cooperation procedure begins in the same way as the consultation procedure. The Commission makes a proposal to the Council, which sends it for its first reading to the EP (and to ECOSOC). Parliament gives its opinion, for which there is at this stage no time limit, then the Council adopts a common position.

  In doing so, the Council acts by qualified majority: but it may only amend the Commission's proposal unanimously. The Common position (with the Council's explanation for its reasons) then goes back to the Parliament.

At this second reading stage, Parliament has three months to act.

- If it fails to do so, or if it approves the common position, the Council must adopt the measure on that basis.

- If it rejects the common position, by an absolute majority of its members (not just those voting), the Council may only proceed to adopt the measure unanimously. Council has three months to do so.

- If it amends the common position within the three month period, the proposal is referred back to the Commission. Amendments must be passed by an absolute majority of MEPs and may only be tabled by committees, political groups or 23 MEPs.

The only amendments which the Parliament will accept are those which either seek to restore the Parliament's first reading position, or represent a compromise between the Council and the EP.

If the Parliament amends the proposal the Commission has one month in which to re-examine the proposal. It has to take the Parliament's amendments into account, although it is not obliged to accept them: if it rejects them, however, it must send them to the Council with its comments.

The Council may then, by qualified majority, adopt the Commission's re-amended proposal within three months. If it wishes to amend the Commission's re-examined proposals, or to adopt any of the EP's amendments which the Commission did not take up, it may only do so unanimously.

If the Council does not adopt the proposal within three months of receiving it back from the Commission, it is deemed to be adopted. The same applies if the Council fails to adopt a measure within three months after the EP rejects a common position. The significance of this lies in the fact that, until the measure is adopted, the Commission may alter the proposal.

This provision, added at Maastricht, further strengthens the role of the Parliament in certain areas.

3.5.3   Article 189b EEC

At second reading (the initial stages being the same as under the co-operation procedure), if the EP accepts the common position or takes no decision within three months, the Council may adopt the measure. If, however, the EP intends to reject the measure, or proposes amendments, different provisions come into operation.

- Rejection of the common position

  Parliament must inform the Council if it rejects the common position, and the Council may agree to a meeting of the conciliation committee (see Chapter 2, para 2.2.7). Whether or not the Council agrees, the EP may, by an absolute majority, reject the common position or proposed amendments. If Parliament rejects the common position, it is deemed not to have been adopted: for the first time Parliament has a veto. This power was used for the first time in March 1995, to reject the proposed biotechnology patents directive.

- Amendment of the common position

Proposed amendments to the common position are forwarded to the Commission for its opinion and then to the Council. The Council may adopt the measure, with Parliament's amendments, within three months.

The majority required in Council is:

(a)   a qualified majority for amendments on which the Commission has not given a negative opinion;

(b)   unanimity for amendments on which the Commission has expressed a negative opinion.

If the Council does not adopt all of the Parliament's amendments, the President of the Council must convene a meeting of the Conciliation committee, in agreement with the President of the EP.

The majority required on the Consultation Committee is designed to maintain the balance between the institutions. It must consist of a qualified majority of Council members (or their representatives) and a majority of the Parliament's representatives (who will be equal in number to the Council Members).

If the committee approves a joint text within six weeks, Council and the EP have a further six weeks in which to approve it by qualified and absolute majority respectively. If either of them does not do so, the measure is deemed not to have been adopted. Again, the EP is given a veto.

If the conciliation committee fails to approve a joint text within six weeks, the Council may within six weeks confirm its original decision (acting by qualified majority) or the measure is deemed not to have been adopted.

3.6   Direct effect

Community law confers rights on individuals, and some provisions of Community law are directly applicable. This means that Community legislation is more readily enforceable than if the only way to oblige Member States to have regard to it was by actions under Article 169 or Article 171.

The national courts in the Member States are obliged to protect these individual rights. There is no need for implementing legislation. But for this to happen, the relevant law has to be in a form which the national courts can handle: it must be *justiciable*. The cases show what the Court of Justice believes should be present in a Community measure before the national courts will be obliged to uphold it.

The concept of direct effect of the provisions of the Treaty was developed by the ECJ in Case 26/62, *van Gend en Loos v Nederlandse Administratie der Belastingen* (1963). The court held that provided it is:

3.6.1   Direct effect of treaty provisions

* *unconditional* and unqualified; and

* *sufficiently precise* and clear,

a Treaty article may be invoked directly in the national courts, overriding conflicting national laws. The latter requirement will not be satisfied if it leaves substantial discretion to the Member States.

* Unconditional

   The first of these requirements will not be met if the right the measure grants depends on the *judgment or discretion* of an independent body. It is explored in the court's decision in Case 10/71, *Ministère Publique Luxembourg v Muller* (1971). This concerned the effect of Article 90(2), which states:

   'Undertakings entrusted with the operation of services of general economic interest or having the character of a revenue-producing monopoly shall be subject to the rules contained in this Treaty, in particular to the rules on competition, *in so far as the application of such rules does not obstruct the performance, in law or in fact, of the particular tasks assigned to them. The development of trade must not be affected to such an extent as would be contrary to the interests of the Community.'* [Emphasis added.]

   The court decided that the two conditions imposed by Article 90(3) were vague and could not be applied to a particular case without guidance from implementing measures. The Council would have to make secondary legislation to give substance to them before the Article could be considered unconditional and the courts could be expected to apply them.

   A provision may still be considered unconditional if an independent body has discretion over it, but that discretion is subject to judicial control (Case 41/74, *van Duyn v Home Office* (1974)).

- Sufficiently precise

  The provision of Community law must give the national court a clear indication of what it requires. The court considered this in Case 43/75, *Defrenne v SABENA* (1976). The case concerned Article 119, which requires men and women to receive equal pay for equal work (on which, see further Chapter 14, para 14.7).

  The Treaty prohibits both direct, overt discrimination and indirect, covert discrimination. However, the court distinguished the two: the first is precisely formulated, enabling courts to recognise it when they see it, but the other is more subtle and not so readily identified. Implementing legislation was required before the national courts could apply the prohibition of indirect discrimination directly.

3.6.2 Regulations

Regulations are directly applicable under Article 189. They automatically become part of national law without the need for implementation. They may, however, fail the 'sufficiently precise' and 'unconditional' tests. Direct applicability is not the same thing as direct effect.

Some regulations may require institutions to take steps to implement them. This is true, for example, of Regulation 19/65, which delegates to the Commission the power necessary to enforce and operate the competition rules.

Where a regulation is directly effective, the court has held that national legislatures must not pass implementing legislation (Case 34/73, *Variola v Amministrazione Italiana delle Finanze* (1973)). If national implementing legislation is needed, it must be consistent with the meaning of the regulation.

3.6.3 Directives

In the 1970s the principle of direct effect was extended to cover directives too. This happened in a series of cases starting with *van Duyn* and leading up to Case 148/78, *Publico Ministero v Ratti* (1979).

The importance of this development is that directives have to be implemented in national law: if the Member State is tardy or delinquent about doing so, it could deprive people of their rights. As the court stated in *Ratti*:

> '... a Member State which has not adopted the implementing measures required by the Directive in the prescribed periods may not rely, as against individuals, on its own failure to perform the obligations which the Directive entails.'

The application of the doctrine to directives raises an important new issue: does a measure have *horizontal* direct effect (against other individuals) as well as *vertical* direct effect (against the state)? This distinction is explored below.

It is also necessary to consider the right of the person who is supposed to enjoy rights under Community law to claim damages for the Member State's failure to implement a directive properly, and the role of directives in the interpretation of national implementing legislation.

The conditions under which a directive can have direct effect are:

3.6.4 When is a directive directly effective?

- the directive has not (or has not properly) been implemented and the time limit for implementation has passed;

- the provision is clear and precise; and

- the provision relied on is unconditional.

Article 189 provides that directives must be implemented in Member States' national laws. Thus, the principle of direct effect can only benefit an individual against the state, ie vertically rather than horizontally against individuals or corporations.

The reasons for giving directives direct effect are rooted in the notion that the state may not benefit from its failure to act. This does not support the principle that directives might be invoked against individuals.

3.6.5 Vertical v horizontal direct effect

In Case 152/84 *Marshall v Southampton and South West Hampshire Area Health Authority (Teaching)* (1986) the court ruled out the possibility of horizontal direct effect. It ruled that 'a directive may not of itself impose obligations on individuals' because:

- by the clear terms of Article 189 of the Treaty, directives are stated to be addressed to and binding on Member States only; and

- the true juridical basis for the direct effect of directives is the estoppel principle ie the notion that an individual may rely on a directive, as a 'sword' or a 'shield', where the Member State has failed on its treaty obligations to implement the directive accurately and within the time limit set out in the directive.

This rules out the possibility of an individual having any direct obligation under a directive. If directives were given horizontal direct effect, the distinction drawn in Article 189 between directives and regulations would be meaningless. Moreover, national judiciaries which were already expressing discomfort with the way the court was developing the doctrine of direct effect would be further alienated.

Member States' courts may, however, still be bound to interpret national law so that it reflects the terms of a relevant directive (see below, para 3.6.7).

| 3.6.6 | Against whom can directives be invoked? |

The notion of direct effect raises at least one problem: identifying the state. Clearly, national governments are included, but if this was the end of the matter, the value of direct effect would be very limited.

The *Marshall* case concerned a health authority's policy requiring female employees to retire at the age of 60 while male employees could stay on to 65. The plaintiff complained that this was contrary to Article 5(1) of Directive 76/207/EEC, which provides that men and women should be guaranteed the same conditions governing dismissal. The directive had not, however, been implemented by the UK within the relevant time limit.

The Court of Appeal had described the defendant in the case as 'an emanation of the state', which permitted the European Court to dispose of the problem of whether the terms of a directive should be invoked against it. Similarly, in Case 222/84, *Johnston v Chief Constable of the Royal Ulster Constabulary* (1986), the European Court held that the Chief Constable of the RUC was bound by the Equal Treatment Directive even though he was not strictly speaking a branch of the government.

Subsequently, the expression 'Member State' has received a more flexible interpretation. After a string of cases in which the courts wrestled with the problem, and the additional difficulty that UK law contains no satisfactory definition of the state, the Court of Appeal obtained a ruling from the European Court which puts the matter beyond doubt. In Case 188/89, *Foster v British Gas* (1990) the court held that it embraces any body which provides a public service, whether in the public or the private sector.

Foster indicates that the court considers mere control to suffice. It also indicates that the court considers that there is an alternative criterion, covering bodies not actually under state control but responsible under a measure adopted by the state for providing a public service under the state's control. On the basis of the court's answer to the questions referred to it, the House of Lords held that British Gas *prior to privatisation* met the relevant tests.

A directive cannot, however, be invoked against a body under the control of the state in terms merely of ownership.

The Court of Appeal held in *Doughty v Rolls-Royce plc* (1992) that the power of control was only one of a series of cumulative criteria.

These cases also provide guidance on the vertical direct effect of directives. An individual may rely on a directive to sue the state or to defend proceedings brought by the state. The state cannot, however, invoke a directive to impose obligations on an individual, at least where the directive has not been implemented into national law.

In Case 14/86, *Pretore di Salo v Persons Unknown* (1989) and Case 80/86, *Officier van Justitie v Kolpinghuis Nijmegen BV* (1989) the authorities were trying to use directives to impose criminal liability on individuals.

In the *Kolpinghuis Nijmegen* case a trader was prosecuted for stocking adulterated mineral water, contrary to Dutch law and Directive 80/777/EEC. The directive had not at the relevant time been implemented in Dutch law, and the court ruled that it could not of itself establish criminal liability (or, for that matter, introduce a civil penalty such as nullity) against an individual.

The European Court may have had in mind the importance of legal certainty in criminal proceedings: if there is no national implementation of the directive, and no obligation on the Commission to publish the directive in the Official Journal (where, naturally, it would come to the attention of the criminal classes) it is not easy for an individual to ascertain their legal position under a directive.

Where the proceedings concern civil law, however, the position may differ. Nevertheless, allowing Member States to rely on the terms of unimplemented directives even in civil proceedings would conflict with the doctrine of estoppel.

In Case 91/92, *Paula Faccini Dori v Recreb Srl* (1994) the court confirmed the basic principles concerning national courts' enforcement of Community law. It refused to extend the principle to situations involving two private parties, since that would mean that the Community had power to create immediate obligations for legal and natural persons by means of directives. That power could only exist where the Treaty gave the institutions the power to adopt directives.

By Article 5, Member States are required to take all appropriate measures, whether general or particular, to ensure the fulfilment of the obligations arising out of the Treaty or resulting from actions taken by the institutions of the Community. They shall facilitate the achievement of the Community's tasks.

3.6.7   Interpretation

Member States must abstain from any measure which could jeopardise the attainment of the objectives of the Treaty.

The obligation applies to the authorities of the Member States including national courts.

- The *von Colson – Harz* doctrine

  In Case 14/83 *von Colson and Kamman v Land Nordrhein Westfalen* (1984) and Case 79/83 *Harz* (1984) the ECJ held that the national courts must interpret their national laws in the light of any relevant directives. This subtle approach achieves the same result as horizontal direct effect without the need for national courts to embrace that unwelcome doctrine.

  The doctrine is based on Article 5 of the EC Treaty, which places a duty on all the authorities of a Member State to:

  '... take all appropriate measures, whether general or particular, to ensure fulfilment of the obligation arising out of the Treaty or resulting from action taken by the institutions of the Community.'

  It is subject, the court said, to the proviso that the doctrine can apply only insofar as the national authority in question is given discretion to do so under national law. And there is an overriding requirement that the principles of legal certainty and non-retroactivity are respected (see para 3.4.4).

- The doctrine in the UK courts

  However, the UK courts have put up stiff opposition to this notion. Although s 2(4) of the European Communities Act 1972 requires the courts to give precedence to Community law to construe domestic law to comply with it.

  In *McCarthys Ltd v Smith* (1979) Lord Denning considered that where an oversight resulted in an inconsistency, '... then it is our bounden duty to give effect to Community law'. In *Garland v British Rail Engineering Ltd* (1983) Lord Diplock implied that the courts should strive to achieve such a result, 'however wide a departure from the prima facie meaning of the language might be needed in order to achieve consistency'. Both acknowledged that where there was a deliberate inconsistency, domestic law would prevail.

  In *Pickstone v Freemans plc* (1989) the respondents claimed that their work was of equal value to that of other employees. The complication was that there was a man doing the same work as the respondents, and it was not clear from the legislation whether this precluded the respondents from claiming equal pay with the comparators.

The relevant law was contained in the Equal Pay Act 1970, as amended by the Sex Discrimination Act 1975 and by the Equal Pay (Amendment) Regulations 1983. The Regulations arose from the European Court decision in Case 61/81 *Equal Pay for Equal Work: Commission v United Kingdom* (1982). They amended s 1(2)(c) of the 1970 Act to modify any term in a woman's contract of employment that was less favourable than a term of a similar kind in the contract of a man:

'... where a woman is employed on work which ... is, in terms of the demands made on her (for instance under such headings as effort, skill and decision), of equal value to that of a man in the same employment.'

The House of Lords could have construed the provision literally and concluded that the regulations were in breach of the UK's obligations under Article 119 and the relevant directive (the Equal Pay Directive, Directive 75/117/EEC). But, since the amendment had been made by regulations, their Lordships were able to refer to Hansard to ascertain the terms in which they were introduced into Parliament. With their readiness to read certain words into the provision, their Lordships were able to find that the regulations had been introduced to give full effect to the relevant Community law. The comparison was valid, notwithstanding the employment of a man in the same position as the women.

This *purposive* approach to construing domestic legislation was also adopted in *Litster v Forth Dry Dock & Engineering Co Ltd (in receivership)* (1990). This case involved a claim based on Directive 77/187, the 'acquired rights' directive which is intended to protect the rights of employees when their employer is taken over. The directive was implemented in the UK in the Transfer of Undertakings (Protection of Employment) Regulations 1981 (known as the TUPE regulations).

The House of Lords (similarly constituted to the judicial committee which heard the *Pickstone* case) decided that the regulations should be read in such a way as to comply with the *von Colson* decision, '... even though, perhaps, it may involve some departure from the strict and literal application of the words which the legislature has elected to use' (*per* Lord Oliver).

However, the House of Lords has also set a limit to the application of this rule. In *Duke v GEC Reliance Ltd* (1988) it held that the *von Colson – Harz* principle applies only to national legislation enacted specifically to implement the directive in question. In that case, s 6(4) of the Sex Discrimination Act 1975 could not be interpreted in the light of the Equal Treatment Directive (see Chapter 14, para 14.9) since it was not enacted for that purpose. Their Lordships held that the doctrine was (*per* Lord Templeman):

'... no authority for the proposition that a Court of a Member State must distort the meaning of domestic statute so as to conform with community law which is not directly applicable.'

The court also held that the doctrine could only apply if the directive is directly effective. Both parties were private individuals, so the directive was not directly effective and their Lordships would not manipulate the 1975 Act to make it conform (*per* Lord Templeman).

The ECJ in *Marshall* and in *Johnston* applied no such qualifications to the doctrine of direct effect. The House of Lords in *Duke* is therefore at odds with the European Court.

- *Marleasing*

  In Case C-106/89 *Marleasing SA v La Comercial Internacional de Alimentacion SA* (1992) the narrow directive was held to be applicable in place of the wider national law. This goes some way towards mitigating the effect of the House of Lords' judgment in *Duke*.

  The case concerned a Spanish company allegedly formed to defraud the creditors of one of its founders. Marleasing (one of the creditors) argued that the formation of the company was a nullity: it amounted to a contract without cause and was void under the Spanish civil code. The defendant relied on Article 11 of Directive 68/151 which did not include this as one of the grounds for a declaration of nullity.

  Spain should have implemented the directive at the time of its accession, but had not done so by the time the matter came before the Spanish court. The matter was referred to the ECJ under Article 177.

  Advocate General van Gerven decided that the list of grounds for nullity of a company in the directive was exhaustive. He also considered that the provision was unconditional and sufficiently precise so that it could be directly applicable. However, both the Advocate General and the court, referring with approval to the *von Colson* decision and recognising that the provisions of a directive do not have direct effect between individuals, held that:

'... it is the national provisions themselves which, interpreted in a manner consistent with the Directive, have direct effect.'

In Case C-322/88 *Grimaldi* (1991) the European Court held that national courts were bound to consider non-binding recommendations when interpreting the provisions of national law. The Advocate General applied this reasoning by analogy in the Marleasing case and the court held:

'... that, in applying national law, whether the provisions in question were adopted before or after the directive, the national court called upon to interpret it is required to do so, so far as possible, in the light of the wording and the purpose of the Directive in order to achieve the result pursued by the latter and thereby comply with the third paragraph of Art 189 EEC.'

The court clearly stated that EC law should take precedence over national law, whether it predated the directive or not. National courts should not, as far as possible, reach a result contrary to that intended by the directive.

This may apply even if the implementation date has not yet passed (*von Colson*).

The Court of Appeal has questioned the *Marleasing* approach. In *Webb v EMO* (1992) it held that the British courts should not distort the meaning of a statute to give effect to a directive having no effect between individuals (Glidewell LJ). But the House of Lords held that the national court must construe national law in accordance with the terms of the directive only if it is possible to do so.

The outcome is unclear, but it probably means that the court's first duty is to seek to reconcile the texts even where it would normally prefer an interpretation which makes the two inconsistent.

The third matter to be considered is the liability of the state for damages if it fails properly to implement a directive. This possibility, which greatly increases pressure on Member States to act in a timely fashion, was first explored by the court in Joined Cases 6/90 and 9/90, *Francovich and others v Italian Republic* (1993).

3.6.8   State liability

- *Francovich*

    In *Francovich* the Member State was held liable for damages to individual plaintiffs for failing to implement a directive. This applies *irrespective of direct effect*.

The ECJ held that where:

- the objective sought by the directive included the creation of rights for individuals;
- the scope of those rights was identifiable from the terms of the directive;
- there was a causal link between the damage suffered and the state's failure to fulfil its obligations,

Community law conferred on individuals the right to obtain compensation from the state.

The case concerned Directive 80/987, which provides that Member States must establish institutions to guarantee payment of employees' outstanding claims in the event of their employer becoming insolvent. The directive had to be implemented by 31 October 1983, and in Case 22/87, *Commission v Italy* (1989) the ECJ held that Italy had failed to comply with that obligation.

Mr Francovich was not paid his full salary by his employer. He brought proceedings claiming 6 million lire from his employer, and when he was unable to satisfy his claim he brought proceedings against the Republic claiming either the payment to which he was entitled under the Directive or damages.

The European Court held that the Directive as a whole was not sufficiently precise and unconditional for him to be able to rely on it. It did not identify the institution responsible for making the payment, though in other respects it appeared to satisfy the requirements. The state could not be regarded as the relevant institution simply because it had not implemented the directive in time. There was therefore no directly effective right to payment.

However, the court held that the full effectiveness of Community rules would be jeopardised if individuals could not obtain compensation for loss suffered as a result of breaches of Community law by Member States. The principle of state liability is inherent in the Treaty, particularly Article 5.

Further, the court held that it was particularly important to provide for claims for compensation where the full effectiveness of the Community rules depended on the action of a Member State. Absent any right to claim compensation, individuals would not be able to enforce the rights given them by the Community legislation before the national courts.

- Individual protection post-*Francovich*

  The court has subsequently received Article 177 references arising from cases where national laws were wrongfully enforced regardless of higher-ranking Community rights. In one instance, plaintiffs are claiming damages in the High Court in England following the *Factortame* decision: in another, Case 46/93, *Brasserie du Pêcheur v Germany* (see (1994) 11 Student Law Review p 33) a French brewery is claiming damages for loss suffered when exports of its products were stopped under the Reinhetsgebot, the German beer purity law considered by the court in Case 178/84, *Commission v Germany* (1987). These cases mark a significant extension of the principle of state liability laid down in *Francovich*.

- What compensation is available?

  The compensation which may be available depends on the nature of the infringement of Community law. The court held that where the infringement comprises the failure to implement a directive, the following conditions would apply:

  - the result to be achieved by the Directive must involve rights conferred on individuals;
  - the content of those rights must be identified on the basis of the Directive;
  - there must be a causal link between the Member State's failure to implement the Directive and the damage suffered by the persons affected.

  The laws of the Member State concerned will specify which courts are competent to hear claims, and will regulate the procedure: but they may not impose conditions which make it harder to bring such claims than claims founded on the domestic law of the Member State (Case 199/82 *San Georgio*, (1983).

  In the present case, these features were present and the court held that the national court had to ensure the rights of the employees to compensation for non-implementation of the Directive.

The *Francovich* decision is particularly important in horizontal direct effect cases. In *Duke*, for example, the plaintiff could have been enabled to sue the government for compensation for its failure to implement the Directive: it had already been held in Marshall that the terms of the Equal Treatment Directive made it directly effective.

3.6.9   **The significance of** *Francovich*

Moreover, the *Francovich* judgment goes much further than merely establishing a right to damages where a Member State fails to implement a directive properly. It lays down a general principle of Community law that Member States are required to make good any damage caused to individuals by infringements of Community law for which they (the Member States) are responsible.

In *Bourgoin v MAFF* (1967) the Ministry of Agriculture, Fisheries and Food imposed an effective import ban on turkeys from France. The court held the ban contrary to Article 30 and French producers sued the Ministry for their losses.

The Court of Appeal held (by a majority) that a breach of Article 30 would in English law afford a right to a judicial review and a declaration of invalidity, but not a claim for damages. Such a claim would lie (if at all) only under the heading of the tort of misfeasance.

This may be within the powers of the national courts laid down in *Francovich* to set the conditions of substance, form and procedure according to which damages may be obtained. Arguably, it does not deny the existence of the right to claim damages against the state.

3.6.10   Decisions

Community decisions also have direct effect (Case 9/70, *Grad v Finanzamt Traunstein* (1970)). The basis for this ruling is much the same as that for directives: if someone to whom a decision is addressed fails to comply with it, other people affected by it should be able to rely on its binding nature and enforce it against the person who has failed to act.

It seems that decisions addressed to Member States will not, however, create individual rights (Case 175/84, *Bulk Oil v Sun International* (1986)). Otherwise, an individual seems able to invoke a decision against a person to whom the decision is addressed, provided it is unconditional and sufficiently precise and that any time limit for complying with it has expired.

Legislation

The primary legislation of the Community is contained in the Treaties establishing the Community and treaties made by the Community with other countries.

Primary legislation

Secondary legislation of the Community comprises:

Secondary legislation

- Regulations, which are generally applicable, binding in their entirety and directly applicable.

- Directives, which bind the Member States to achieve the specified ends but leave them to determine the means.

- Decisions, binding in their entirety on their addresses.

- Recommendations and opinions of no binding force.

In addition there is also a category of tertiary legislation comprising acts adopted by Ministers in Council, the caselaw of the ECJ, general principles of law (such as the principles of proportionality and alternative means), and principles of public international law. Laws which are directly applicable may be used in national courts, either as the basis of a claim or as a defence.

Directives are intended to be implemented by national legislation. It does not have to be transposed word for word (Case 363/85, *Commission v Italy*). Failure to comply by the due date is a breach by the Member States of its obligations.

Directives

Interpretation of directives is difficult for common lawyers. The style is open, and the preamble is an important aid to construction. Reference to the Treaty article under which secondary legislation is made is also important, as this indicates the purpose of the law.

The existence of 11 different language versions gives further scope for problems (Case 29/69, *Stander v Ulm*). In Case 283/81, *CILFIT v Italian Ministry of Health*, the Court of Justice stressed that this required national courts to consider carefully before deciding not to make a reference for a preliminary ruling under Article 177.

General principles of law – elements of tertiary Community law – will also be applied. These include equality, legal certainty, legitimate expectation, proportionality, natural justice, and respect of human rights.

Directives are made by three methods:

- Consultation. Parliament must be consulted on a variety of different types of legislation, including directives. Its views carry no formal weight. If the Council or the Commission substantially modifies a proposal, it may ask to be reconsulted, or in some cases reconsultation may be required.

- Co-operation. This procedure gives the Parliament a second reading, and applied most importantly to single market legislation (though the Maastricht Treaty has changes this). Parliament gives its opinion on the original proposal, and the Council then adopts a common position. Parliament then has a second reading, which must be completed within three months, and may approve, reject or amend the common position.

- Conciliation and veto. This new procedure, introduced by TEU, changes the procedure if Parliament rejects or amends the common position on second reading. The Council may agree to a meeting of the conciliation committee to resolve differences: but Parliament may reject the common position or amendments, giving it a veto.

Direct applicability

Some provisions of Community law are directly applicable, conferring enforceable rights on individuals and legal persons. National counts must protect these rights without any need for implementing legislation. In Case 26/62, *Van Gend en Loos*, the Court laid down the conditions for a Treaty article to be directly applicable: it must be:

- unconditional and unqualified;

- sufficiently precise and clear.

Otherwise, the national courts will require something further, such as Community secondary legislation or national implementing legislation, to assist them.

Regulations are automatically directly applicable. Directives, though intended to be implemented by national legislation, may have direct effect: Case 41/74, *van Duyn v Home Office* if a Member State fails to comply with its obligations under a directive individuals may be deprived of rights. A directive (or a provision in a directive) may have direct effect if:

- it has not (or has not properly) been implemented with the time limit);

- it is clear and precise;

- it is unconditional.

Direct effect may be horizontal or vertical. Vertical direct effect means effective against the state, which cannot be allowed to benefit from its failure to implement the directive. Horizontal direct effect would enable individuals to invoke the directive against other individuals, which is normally not permitted (Case 152/84, *Marshall*).

However, in *Marshall* the Court decided that the defendant health authority was an 'emanation of the State' and a directive was directly effective against it. The same principle was applied to a Chief Constable (Case 222/84 *Johnston*) and in Case 188/89, *Foster v British Gas*, the Court held that any body which provides a public service, whether in the public or the private sector, could constitute an emanation of the state.

A private party may not, however, rely on the terms of an unimplemented directive against another (Case 91/92, *Dori*).

EC legislation also affects the interpretation of national law. The Court has held that national courts must interpret national laws in the light of relevant directives (Case 14/83, von *Colson* and Case 79/83, *Harz*). This achieves horizontal direct affect.

UK courts have been reluctant to accept this notion: see *McCarthys v Smith* (1979), *Garland v British Engineering* (1983) and *Pickstone v Freemans* (1989), where the House of Lords adopted a purposive construction of the UK regulations. In *Litster* the House of Lords decided that it must read the Regulations in the light of the directive, notwithstanding that this might lead to a departure from the strict words use by Parliament. However, this approach is only adopted where the UK legislation is adopted to comply with a directive (*Duke v GEC Reliance*). The ECJ has modified this approach somewhat in Case 106/89, *Marleasing*, where it upheld the narrow directive and ruled that the national legislation was unlawful.

If the state fails to implement a directive, it may be liable in damages: Joined Cases 6/90 and 9/90, *Francovich*. There, irrespective of direct effect, a directive which was designed to confer rights on individuals, the scope of which was identifiable from the directive, allowed the individual to claim damages from the state where there was a causal link between the damage and the state's failure to meet its obligations.

Horizontal and vertical direct effect

Sabena = horizontal

Supremacy of EC law

Damages for non-implementation

Chapter 4

Actions for Annulment

Judicial review of the acts of the Council and the Commission is provided for in the Treaty in three ways:

(a) Article 173 empowered the Court to review the legality of all acts of the Council and the Commission, except recommendations and opinions. This power has since been extended.

(b) Article 175 allows Member States and institutions of the Community to bring infringement actions before the Court, where the Council or the Commission has failed to act.

(c) Article 184 allows the legality of Regulations to be challenged, in limited circumstances.

Article 173 requires the Court to review the legality of the acts of the Council and the Commission, other than recommendations and opinions. The Court has jurisdiction in cases brought by the Council, the Commission, the Member States and (in certain circumstances) other persons, natural or legal.

Article 173 provides that:

> 'The Court of Justice shall review the legality of acts adopted jointly by the European Parliament and the Council, of the Commission and of the ECB, other than recommendations and opinions, and of acts of the European Parliament intended to produce legal effects *vis-à-vis* third parties.

> It shall for this purpose have jurisdiction in actions brought by a Member State, the Council or the Commission on grounds of lack of competence, infringement of an essential procedural requirement, infringement of this Treaty or of any rule of law relating to its application, or misuse of powers.

> The Court shall have the same jurisdiction in actions brought by the European Parliament and by the ECB for the purpose of protecting their prerogatives.

> Any natural or legal person may, under the same conditions, institute proceedings against a decision addressed to that person or against a decision which, although in the form of a regulation or decision addressed to another person, is of direct and individual concern to the former.

The proceedings provided for in this Article shall be instituted within two months of the publication of the measure, or of its notification to the plaintiff, or, in the absence thereof, of the day on which it came to the knowledge of the latter, as the case may be.

The grounds on which acts may be reviewed (which were not changed by Maastricht) are:

- lack of competence (ie absence of legal power to adopt an act, which is rare);

- infringement of an essential procedural requirement (minor infringements will not suffice);

- infringement of the Treaty or of any rule of law relating to its application (including such general principles as the right of the parties to be heard, legal certainty, proportionality, and equality); and

- misuse of power.

These are examined in greater detail below.

4.2.1	Extended jurisdiction

The Court's jurisdiction was significantly increased by the Maastricht amendments to the Treaty. Originally, its competence extended only to the acts of the Council and the Commission, though even before Maastricht it had carved out some additional areas for judicial review.

The Court decided first that it could consider 'all measures adopted by the institutions, whatever their nature or form, which are intended to have legal effects' (Case 22/70, *Commission v Council* (*the ERTA* case) (1971). This included decisions of the European Parliament which had the necessary effect: Case 294/83, *Les Verts v European Parliament* (1986). This is now recognised in the revised Article.

The amendments also accommodate the conciliation and veto procedure laid down in Article 189b, which allows the Council and the Parliament to adopt measures jointly. These are expressly brought within the scope of judicial review.

Finally, the amended Article gives *locus standi* to the European Parliament and the European Central Bank, but only for 'protecting their prerogatives'.

4.2.2   Grounds for review

There are, as we saw, four grounds for review of Community measures.

- Lack of competence

This ground applies where the institution concerned has exceeded its powers under either the Treaty or parent legislation by which the power was delegated to it. There are few examples.

(a) Cases 281, 282-5 and 287/85, *Germany and others v Commission* (1987) concerned the power of the Commission to adopt a decision under Article 118 of the Treaty. This article is concerned with promoting co-operation between Member States in the social field, but the decision set up a prior communication and consultation procedure on migration policies relating to non-Member States. The applicants argued that this was not within the social field and the Commission had therefore exceeded its powers. The Court decided that it could be said to be within this field.

(b) In Case 61/86, *UK v Commission, Re Clawback on Export of Sheep* (1986) the Court found two Commission regulations partly void because the Commission had exceeded the powers delegated to it by the Council.

Where the Commission's powers are delegated to it, this will determine the shape of its freedom of action: in Cases 279-280/84 and 285-286/84, *Walter Rau Lebensmittelwerke v Commission*, the *Christmas Butter Scheme* case (1987), the Commission had wide implementing powers, whereas in Case 264/86, *France v Commission, Re Runa Producers* (1989), its powers were very narrow.

• Infringement of an essential procedural requirement

This ground is concerned with the situation where an institution fails to respect the procedure set out in the Treaty, contravenes its own rules of procedure, or fails to comply with the requirements of Article 190 of the Treaty by not giving an adequate statement of reasons.

It is an essential procedural requirement for the Parliament ought to be consulted about a legislative proposal where the Treaty requires this (Case 138/79, *Roquette Frères v Council* (1989)).

A Council Directive was annulled in Case 68/86, *UK v Council* (1988) because the Council had adopted it under its written procedure, which the Council's rules of procedure said could only be used where all Council members agreed to its use.

• Infringement of the Treaty or rule of law

This heading gives the Court wide powers to strike down measures which do not comply with the general principles of law which the Court has articulated. These are not set out in the Treaty, and the only limit to their scope (according to Beaumont and Weatherill) is 'judicial self-restraint'. The headings are set out in Chapter 3: see para 3.4.4.

- Misuse of powers

  The Court considers that 'a decision may amount to a misuse of powers if it appears, on the basis of objective, relevant and consistent facts, to have been taken for purposes other than those stated' (see Cases 18, 35/62 *Gutmann v Commission* (1966), and Case 69/83, *Lux v Court of Auditors* (1984)). This is very difficult in practice to prove, so the provision is rarely used.

4.2.3   What is reviewable?

Recommendations and opinions, expressly excluded from the review process by Article 173, have no binding force under Article 189: so the Court decided, in the ERTA case, that it could review all measures adopted by the Council or the Commission which are intended to have legal effects. The alternative view, that Article 173 would only permit it to review measures of the other types specified in Article 189, namely directives, regulations and decisions, would have been too narrow to enable the Court to perform its duties under Article 164.

The cases reveal what sort of measures the Court has considered it could review:

(a) In the *ERTA* case the Court held that certain proceedings of the Council could be reviewed. The Commission was challenging something the Council's conclusions about the attitude the Member States should adopt in the negotiations concerning a European agreement being made under the auspices of the United Nations Economic Commission for Europe. The Court concluded that this was a matter within the competence of the Community: the Council was prescribing a course of action intended to be binding in the Member States. The measure was therefore reviewable under Article 173.

(b) In Cases 8-11/66, *Cimenteries v Commission* (1967), the Court held that a Commission notice, communicated by registered letter, was reviewable. The cement market was divided by agreement between some 74 undertakings in 1956. In 1962 the agreement was notified to the Commission (since Regulation 17/62 had just come into operation: see Chapter 13 para 13.2.2). The Commission decided that a notice should be sent, which would have the effect of removing the immunity from fines for operating a restrictive agreement which the parties had obtained by notifying the agreement. The parties challenged the validity of the Commission's act.

The notice reflected the Commission's preliminary conclusion that the agreement breached Article 85(1) of the Treaty, but was not a final decision (which would certainly have been reviewable). But the Commission was not likely to change its mind, and one attraction of using the notice was that the threat of fines would probably secure compliance without the need for a formal decision. Since it effectively substituted for a reviewable act, and produced binding legal effects, it was reviewable.

(c) In Case 60/81, *IBM v Commission* (1981) the Court decided that it could not review a letter sent to the subject of a competition investigation, containing a statement of objections and requiring a reply within a stated time. It distinguished the Cimenteries case since the statement of objections did not affect IBM's immunity from fines: it was simply part of the process of preparing the final decision, which would be reviewable.

(d) Case T-64-89, *Automec v Commission* (1990), concerned BMW's dealership agreement in Italy. A dealer refused supplies because he did not comply with the conditions for admission to the BMW network complained, but the Commission did not take the matter up as vigorously as he wished. The CFI decided that the Commission's preliminary observations were not reviewable.

(e) In Case 53/85, *AKZO Chemie v Commission* (1986) the Court decided that where the Commission revealed confidential information provided by the subject of a competition investigation to the complainant, that amounted to taking a definitive decision about the confidential nature of the documents. Although it was only a preliminary stage in the investigation, challenging the eventual decision would not assist AKZO in protecting its rights. The act was therefore reviewable.

(f) In Case 229/86, *Brother Industries v Commission* (1987) the Court held that a memorandum sent to the Member States which said that certain anti-dumping procedures had been discontinued because they had decided that the goods came from Japan, not Taiwan, was not reviewable because it was not legally binding. Brother objected because it would have to pay higher duties if the information in the memorandum was acted on: but there was no obligation on the Member States to abide by this finding of the Commission, so the conditions set by Article 173 were not met.

4.2.4	**Which institutions' acts can be reviewed?**

In *Les Verts* the Court decided that even though the wording of the Article limited it to reviewing acts of the Council and the Commission, nevertheless it could review the allocation by the Bureau of appropriations in the Parliament's budget for political parties' expenses in the 1984 elections. The Court attached much importance to the fact that when the Treaty was written the Parliament did not have powers to adopt measures which would have legal effects *vis-à-vis* third parties.

Note that in the second *Les Verts* case, Case 190/84 *Les Verts v European Parliament* (1988) the Court held that the contested measures had only internal effect and were not reviewable. There, it was the decisions of the financial controller and the accounting officer rather than the decisions in principle of the Parliament which were challenged.

Since the Maastricht amendments, this question of the extent of the Court's jurisdiction under Article 173 is much less important.

4.2.5	**Who may bring actions?**

There are two groups of potential applicants under Article 173: privileged applicants and non-privileged ones. The first group includes the Council, the Commission and the Member States, who have *locus standi* without having to show any interest in bringing the proceedings: the Parliament (the Court considered) had *locus standi* where its own prerogatives were concerned, and the amendments to the Treaty have confirmed this.

The second group, comprising natural and legal persons not in the first group, may challenge decisions that are addressed to them. They must prove that the matter 'is of *direct and individual concern to [them]*' (emphasis added).

We shall now look in detail at the rules governing the standing of non-privileged applicants.

4.2.6	**Non-privileged applicants**

Non-privileged applicants may only challenge decisions, but the Treaty clearly recognises that a decision may take the form of a regulation, and that a decision addressed to someone else may nevertheless be of direct and individual concern to an applicant. This means that by choosing the form of a regulation the Commission cannot prevent a person from challenging the validity of the measure.

There are therefore two important issues to explore here: first, what criteria must be present before a decision can be reviewed; and secondly, when is a regulation to be treated as a decision?

The act which the applicant wants the Court to review must be of direct and individual concern to the applicant. The question of what amounts to direct concern is explored in Case 66/69 (*Alcan Aluminium Raeran SA v Commission* (1970)). The Commission refused a request from the Belgian government for a tariff quota for aluminium, and the Court had to decide whether that was a decision of direct concern to three importers. The Court held that the origin of the applicants' legal position lay in the act of the Member State concerned, which had a discretion first to request a quota and then to open it. The Commission's decision therefore did not directly effect the applicants.

Where a third party whose discretion under the Community measure will determine how the applicant is affected, such as the Belgian government in the *Alcan* case, tells the applicant in advance how it will exercise it, the conditions for review will be met: Case 62/70, *Bock v Commission* (1971). See also Case 11/82 *Piraiki- Patraiki v Commission* (1985) where the French government had demanded stricter quotas than were granted by the Commission, which was taken by the Court as an indication of how the more limited quotas granted would be applied.

The question of when a measure is of individual concern to an applicant is considered in the context of applicants' rights to seek review of regulations, in the following section.

If a regulation is going to be reviewed by the Court on the application of anon-privileged applicant, it will still have to meet the requirements of Article 173: it must be of direct and individual effect on the applicant. Once that requirement is met, it is necessary to consider whether it is a real regulation or merely a decision dressed up as one: that is, whether the applicant has *locus standi* to challenge it.

Initially the Court looked to the Treaty to determine the difference between a regulation and a decision. In the first Article 173 case, Cases 16, 17/62, *Producteurs de Fruits v Commission* (1962) it looked at Article 189 and determined that the key question was whether the measure is one of individual concern to specific individuals. This 'individual concern' test would be satisfied if the measure applies to a fixed and identifiable group of persons, and whether it was called a regulation or a decision it would be reviewable.

But in Case 64/69, *Compagnie Française Commerciale v Commission* (1970) the Court decided that a transitional provision in a regulation which did satisfy the individual concern test was an integral part of a true regulation and could not be reviewed.

4.2.7 When can a decision be reviewed?

4.2.8 When is a regulation a decision?

In subsequent cases the Court has required an applicant to show not only that the measure is one of individual concern but also that the so-called regulation is in fact not truly legislative in nature. Even if all the persons affected by the measure can be identified, if the measure takes effect by virtue of an objective legal or factual situation defined by the measure it will not be considered to be anything other than a regulation. (See Case 162/78, *Wagner v Commission* (1979); Cases 789-90/79, *Calpak v Commission* (1980); Case 45/81 *Moksel v Commission* (1982); Case 147/83 *Binderer v Commission* (1985); Case 26/86, *Deutz und Gelderman v Council* (1987); Case 253/86, *Agro-Pecauria Vicente Nobre v Council* (1988); Case C-244/88, *Usine co-operative de déhydration du Vexin and others v Commission* (1989).)

A non-privileged applicant will therefore have *locus standi* to challenge a regulation only if:

• it is not a legislative measure of general application; and

• the applicant is part of a fixed and identifiable group which is affected by the regulation.

4.2.9 Decisions addressed to others

If a measure is called a decision (ie a measure having individual application) the Court will not in practice enquire into whether that is in fact what it is, or whether it has general application.

If a decision is addressed to the applicant, there is no problem about whether the Court can hear an action under Article 173: if it addressed to someone else, the answer is more difficult.

In Case 25/62, *Plaumann & Co v Commission* (1963), the *Clementines* case (fruit looms large in this area of EC law) the Court held that a measure would be of individual concern to persons other than those to whom it is addressed:

'... if that decision affects them by reason of certain attributes which are peculiar to them or by reason of circumstances in which they are differentiated from all other persons and by virtue of these factors distinguishes them individually just as in the case of the person addressed.'

However, in Cases 106, 107/63, *Toepfer v Commission* (1965) the number and identity of the persons affected had become fixed and ascertainable. The Commission knew that the decision would affect precisely those persons and no others, so the Court admitted the application.

The 'fixed and ascertainable' rule has been departed from, or at least relaxed, in a couple of subsequent cases (see Case 294/81 *Control Data v Commission* (1983) and Case 11/82

Piraiki-Patraiki v Commission (1985)). These decisions, each of a chamber of only three judges, are probably abberations. In some particular areas, though, the test is not rigorously enforced.

- In competition investigations, complainants are given the right to seek review of the Commission's acts even though the test might not be satisfied (see for example Case 26/76, *Metro v Commission* (1977)).

- Under Article 93(2), natural and legal persons can challenge state aids: complainants will have locus standi if their position on the market is significantly affected by the aid under investigation (Case 1698/84, *COFAZ v Commission* (1986)). Trade associations will not be allowed to make applications.

- Where a complaint is made that imported goods are being unfairly subsidised, the complainant may bring an action to annul a Commission decision not to investigate (Case 191/82, *Fediol v Commission* (1983)) or to terminate its investigation (Case 187/85, *Fediol v Commission* (1988)).

There is a short time limit for bringing actions for annulment under Article 173. Two months are given from the date of publication of the measure, or from its notification to the applicant, or its coming to the attention of the applicant.

The limit is strictly enforced in the absence of unforeseeable circumstances or *force majeure*. However, the two months is only a basic limit:

- It is extended first to take account of the applicant's distance from the Court: in the UK this means 10 days are added to enable applicants to get to Luxembourg.

- If the measure is published in the *Official Journal*, the time limit is also extended by 15 days.

The time-limit may be circumvented: a Member State may bring annulment proceedings outside the time-limit in an action brought against it by the Commission for failure to comply with Community obligations. And in *BASF* (see Chapter 2, para 2.5.6) the CFI decided that the defects in the Community measure concerned were such that the decision was in fact non-existent.

4.2.10   Time limits

Article 186 gives the President of the Court power to grant interim measures. An application for annulment may be accompanied by an application for interim measures, including the suspension of the measure concerned (notwithstanding that Article 185 makes clear that actions before the Court do not have automatic suspensory effect).

4.2.11   Interim measures

4.2.12   **Consequences of annulment**

The result of a successful Article 173 application is that the Court will declare the measure void. Part only of a measure may be declared void (Cases 56, 58/64, *Consten/Grundig v Commission* (1966)).

4.3   **Article 175**

The mirror-image of Article 173, which requires the institutions to act within their powers, is Article 175, under which the institutions can be required to take action. It provides (as amended at Maastricht):

> 'Should the European Parliament, the Council or the Commission, in infringement of this Treaty, fail to act, the Member States and the other institutions of the Community may bring an action before the Court of Justice to have the infringement established.
>
> The action shall be admissible only if the institution concerned has first been called upon to act. If, within two months of being so called upon, the institution concerned has not defined its position, the action may be brought within a further period of two months.
>
> Any natural or legal person may, under the conditions laid down in the preceding paragraphs, complain to the Court of Justice that an institution of the Community has failed to address to that person any act other than a recommendation or an opinion.
>
> The Court of Justice shall have jurisdiction, under the same conditions, in actions or proceedings brought by the European Central Bank in the areas falling within the latter's field of competence and in actions or proceedings brought against the latter.'

At very least, Article 175 requires the institution concerned to define its position. The position statement is itself reviewable under Article 173, at least at the instance of privileged applicants.

Privileged applicants are given standing under the first paragraph of the Article: non-privileged applicants are covered by the third paragraph. The Court has applied the same tests relating to *locus standi* and the type of measures which can be the subject of a challenge, as in the case of annulment proceedings under Article 173 (see Case 15/70, *Chevally v Commission* (1970)).

The procedure is set out in the second paragraph of Article 175: the institution concerned has two months in which to define its position. If it has no obligation to act – perhaps because it is a matter of discretion – note that there is no obligation on it to define its position as it has not infringed against the treaty.

The institution may define its position by saying that it is not going to act or that it proposes to act, perhaps in a different way from that the applicant wanted. Article 175 is only concerned with a failure to take a decision or to define a position: the adoption of a measure other than that desired cannot be challenged under this provision (see Case 247/87 *Star Fruit Co v Commission* (1989)).

If the applicant does not like the position defined by the institution, its remedy lies under Article 173. Article 175 is not available as a means of avoiding the strict time-limits set in Article 173. In particular, an applicant seeking the revocation of an act of an institution may not use Article 175 to challenge the institutions decision not to revoke: it must use Article 173 to challenge the validity of the objectionable act.

If the institution concerned passes the necessary measure while the Article 175 application is before the Court, no judgment will be given. Article 176 provides that the Court can only require the institution concerned to take the necessary measure to comply with the judgment: if it has already done so, the subject matter of the action is non-existent.

In Case 13/85 *Parliament v Council* (1985) the EP brought an action against the Council for failing to fix a framework for the Common Transport Policy and to take certain other specific related measures. The EP informed the Council of its intention to bring an action, and the reply from the Council did not appear to the EP to constitute a definition of the Council's position.

The Court decided that the EP's application was admissible and concluded that a failure by an institution to take several decisions or a series of decisions which the Treaty obliges that institution to take may be challenged. The institutions failures must be stated with sufficient precision to enable the institution concerned to comply with the Court's decision, as required by Article 176.

In the present case, however, the Court decided that the applicant had failed to do this. The Council had a broad discretion over aspects of the Common Transport Policy, and could decide what it should consist of and what the priorities should be. The EP had failed to state what measures were necessary and in what order they should be dealt with.

If the Court merely judged that there had to be a CTP, the judgment would be of no help to the institution concerned (the Council) because it would have no idea what it had to do to comply with Article 176. On the other hand, the Court could not in its judgment elaborate on the detail of the CTP.

However, the EP had specifically requested the Council to take certain measures required by the Treaty. If the Court ordered the Council to take these steps it would know what was required of it, and, furthermore, the Council's discretion in this area is more limited than in other areas of the CTP. The Court therefore upheld the EP's application as far as it related to these aspects.

In its judgment the Court also noted that Article 176 does not prescribe a time limit for compliance. It held that the institution concerned has 'a reasonable time' to do so.

4.4 Article 184

Article 184 provides a way for applicants to argue in proceedings brought before the Court under some other Treaty provision that a regulation is inapplicable. It says:

> 'Notwithstanding the expiry of the period laid down in the fifth paragraph of Article 173, any party may, in proceedings in which a regulation adopted jointly by the European Parliament and the Council, or a Regulation of the Council, Commission, or of the European Central Bank is at issue, plead the grounds specified in the second paragraph of Article 173 in order to invoke before the Court of Justice the inapplicability of that Regulation.'

There must be a connection between the main action and the plea that the Regulation is inapplicable (Case 32/65, *Italy v Council and Commission* (1966)).

4.4.1 Non-privileged applicants

The value of Article 184 is that it enables a party to put in issue the validity of a Regulation without having to show that it is in fact a decision. This can be done in the context of proceedings relating to the validity of a measure implementing that Regulation, and it can be done even though the time for challenging the Regulation under Article 173 has passed.

Thus, if a motor vehicle manufacturer were to have exemption withdrawn from its dealer agreement under the provisions of the block exemption (Regulation 123/85), perhaps on the grounds that price differentials were too great, it could challenge not only the validity of the specific decision withdrawing exemption (under Article 173) but also the validity of the block exemption regulation.

4.4.2 Privileged applicants

Privileged applicants get a second go at challenging regulations under Article 184. If they miss the time limit under Article 173 they can seek to establish illegality under Article 184 instead.

4.4.3 Effect

A successful application under Article 184 does not render the measure concerned void. It makes it inapplicable to the applicant, so any implementing measures taken against the applicant – such as the hypothetical decision to withdraw exemption from a motor vehicle dealer agreement – would be liable to be declared void by the Court. But the institution whose Regulation was attacked would probably soon replace it with a good one, so the advantage would be short-lived.

The Article speaks only of Regulations, but the Court has extended its scope to take in other measures of general application (Case 92/78, *Simmenthal v Commission* (1979)).

4.4.4   Scope

The wording of the Article does not help determine whether a Member State can bring proceedings under Article 184. If the Commission claims a Member State has failed to comply with a measure made under a regulation which the Member State considers illegal, it may be able to use the provision to challenge the basic regulation.

Actions for Annulment

Article 173 requires the Court to review the legality of the acts of the Council and the Commission, other than recommendations and opinions. The Court has jurisdiction in cases brought by the Council, the Commission, the Member States, and (in certain circumstances) other persons, natural or legal.

Article 173

Originally, the Commission's competence extended only to the acts of the Council and the Commission. The Court extended this to 'all measures adopted by the institutions, whatever their nature or form, which are intended to have legal effects' (*ERTA*), including decisions of the European Parliament which had the necessary effect (*Les Verts v European Parliament*).

Article 173 was revised by TEU to recognise these developments, to accommodate the conciliation and veto procedure, and to give limited *locus standi* to the European Parliament and the European Central Bank.

The grounds on which acts may be reviewed are:

- Lack of competence, where the institution concerned has either exceeded its powers under either the Treaty or parent legislation by which the power was delegated to it.

- Infringement of an essential procedural requirement, where an institution fails to respect the procedure set out in the Treaty (eg failure to consult the Parliament (*Roquette Frères v Council*)), contravenes its own rules of procedure (eg wrongly using a written procedure to adopt a directive: *UK v Council*), or fails to comply with the requirements of Article 190 of the Treaty by not giving an adequate statement of reasons.

- Infringement of the Treaty or of any rule of law relating to its application (including such general principles as the right of the parties to be heard, legal certainty, proportionality, and equality).

- Misuse of power, where 'a decision may amount to a misuse of powers if it appears, on the basis of objective, relevant and consistent facts, to have been taken for purposes other than those stated' (*Gutmann v Commission, Lux v Court of Auditors*).

The Court decided, in the *ERTA* case, that it could review all measures adopted by the Council or the Commission which are intended to have legal effects. These include certain proceedings of the Council and a Commission notice, communicated by registered letter (*Cimenteries v Commission*). In *Automec*, the CFI decided that the Commission's preliminary observations concerning a competition complaint were not reviewable. Applicants may be:

- *privileged applicants* which include the Council, the Commission and the Member States, who have *locus standi* without having to show any interest in bringing the proceedings. The Parliament has *locus standi* where its own prerogatives were concerned.

- *non-privileged applicants* which include natural and legal persons not in the first group and may challenge decisions that are addressed to them. They must prove that the matter 'is of *direct and individual concern* to [them]' (emphasis added). They may only challenge decisions, but the Treaty recognises that a decision may take the form of a regulation, and that a decision addressed to someone else may nevertheless be of direct and individual concern to an applicant. A non-privileged applicant will have *locus standi* to challenge a regulation if it is not a legislative measure of general application: and the applicant is part of a fixed and identifiable group which is affected by the regulation.

In *Plaumann & Co v Commission* the Court held that a measure would be of individual concern to persons other than those to whom it is addressed:

'... if that decision affects them by reason of certain attributes which are peculiar to them or by reason of circumstances in which they are differentiated from all other persons and by virtue of these factors distinguishes them individually just as in the case of the person addressed.'

However, in *Toepfer v Commission* the number and identity of the persons affected had become fixed and ascertainable. The Commission knew that the decision would affect precisely those persons and no others, so the Court admitted the application.

The time limit for bringing an action is two months from the date of publication of the measure, or from its notification to the applicant, or its coming to the attention of the applicant.

An application for annulment may be accompanied by an application for interim measures, including the suspension of the measure concerned.

Article 175 enables actions to be taken to require the institutions to take action. Privileged and non-privileged applicants are given the same *locus standi* as under Article 173.

The institution concerned has two months in which to define its position. It may do so by saying that it is not going to act or that it proposes to act, perhaps in a different way from that the applicant wanted. Article 175 is only concerned with a failure to take a decision or to define a position: the adoption of a measure other than that desired cannot be challenged under this provision (see *Star Fruit Co v Commission*).

Article 184 provides a way for applicants to argue in proceedings brought before the Court under some other Treaty provision that a regulation is inapplicable. There must be a connection between the main action and the plea that the Regulation is inapplicable (*Italy v Council and Commission*).

Non-privileged applicants may put in issue the validity of a Regulation without having to show that it is in fact a decision. This can be done in the context of proceedings relating to the validity of a measure implementing that Regulation, and it can be done even though the time for challenging the Regulation under Article 173 has passed.

Privileged applicants get a second go at challenging regulations under Article 184. If they miss the time limit under Article 173 they can seek to establish illegality under Article 184 instead.

A successful application under Article 184 does not render the measure concerned void. It makes it inapplicable to the applicant, so any implementing measures taken against the applicant would be liable to be declared void by the Court.

Article 184 speaks only of Regulations, but the Court has extended its scope to take in other measures of general application (*Simmenthal v Commission*). If the Commission claims a Member State has failed to comply with a measure made under a regulation which the Member State considers illegal, it may be able to use the provision to challenge the basic regulation.

Chapter 5

Direct Actions

Actions may be brought against Member States under five provisions of the Treaty:

- Article 169, which allows the Commission to deal with infringements by Member States;

- Article 170, which allows Member States to take action;

- Article 93(2), under which the Commission or a Member State may take infringement proceedings relating to state aids;

- Article 100a(4) (and the related 100b(2)), relating to derogations from the single internal market; and

- Article 225, relating to distortions to competition due to states taking essential security measures.

No proceedings under these last two heads have been brought.

Article 169 provides:

> 'If the Commission considers that a Member State has failed to fulfil an obligation under this Treaty, it shall deliver a reasoned opinion on the matter after giving the State concerned the opportunity to submit its observations.
>
> If the State concerned does not comply with the opinion within the period laid down by the Commission, the latter may bring the matter before the Court of Justice.'

Note that despite the wording of the Article the Commission is not under a duty to deliver a reasoned opinion if it thinks that a Member State is in breach. It has a discretion at each stage of the procedure: no action will lie against the Commission for failure to start or see through Article 169 proceedings (Case 247/87, *Star Fruit Co v Commission* (1989)).

An example of the use of the Article 169 procedure is the *German Beer* case (Case 178/84 *Commission v Germany* (1987)). German law prohibited the marketing of foreign beers unless they complied with strict purity laws (Rheinheitsgebot). The Commission successfully brought infringement proceedings against Germany under Article 169, for failure to fulfil obligations under Article 30 of the Treaty which prohibits measures having an effect equivalent to restrictions on imports. (See further below, Chapter 12.)

While Article 169 will usually be brought to bear on legislation which does not comply with the requirements of the Treaty (or failures to implement Community requirements), it is possible for a Member State to be in breach of its obligations because of a decision of a court. In one instance, the Commission began proceedings against France when the Cour de Cassation in apparent breach of Community law failed to overturn a lower court's decision.

There are four stages to proceedings under Article 169:

- Informal discussions between the Commission and the Member State

  Usually, an alleged violation will be the subject of a complaint to the Commission from an individual or company: otherwise, the Commission's own inquiries may bring possible infringements to light.

  Many cases are settled at the informal stage, by the Member State changing the offending legislation or persuading the Commission that it is not infringing the Treaty. The initial approach will be made by the Commission to the permanent representative to the Community of the Member State in question, asking for a response form the national government within a specified period.

- Formal notice from the Commission

  If the matter is not resolved at the informal stage, a letter of formal notice may be sent by the Commission (signed by a Commissioner) to the foreign minister of the Member State concerned.

  The scope of the case against the Member State is set in the letter, so the Member State knows what it has to reply to. It cannot subsequently be widened in the reasoned opinion. Case 51/83 *Commission v Italy* (1984) concerned Italian laws on the import of animal gelatin: the Commission's letter of formal notice dealt only with gelatin for use in sweets, but in the reasoned opinion it tried to extend the procedure to cover gelatin used in preserved meat products and ice cream. The Court held the action relating to these extra products inadmissible since the Italian government had not been given a fair hearing as far as they were concerned.

  Most of the cases which are not resolved at the informal stage are resolved after the Commission sends a letter of formal notice. In the minority of cases, the Commission will proceed to issue a reasoned opinion.

- The Commission's reasoned opinion

  The reasoned opinion sets out how the Commission thinks that the Member State has failed to meet its obligations under Community law. It establishes the legal arguments in the same way as the letter of formal notice establishes the subject matter of the violation, and any subsequent application to the Court must be founded on the same grounds and submissions as the reasoned opinion (Case 290/87, *Commission v Netherlands* (1989)).

  The Court has also made clear just how reasoned the opinion has to be: it '... must be considered to contain a sufficient statement of reasons to satisfy the law when it contains ... a coherent statement of the reasons which led the Commission to believe that the State in question has failed to fulfil an obligation under the Treaty'.

  There is no requirement that the Commission rebuts arguments in its defence which the Member State may have raised.

  The Member State then has a period of grace in which to comply with the reasoned opinion. In Case 74/82, *Commission v Ireland* (1984), the offending Member State was given five days to change a law which had been applied without complaint for 40 years, and the Court decided this was not long enough. (The Commission did in fact give an extension, and the case was considered admissible.) Any measures necessary to comply must be taken within the grace period: it is not good enough to do so after the time limit has expired but before the Court gives judgment. Apart from anything else, this serves to establish the state's liability to persons who may have accrued rights as a result of the failure (see Case 240/86, *Commission v Greece* (1984)).

  About half the cases in which reasoned opinions are given are resolved at this stage. The remainder may be referred to the Court (the Commission has discretion over whether to do so).

- Reference to the Court

  The Court conducts a hearing on all the issues raised in the case: it does not simply review the Commission's opinion. The burden of proof is on the Commission. As a preliminary matter, the Court may declare the case inadmissible if it thinks the Member State has not been given a sufficient opportunity to end the alleged infringement.

In determining whether this is the case, the Court will consider not only how long the Member State was given to respond to the formal notice and the reasoned opinion, but also the duration of the informal stage. If this was extensive, shorter periods for the formal stages will be acceptable since the Member State is aware of the nature of the alleged infringement.

For example, in two cases brought by the Commission against Belgium the Court took different views on this matter. In Case 85/85 (1986) the Belgian government was given only 15 days to respond to the formal notice and the same time to respond to the reasoned opinion. However, it had been made fully aware of the nature of the allegations during an extensive informal stage, so the Court considered the case admissible. In Case 293/85 (1988) periods of eight and 15 days for the two formal pre-litigation stages were considered insufficient because the Belgian government was not fully informed of the views of the Commission before proceedings were brought against it.

Even after the Commission has reached the stage of Court proceedings, the case may still be settled without the ECJ having to give a judgment.

The Court has rejected defences based on internal legislative difficulties: Case 58/81, *Commission v Luxembourg* (1982), and see Cases 227-30/85, *Commission v Belgium* (1988), where the Belgian government argued that it could do nothing to force the regional governments of Wollonia and Flanders to comply with EC directives. The principle is that it is the state which is in breach of its Treaty obligations, not the central government. The state is responsible for any default on the part of its agencies.

Force majeure can be pleaded, but the Court adopts a very restrictive view of it. In Case 101/84, *Commission v Italy* (1985), the Court refused to accept a plea based on the destruction by bombing of the Italian Ministry of Transport's vehicle register. Such an excuse would only hold water for as long as it would take a normal diligent administration to replace equipment and collect and prepare the data. There, the bomb attack was in 1979 and the Court clearly thought that the government should have got back to normal by 1984.

Member States may also be held to account under Article 169 for the acts or defaults of nationalised industries and even of private bodies if they are sufficiently under government control. In Case 149/81, *Commission v Ireland*

(1982) – the 'Buy Irish' case – the campaign was directed by the Irish Goods Council, a limited company though one funded largely by the government and having a management committee appointed by the Minister. That was sufficient for the Court to decide that Article 30 applied, and (as we shall see in Chapter 7) prohibited the initiative.

The fact that another Member State, or an institution, is in breach of the Treaty does not justify a Member State's breach (Cases 90, 91/63, *Commission v Luxembourg and Belgium* (1964)). Nor does it help if the Council has before it a legislative proposal which would end the infringement (Case 220/83, *Commission v France* (1986)) and other cases arising out of the same facts.

If a Member State is in breach of its Treaty obligations, it will not suffice to change administrative practice so that the offending law is not enforced (Case 167/73, *Commission v France* (1974)).

Failure to co-operate with the Commission can be grounds for a finding by the Court of a breach of Article 5 of the Treaty, which requires Member States to facilitate the achievement of the Community's tasks.

Under Article 170:

5.1.2   Article 170

'A Member State which considers that another Member State has failed to fulfil an obligation under this Treaty may bring the matter before the Court of Justice.

Before a Member State brings an action against another Member State for an alleged infringement of an obligation under this Treaty, it shall bring the matter before the Commission.

The Commission shall deliver a reasoned opinion after each of the States concerned has been given the opportunity to submit its own case and its observations on the other party's case both orally and in writing.

If the Commission has not delivered an opinion within three months of the date on which the matter was brought before it, the absence of such an opinion shall not prevent the matter from being brought before the Court of Justice.'

The Commission's involvement means that either the complaint will be dealt with under Article 169, or may proceed under Article 170 after a delay of three months. Just as the Commission must prove its case before the Court under Article 169, so the Member State bringing the action must carry the burden of proof in Article 170 actions.

The procedure has been very rarely invoked – not surprisingly, given the cost (which in Article 169 proceedings is borne by the Commission), the burden of proof and the attendant diplomatic embarrassment. In one of two cases initiated under Article 170 before 1990, Case 58/77 *Ireland v France* the parties settled: in the other, Case 141/78, *France v UK* (1979) the ECJ held that the UK law on fishing net mesh sizes breached Community law.

5.1.3   Enforcement

Article 171 originally provided:

'If the Court of Justice finds that a Member State has failed to fulfil an obligation under this Treaty, the State shall be required to take the necessary measures to comply with the judgment of the Court of Justice.'

The Court's judgments are *declaratory*. They are binding on the Member State concerned, but could not be enforced by financial or other penalties. Under the Maastricht amendments, however, a new paragraph has been added:

'2   If the Commission considers that the Member State concerned has not taken such measures it shall, after giving that State the opportunity to submit its observations, issue a reasoned opinion specifying the points on which the Member State concerned has not complied with the judgment of the Court of Justice.

If the Member State concerned fails to take the necessary measures to comply with the Court's judgment within the time-limit laid down by the Commission, the latter may bring the case before the Court of Justice. In so doing it shall specify the amount of the lump sum or penalty payment to be paid by the Member State concerned which it considers appropriate in the circumstances.

If the Court of Justice finds that the Member State concerned has not complied with its judgment it may impose a lump sum or penalty payment on it.

This procedure shall be without prejudice to Article 170.'

Before the Maastricht amendments came into operation the only course for the Court if a Member State did not comply with a judgment was to start fresh infringement proceedings, going through the entire Article 169 procedure again. It was simply not effective.

Article 171 does not specify how long Member States have in which to comply. In Case 69/86, *Commission v Italy* (1987) the Court stated that 'the action required to give effect to a judgment must be set in motion immediately and be completed in the shortest possible period'.

5.1.4   Article 93(2)

The purpose of the provisions on State aids is to ensure that Member States do not distort the operation of the common market by giving financial assistance to domestic industries, and the basic prohibition is contained in Article 92(1). Some aids will be permitted, but if aid is given in breach of Article 92 or is being misused Article 93(2) permits the Commission to decide that the Member State must abolish or alter that aid within a set time scale.

If the State fails to comply, the Commission or any other interested State may refer the matter to the Court of Justice. Failure to notify new or substantially altered aid to the Commission is a matter for action under Article 169.

Article 93(2) provides that means to resolve doubts about the compatibility of aid with the Treaty. The State granting the aid gets a chance to present its case, as do other interested States, and also undertakings affected by the aid.

By Article 186:

> 'The Court of Justice may in any case before it prescribe any necessary interim measures.'

5.1.5   Interim measures in infringement proceedings

This power is not limited to infringement proceedings: its application in other areas of the Court's jurisdiction is dealt with later.

Under the Court's rules of procedure (Article 83(2)) the application for interim measures must 'state the subject-matter of the proceedings, the circumstances giving rise to urgency and the pleas of fact and law establishing a *prima facie* case for the interim measures applied for'. The application is normally heard by the President of the Court, but he may refer it to the Court.

In Case 154/84R *Commission v Italy* (1985) the Commission sought an order requiring Italy to give Aer Lingus provisional authorisation to operate a service between Manchester and Milan. The Commission needed to show that 'serious and irreparable damage' would be caused if the order were not given, and the Court held that this had not been shown. Aer Lingus had not previously run this service, so the loss was the anticipated profit and that did not establish urgency.

In Case 246/89R, *Commission v UK* (1989) the Commission sought an interim order requiring the UK to suspend the nationality requirements of the Merchant Shipping Act 1988 as they applied to nationals of other Member States and to fishing boats which had formerly fished as British registered vessels. The President of the Court acknowledged that it may be necessary for the UK to ensure that there is a 'genuine link' between vessels entitled to fish the UK quota and the British fishing industry: but it was another matter to conclude that this meant that a derogation from the normal rules of discrimination on the grounds of nationality should be granted. Loss of registration would mean the loss of the ability to fish, which clearly entailed serious damage. There was no way to oblige the UK to compensate the owners of the vessels for this loss, so it would also be irreparable. The interim measures were therefore granted.

Direct Actions

Article 169 allows the Commission to deal with infringements by Member States. There are four stages:

- Many cases are settled by *informal discussions*. The Member State may change the offending legislation or persuade the Commission that it is not infringing the Treaty.

- If the matter is not resolved at the informal stage, a *letter of formal notice* may be sent by the Commission. The scope of the case against the Member State is set in the letter, so the Member State knows what it has to reply to. It cannot subsequently be widened in the reasoned opinion (*Commission v Italy*).

- The Commission's *reasoned opinion* sets out how the Commission thinks that the Member State has failed to meet its obligations under Community law. It establishes the legal arguments and '... must be considered to contain a sufficient statement of reasons to satisfy the law when it contains ... a coherent statement of the reasons which led the Commission to believe that the State in question has failed to fulfil an obligation under the Treaty'.

- On a reference to the Court, it conducts a hearing on all the issues raised in the case. The Court has rejected defences based on internal legislative difficulties (*Commission v Luxembourg*). *Force majeure* can be pleaded, but the Court adopts a very restrictive view of it (*Commission v Italy*). Member States may also be held to account under Article 169 for the acts or defaults of nationalised industries and even of private bodies if they are sufficiently under government control (*Commission v Ireland*).

The Commission has a discretion at each stage of the procedure: no action will lie against the Commission for failure to start or see through Article 169 proceedings.

Article 170 allows Member States to take action against other Member States which are in default. The matter must first be brought before the Commission, which considers the cases of the two parties and prepares a reasoned opinion. If this is not competed within three months, the Member State which raised the matter may take it to the Court. Article 170 is rarely invoked.

Article 93(2) deals with state aids. Some aids will be permitted, but if aid is given in breach of Article 92 or is being misused Article 93(2) permits the Commission to decide that the Member State must abolish or alter that aid within a set time scale.

If the state fails to comply, the Commission or any other interested state may refer the matter to the Court of Justice. Interim measures are available in infringement proceedings (*Commission v Italy, Commission v UK*).

Chapter 6

Judicial Review and Article 177

Article 177 provides a bridge between the Community legal order and the national courts. Following the Maastricht amendments, it provides:

'The Court of Justice shall have jurisdiction to give preliminary rulings concerning:

- the interpretation of this Treaty;

- the validity and interpretation of acts of the institutions of the Community and the European Central Bank;

- the interpretation of the statutes of bodies established by an act of the Council, where those statutes so provide.

Where such a question is raised before any court or tribunal of a Member State, that court or tribunal may, if it considers that a decision on the question is necessary, to enable it to give judgment, request the Court of Justice to give a ruling thereon.

Where any such question is raised in a case pending before a court or tribunal of a Member State, against whose decisions there is no judicial remedy under national law, that court or tribunal shall bring the matter before the Court of Justice.'

Article 177 enables national courts or tribunals to seek the Court of Justice's advice on matters before them. Only courts or tribunals, not the parties to the litigation, can make such references, though the parties can ask the national court to put a question of EC law to the Court.

It provides a way to mount an indirect challenge to Community legislation in the national courts, since only the Court of Justice can declare Community legislation invalid. Once the Community legislation is incorporated into national legislation, a challenge to the Community legislation can be achieved via a challenge at national level to the national implementing act.

It has given rise to about half the cases that have come before the Court, and many important developments in Community law have come about this way. For example, the doctrine of direct effect was established in Case 26/62, *Van Gend en Loos* (1963) and the doctrine of supremacy of directly effective Community provisions was laid down in Case 6/64, *Costa v ENEL* (1964). Both were Article 177 cases.

Most of the cases referred under Article 177 concern interpretation rather than validity of Community acts: the provision ensures uniform interpretation of Community legislation.

6.2   **The Court's jurisdiction**

The first point to note about the Court's jurisdiction is that it does not decide the case. Nor does it investigate facts: it is not set up to do so, nor does it have the necessary authority. It can only answer the questions put to it, and hand the answer back to the referring court.

The national court, for its part, must establish the facts. The facts will determine what questions of EC law need to be referred. Once the answer is received, the national court will decide the case in the light of what the Court of Justice has said.

The first paragraph of Article 177 defines the Court's jurisdiction. The meaning of 'acts of the institutions of the Community' has proved slightly controversial:

- Legally binding provisions within the meaning of Article 189 are clearly covered. This includes regulations, directives and decisions.

- Non-binding recommendations and opinions (also within the meaning of Article 189) (Case C-322/88, *Grimaldi v Fonds des maladies professionelles* (1989)).

- International agreements entered into by the Community under powers given by the Treaty (Case 181/73, *Haegman v Belgium* (1974), which concerned the Association Agreement between the Community and Greece). In Case 270/80, *Polydor v Harlequin Record Shops* (1982), to which we shall refer when we consider intellectual property law in the Community.

- Decisions made by legislative bodies set up under international agreements made by the Community (Case C-192/89, *Sevince v Staatsecretaris van Justitie* (1990), where the decisions of the Association Council established under the Association Agreement between the Community and Turkey were interpreted by the Court). But the Court has refused to interpret the statutes of bodies established by agreement between the Member States (Case 44/84, *Hurd v Jones* (1986), which concerned the Statutes of the European School).

The Court's jurisdiction does not extend to interpreting national laws. It cannot therefore determine the compatibility of national law with Community legislation: all it can do is tell the national courts what the Community law says, and leave the interpretation of the national law to them. If a national court asks whether the provisions of national law are compatible with Community law, the Court will simply provide an interpretation of the relevant Community provisions.

Where a Member State applies Community law to situations not required to be covered by it, as where Belgium applied the Community provisions regarding the spouses of nationals of other Member States working in Belgium to non-EC nationals too, the Court will rule on the meaning of the Community provisions (Case C-297/89 and Case C-197/89, *Dzodzi v Belgium* (1990)).

The meaning of Article 177 para 2 seems clear: but it begs the question, whether a body counts as a court or tribunal. Several decisions of the Court clarify this issue.

6.3   What courts and tribunals may refer questions?

- If the parties agree to submit disputes to arbitration, the arbitrator is not a court or tribunal (Case 102/81, *Nordsee v Reederei Mond* (1982)).

- If national law imposes arbitration on parties who cannot agree, and the composition of the arbitration board is not wholly within the parties' discretion, the board is a tribunal (Case 109/88, *Handels-og Kontorfunktionærernes Forbund i Danmark v Dansk Arbejdsgiverforening* (1981)).

- If national law requires disputes to be settled before it, a body will be considered a court or tribunal. The composition of such a body must be at least partly controlled by the law or public authorities (see Case 61/65, *Vaasen v Beambtenfonds Mijnbedrijf* (1966)).

- It is not necessary that a body be considered a court according to the laws of the Member State concerned (Case 246/80, *Broekmeulen v Huisarts Registratie Comissie* (1981)).

- If the body concerned exercises functions preliminary to its judicial functions, for example, investigating an alleged offence, the Court will accept a reference even during the preliminary stage (Case 14/86, *Pretore di Salo v Persons Unknown* (1987)).

Article 177 provides for the making of references in two distinct situations:

6.4   When are references to be made?

- If a national court or tribunal considers that a decision on the subject is necessary to enable it to give judgment; and

- Where there is no judicial remedy against the decision of the national court or tribunal before which the question is raised (ie there is no appeal against the decision of that body).

We shall now examine these two situations in turn.

6.4.1   Discretionary references

Originally, the Court did not think that it was for it to decide whether a ruling was actually needed for the national court to decide the case. There was a clear separation of functions between the national courts and the Court of Justice. The sovereignty of the judicial office is preserved by leaving it to the national judge to decide whether to refer.

However, the Court will sometimes differ from the national court in its view of the need for a ruling. If no reference is made, the Court has no chance to express a view: but if a reference is made, the Court may in certain circumstances decline to give a ruling.

- The Court will only give a ruling on a reference where the national court is going to give judgment in proceedings which are intended to lead to a judicial decision. In Case 130/80, *Borker* (1980) the Court declined to rule on a reference from the bar council of Paris. The council was under no duty to try the case before it: it was considering a request for a declaration in a dispute between a member of the Paris bar and the courts of a Member State.

- If the national proceedings have already terminated when the Court is asked for a reference, it is under no duty to give a ruling (Case C-159/90, *Grogan v Society for the Protection of the Unborn Child* (1991) and Case 338/85, *Pardini v Ministerio del Commercio con L'Estero* (1988)).

- The Court will not rule in proceedings which do not relate to a real dispute. If the parties have merely colluded between themselves to litigate in order to obtain a ruling on Community law, the Court will not get involved (Case 104/79, *Foglia v Novello* (1980)), which was an elaborate attempt to challenge the validity of French tax on liqueur wines. Similarly, in Joined Cases C-297/88 and C-197/89, *Meilicke v ADV/ORGA F A Meyer AG* (1990) the Court declined to answer a lengthy series of complex questions about the second company law directive raised in an action brought by a company law specialist which appeared to be designed to get the Court's ruling on the views put forward in one of his own books.

The Court put the matter clearly in Case 244/80, *Foglia v Novello (No 2)* (1981) (when the Italian court came back with some more questions):

'... the duty assigned to the Court by Article 177 is not that of delivering advisory opinions on general or hypothetical questions but of assisting in the administration of justice in the Member States. It accordingly does not have jurisdiction to reply to questions of interpretation which are submitted to it within the framework of procedural devices arranged by the parties in order to induce the Court to give its views on certain problems of Community law which do not correspond to an objective requirement inherent in the resolution of a dispute.'

* There must be a point of Community law relevant to the resolution of the dispute. In Case 298/84, *Jorio v Azienda Autonoma delle Ferrovie dello Stato* (1986) the Court found no causal connection between the questions about free movement of workers and discrimination, and the national measure which permitted only first-class passengers to use express trains.

* Where the Court is asked to rule on the compatibility of the law of *another* Member State with Community law (as in the *Foglia* case) it will be particularly careful, since such disputes can be artificial. The court making the reference might not be able to do anything with the interpretation. However, if there is a genuine dispute the Court will be prepared to give the referring court the ruling it needs to assess the compatibility of that other Member State's law with Community law.

* However, the Court has given rulings which appear to be advisory in some cases. In Cases 98, 162, 258/85 *Bertini v Regione Lazio* (1986) the Court was asked whether Community law required Italian medical schools to establish a fixed student intake. Quite what this had to do with the dispute before the Italian court, which concerned the alleged unlawful dismissal of surgeons, was not clear (and the Commission and the Italian government both urged the Court not to entertain the reference): the Third Chamber expressed regret that the Italian court had not said why it wanted a ruling, but nevertheless gave one, stating that it had to respect the national court's view that a ruling was necessary. It is also pertinent to note that there was a genuine dispute there, not a procedural contrivance as in *Foglia*.

In the UK, a decision not to refer is a point of law appealable to a higher court.

In theory, if the courts of a Member State persistently failed to make references, there might be grounds for an Article 169 enforcement action. In practice, though, higher courts set down guidelines such as those promulgated by Lord Denning MR in *Bulmer v Bollinger* (1974), lower courts are not browbeaten into refraining from making references.

6.4.2	Timing	The timing of a reference is a matter for the discretion of the national court (see *Pretore di Salo*). However, the Court does like national courts to establish the facts and resolve questions of national law first, otherwise the question posed may be deficient.

6.4.2   Timing

The timing of a reference is a matter for the discretion of the national court (see *Pretore di Salo*). However, the Court does like national courts to establish the facts and resolve questions of national law first, otherwise the question posed may be deficient.

6.4.3   Precedent

A national court can refer a matter to the ECJ even though the same question has already been asked in proceedings involving different parties. The fact that a measure has been held to be invalid by the Court in an Article 177 reference is sufficient reason for another national court to consider it void: but that does not prevent the second national court referring the matter to the ECJ (see Case 66/80, *International Chemical Corporation v Amministrazione della Finanze dello Stato* (1981)).

6.4.4   Multiple references

More than one preliminary ruling may be sought in the same case. The national court might have difficulties understanding or applying the Court's ruling, encounter a new problem of interpretation, or submit new considerations which might make the Court change its mind. However, a new reference cannot be used as a way to challenge the validity of the Court's ruling (Case 69/85, *Wünsche v Germany* (1986)).

6.4.5   National rules and references

The Court will not entertain a reference if the decision to refer is quashed by a superior national court. However, the mere fact that the decision to refer is appealed will not stop the Court of Justice giving a ruling (Case 13/61, *de Greus v Boschvan Rijn* (1962)).

National rules cannot prevent a court or tribunal from referring a question to the Court and require it instead to follow a decision of a higher national court on the same question of Community law (Case 166/73, *Rheinmühlen v Einfuhr- und Vorratstelle Getreide* (1978)).

6.4.6   National Courts of last resort

Where there is no judicial remedy against the decision of a national court, different rules apply. The Treaty says such courts 'shall' refer the matter: other language versions of the Treaty use more imperative wording.

This applies not only to the highest courts in the Member States (eg the House of Lords in the UK) but also to lower courts from which there is no appeal. *Costa v ENEL* was a reference from the Guidice Conciliatore in Milan, which had jurisdiction because of the small amount of money involved and from whose decision no appeal was possible.

Article 177 appears to give national courts of last resort no discretion over whether to refer a question of Community law to the Court of Justice. But the Court itself has given national courts a little leeway here:

- Similar case already decided

  One of the early cases referred by the Court under Article 177 was Case 26/62, *Van Gend en Loos* (1963) (see above, Chapter 3, para 3.6.1). Subsequently, the same facts arose in a case involving different parties, Cases 28-30/62, *da Costa v Nederlandse Belastingadministratie* (1963), which was referred to the Court before the *Van Gend en Loos* judgment was given. The Court said:

  'Although the third paragraph of Article 177 unreservedly requires courts or tribunals of a Member State against whose decisions there is no judicial remedy under national law ... to refer to the Court every question of interpretation raised before them, the authority of an interpretation under Article 177 already given by the Court may deprive the obligation of its purpose and thus empty it of its substance. Such is the case especially when the question raised is materially identical with a question which has already been the subject of a preliminary ruling in a similar case.'

- Is a reference needed?

  In Case 283/81, *CILFIT v Italian Ministry of Health* (1982), the Court stated that national courts and tribunals of last resort have the same discretion as other national courts and tribunals to decide whether they need a ruling from the Court. They do not have to refer a question of Community law raised before them 'if that question is not relevant, that is to say, if the answer to that question, regardless of what it may be, can in no way affect the outcome of the case'.

- Question of law already decided

  In the same case, the Court also expanded the *da Costa* principle. This exception was extended to cover the situation where 'previous decisions of the Court have already dealt with the point of law in question, irrespective of the nature of the proceedings which led to those decisions, even though the questions at issue are not strictly identical'.

- *Acte clair*

  Not content with those exceptions, the Court then formulated a third CILFIT exception: even though the question of Community law is relevant to the case, and there is no previous ruling on the same point of law, if the correct application of Community law is 'so obvious as to leave no scope for any reasonable doubt as to the manner in which the question is to be resolved', the national court may refrain from referring the matter to the ECJ.

The Court cautioned that the court or tribunal considering the case must be sure that the matter will be just as obvious to courts in the other Member States and to the ECJ itself. This is not easy to predict – indeed, it may be impossible – so the *acte clair* doctrine may be less sweeping than at first sight it appears.

Each of these exceptions, but especially the final one, derogates from the basic purpose of having a Court of Justice for the European Community: there is scope for a body of national law to develop on the interpretation of Community measures. The House of Lords has (as we shall see) used the various exceptions, particularly *acte clair*, to justify not referring a number of cases.

Weatherill and Beaumont suggest that the development of the *acte clair* doctrine had much to do with the attitude of the supreme courts in France and Germany at the time. In *Syndicat Général des Semoules de France* (1970) the Conseil d'Etat refused to accept the supremacy of Community regulations over later national law: in *Minister of the Interior v Cohn-Bendit* (1980) it refused to accept the direct effect of directives: and in *Re VAT Directives* (1982) and in *Kloppenberg* (1989) (decided in 1985) the German federal fiscal court, the Bundesfinanzhof, also refused to accept direct effect. A properly formulated *acte clair* doctrine could be expected to bring these rebels back into line: a rejection of the doctrine would have reinforced the rebellion. The Court's strategy seems to have been successful.

| 6.4.7 | The question for the Court |

The precise question posed in the reference is very important, as generally the Court is restricted in what it can do by what it is asked. In the UK the parties' lawyers participate in the drafting of the question (or questions – there are usually several), so the result should be a clear statement of the problem. But the Court often finds that the questions asked leave something to be desired.

Often, the question posed by the national court will not make it entirely clear what ruling is being sought. It cannot send the reference back, but will make the best of a bad job.

The Court will work out what the question of Community law involved is. This is particularly important in the context of references which ask whether a national measure is compatible with Community law: the Court cannot answer this question, but will work on the basis that the national court is looking for an interpretation of the relevant provision of Community law, even if it has not specified what that provision is. (See Cases 209-13/84, *Ministère Publique v Asjes* (1986), and Case 35/85, *Procureur de la République v Tissier* (1986).)

In the *Tissier* case, the Court stated:

'It is for the Court, when faced with questions which are not framed in an appropriate manner or which go beyond its functions under Article 177, to extract from all the information provided by the national court, in particular from the grounds of the decision referring the questions, the points of Community law which require interpretation or whose validity is at issue, having regard to the subject-matter of the dispute. In order to provide a satisfactory answer to a national court which has referred a question to it, the Court of Justice may deem it necessary to consider provisions of Community law to which the national court has not referred in the text of its question. However, it is for the national court to decide whether or not the rule of Community law, as interpreted by the Court of Justice pursuant to Article 177, is applicable in the case before it.'

The Court may therefore consider provisions of Community law not referred to in the question. However, it is under no duty to do so.

The Court will if necessary redraft the question to focus on the relevant issues (Case 78/70, *Deutsche Gramophon v Metro-SB-Grossmärkte* (1971)), provided it has enough facts to go on. If the referring court appears to have no idea what it is after, and has posed a number of questions, the Court will select and answer relevant questions. This approach ensures prompt assistance to the national courts (which may make a further reference if needed) and a speedy resolution of the dispute.

If the answer to the question will have no bearing on the case before the national court, the Court of Justice may decline to give one: this would be the case if the Community measure the interpretation of which was in issue had expired before the case was brought in the national court (Case 112/83, *Produits de Maïs v Administration des douanes* (1985)).

The Court has held that it is not necessary for a court of last resort to refer a question of Community law to it under Article 177 if the question arises in interlocutory proceedings (ie before the substantive issues in the case have come to trial). This is so even where there is no appeal against the interim decision in national law, but the parties must be able to insist on the substantive issues going to trial so that the question of Community law may be referred during those proceedings.

6.4.8   Interlocutory proceedings

6.5   Effect of preliminary rulings

Generally, a ruling under Article 177 on the interpretation of measure applies even to existing legal relationships. The Court takes the view that it is clarifying and defining the meaning and scope of the rule 'as it must be or ought to have been understood and applied from the time of its coming into force'. This principle has been stated several times in judgments of the Court: the first in time was Case 61/79, *Amministrazione della Finanze dello Stato v Denkavit Italiana* (1980).

However, the Court will sometimes restrict the effect of a judgment on existing relationships. It will apply the principle of legal certainty, and will typically state that the ruling only applies to those who had started legal proceedings before the judgment was given. Nor will the Court restrict the effects of its rulings in this way in subsequent cases: the restriction will be available, if at all, only in the case in which the ruling was given.

One celebrated case in which the principle was important is Case 43/75, *Defrenne v SABENA* (1976), where the Court decided that Article 119 directly applied the principle of equal pay for equal work. This decision had the potential to open the floodgates for claims for back pay, and to avoid this problem the Court held that its ruling could only be relied on for the period before it was given by workers who had already made their claims.

In Case C-262/88, *Barber v GRE* (1990), another Article 119 case this time involving pensions entitlements, the Court again restricted the effect of its ruling to the period after it was given, save in the cases of existing claimants.

6.5.1   Invalidity

The Court also has discretion to set limits on the temporal extent of its invalidity rulings. In Case 41/84, *Pinna v Craisse d'Allocations Familiales de la Savoie* (1986) the Court stated:

> 'When the Court makes use of the possibility of limiting the effect on past events of a declaration in proceedings under Article 177 of the Treaty that a measure is invalid, it is for the Court to decide whether an exception to that temporal limitation of the effect of its judgment may be made in favour of the party which brought the action before the national court or in favour of any other person who took similar steps before the declaration of invalidity or whether, conversely, a declaration of invalidity applicable only to the future constitutes an adequate remedy even for those persons who took action at the appropriate time with a view to protecting their rights.'

6.6   Interim measures

The general rule here is that a national court cannot declare acts of the institutions invalid. This is the exclusive preserve of the Court of Justice. However, the Court may make an exception where interim measures are sought from the national court while the Court of Justice's ruling is still awaited (see Case 314/85, *Foto Frost v Hauptzollamt Lübeck-Ost* (1987)).

A national court may suspend the operation of a national measure which implements a Community obligation pending the Court of Justice's ruling on the validity of the Community measure (Cases C-143/88 and C-92/89, *Zuckerfabrik Süderithmarschen v Hauptzollamt Itzehoe* (1991)).

National courts may also use interim measures to protect rights under EC law, pending an Article 177 ruling on those rights.

Judicial Review and Article 177

Article 177 provides a bridge between the Community legal order and the national courts. It enables national courts or tribunals to seek the Court of Justice's advice on matters before them.

Only the tribunal can refer a question: the parties may only request a referral. Only the Court of Justice can declare a piece of Community legislation void, so Article 177 provides a way of challenging the validity of such legislation indirectly. Most of the important developments in Community law have come about through Article 177 references, which account for about half the Court's workload.

Most of the references concern interpretation of Community laws. The Court's role ensures uniform interpretation throughout the Community.

The Court of Justice does not investigate facts. It merely answers the question on Community law put to it and hands the matter back to the national court.

The Court's jurisdiction under Article 177 covers legally binding provisions, non-binding recommendations and opinions (*Grimaldi v Fonds des maladies professionelles*), international agreements entered into by the Community under powers given by the Treaty (*Haegman v Belgium*), and decisions made by legislative bodies set up under international agreements made by the Community.

Article 177 provides for discretionary references from lower courts and tribunals and mandatory references from courts from which there is no appeal. In principle, any body before which national law requires issues of law to be settled is a court or tribunal. An arbitrator appointed by agreement between the parties is not a tribunal (*Nordsee v Reederei Mond*) but one imposed on the parties by national law, where the parties have no choice in the appointment, is.

The decision to make a discretionary reference is a matter for the national judge. However, the ECJ may refuse to give a ruling, so it can indicate when it thinks the reference should not have been made. It will only give a ruling on a reference where the national court is going to give judgment in proceedings which are intended to lead to a judicial decision. If the national proceedings have already terminated when the Court is asked for a reference, it is under no duty to give a ruling. The Court will not rule in proceedings which do not relate to a real dispute (*Foglia v Novello, Meilicke v ADV/ORGA F A Meyer AG*).

There must be a point of Community law relevant to the resolution of the dispute. In the UK, a decision not to refer is a point of law appealable to a higher court, but the mere fact that the decision to refer is appealed will not stop the Court of Justice giving a ruling

The timing of a reference is a matter for the discretion of the national court: see *Pretore di Salo*. However, the Court does like national courts to establish the facts and resolve questions of national law first, otherwise the question posed may be deficient.

A national court can refer a matter to the ECJ even though the same question has already been asked in proceedings involving different parties.

Where there is no judicial remedy against the decision of a national court, the court 'shall' refer the matter. This applies to lower courts from which there is no appeal as well as to national supreme courts. The Treaty requirement for a reference will not apply where a similar case or the same question of law has already been decided, where the court does not need a ruling to reach its decision, or if the meaning of the relevant Community law is so clear that no ruling is needed (the *acte clair* doctrine).

The precise question posed in the reference is very important, as generally the Court is restricted in what it can do by what it is asked. The ECJ cannot send a deficient question back, but will try to identify the point of Community law about which it is asked if this is not clear from the question, or it will select questions from those posed in the reference.

Generally, a ruling under Article 177 on the interpretation of measure applies even to existing legal relationships (*Amministrazione della Finanze dello Stato v Denkavit Italiana*). However, the Court will sometimes restrict the effect of a judgment on existing relationships (*Defrenne, Barber*). The Court also has discretion to set limits on the temporal extent of its invalidity rulings.

Chapter 7

The Common Market

While the Community is about a great deal more than just a common market, nevertheless the creation of a common market among the Member States is a central concern of the Treaty of Rome. This in turn entails a number of factors:

- the creation of a customs union between the Member States;

- the prohibition of discriminatory taxation;

- the guarantee of rights of freedom of movement of goods, workers and capital, and the right of establishment and the freedom to provide services;

- the harmonisation of laws which may affect trade between Member States, and the creation of Community legal regimes to replace national systems in certain areas.

As we have seen, Article 2 of the Treaty refers to the creation of the common market, and Articles 2 and 3 refer to common policy-making in certain areas. The objective of completing the single market, or internal market (which means the common market) by the end of 1992 is now contained in Article 8c (Article 7c after the Maastricht amendments), which was inserted into the Treaty by the Single European Act.

In this chapter, we are concerned with the first two elements and the last. In the following chapters, we look at the other elements of the common market.

7.1   Introduction

Article 9 of the Treaty provides that the Community shall be based on a customs union. This involves:

- the prohibition of customs duties on imports and exports and of charges having equivalent effect; and

- the adoption of a common customs tariff in the Member States' relations with third countries.

The liberalisation of trade within the common market has to be seen in the context of the broader liberalisation of trade throughout the world, brought about since the last war through the General Agreement on Tariffs and Trade (which is now becoming the World Trade Organisation). Within GATT, the EC acts as a single entity, and its common customs tariff is intended to be progressively reduced as a result of the successive negotiating rounds of the GATT.

7.2   The Customs Union

7.2.1	The common customs tariff

The first matter to consider is the common customs tariff. Article 3 committed the Community to the establishment of a common customs tariff, and of a common commercial policy towards third countries. Articles 18 to 29 deal with the details. In particular, Article 18 states:

> 'The Member States declare their readiness to contribute to the development of international trade and the lowering of barriers to trade by entering into agreements designed, on a basis of reciprocity and mutual advantage, to reduce customs duties below the general level of which they could avail themselves as a result of the establishment of a customs union between them.'

Within the common customs tariff, the Community is supposed to be a common market. The following provisions are concerned with the abolition of customs duties within the common market area.

7.2.2	Prohibiting customs duties

Articles 12 to 17 of the Treaty (of which, all but Article 12 have long since expired) contain the provisions which achieve the abolition of customs duties. Article 12 provides:

> 'Member States shall refrain from introducing between themselves any new customs duties on imports or exports or any charges having equivalent effect, and from increasing those which they already apply in their trade with each other.'

The following articles dealt with the progressive abolition of those charges which existed at the creation of the Community. Article 16 required the abolition of duties on exports and charges having equivalent effect, by the end of the first stage of integration (four years after signing of the Treaty).

The court has strictly interpreted the provisions of Article 12, which was the subject of *Van Gend en Loos*, the leading case on direct effect. Since it catches not only customs duties in the strict sense, but also measures having equivalent effect, its scope is wide. Two cases illustrate the court's approach:

- In Case 7/68, *Commission v Italy* (1968), a tax on the export of art treasures was considered. The court was not impressed by the Italian government's arguments that the levy was not raised on 'goods' but on cultural articles, and that the tax was designed to prevent exports not to raise money. On the latter, the point that Article 12 (like other provisions of the Treaty) is concerned with effect not purpose or form was stressed.

- In Case 2, 3/69, *Sociaal Fonds voor de Diamantarbeiders v SA Ch Brachfeld & Sons* (1969) the court took a similar view. The requirement in Belgian law that a percentage of the value of imported diamonds be paid into a social fund for the benefit of workers in the industry had the effect of a customs duty. It was an obstacle to the free movement of goods when they crossed a national frontier.

In Case 24/68, *Commission v Italy* (again!) (1969) the court defined the sort of charge which was caught (in that case by Article 16, which relates to exports):

'... any pecuniary charge, however small and whatever its designation and mode of application, which is imposed unilaterally on domestic or foreign goods by reason of the fact that they cross a frontier, and which is not a customs duty in the strict sense, constitutes a charge having equivalent effect ... even if it is not imposed for the benefit of the state, is not discriminatory or protective in effect, and if the product on which the charge is imposed is not in competition with any domestic product.'

In that case, the Italian government sought to justify a charge which it said was for a benefit to the exporter, namely for compiling statistical data on trade flows. The court accepted that if there was a genuine bargain, the charge would be outside the Article 12 prohibition: but it did not consider that this charge was. The trade would have to receive a specific, identifiable benefit: the sum paid would have to be proportionate to the benefit. In this case, the benefit should not be attributed to one individual trader. The benefits to the trader were too general to be excluded.

In Case 170/88, *Ford España v Spain* (1989) a charge purportedly for services rendered clearing the goods through customs was held illegal. Even if there was a specific benefit (which there might have been in that case) the price would have to be fixed according to the cost of providing the service. Instead, the Spanish authorities levied a flat percentage of the declared value of the goods. It could not be considered proportionate.

The same argument has failed when used to justify charges or fees imposed for compulsory veterinary and public health inspections on imported goods (see, for example, Case 87/75, *Bresciani* (1976) and Case 39/73, *Rewe-Zentralfinanz* (1973)).

Where checks are mandatory under Community law, and are imposed as a means of securing free movement of goods, fees levied by the authorities to cover the costs of the checks are compatible with Community law. They must still be proportionate.

If they have no basis in Community law, they will be considered to be charges having equivalent effect. If the relevant Community measure *permits* but does not require the check to be performed, the state in question must bear the cost: if it demands a fee from the trader, that is contrary to Article 12.

Fees may be charged under international obligations to which all Member States are party. If the fees represent the cost of services which are compulsory, they will fall outside Article 12. In Case 89/76, *Commission v Netherlands* (1977) fees chargeable for controls required under the International Plant Protection Convention (1951) were not caught by Article 12.

Again, the fee must be proportionate to the cost of providing the service.

7.3 Discriminatory taxation

Article 95 has much in common with Article 12. Where the earlier provision was concerned with customs duties, the later one is concerned with other fiscal charges which may have the capacity to interfere with inter-state trade. It provides:

> 'No Member State shall impose, directly or indirectly, on the products of other Member States any internal taxation of any kind in excess of that imposed directly or indirectly on similar domestic products.'

Furthermore, no Member State shall impose on the products of other Member States any internal taxation of such a nature as to afford indirect protection to other products.

The purpose of the Article is set out in the court's judgment in Case 171/78, *Commission v Denmark* (1980):

> 'The ... provisions supplement, within the system of the Treaty, the provisions on the abolition of customs duties and charges having equivalent effect. Their aim is to ensure the free movement of goods between the Member States in normal conditions of competition by the elimination of all forms of protection which result from the application of internal taxation which discriminates against products from other Member States. As the Commission has correctly stated, Article 95 must guarantee the complete neutrality of internal taxation as regards competition between domestic products and imported products.'

This encompasses financial charges within a general system which applies systematically to domestic and imported goods. The taxation system may not:

- discriminate against imported products which are the same as or similar to domestic products; or

- be applied to imported products in order to protect the market position of a domestic product which, though not the same or similar, does compete in the same market.

Article 95 goes no further than to prohibit discrimination: it does not try to provide for equality of tax treatment between Member States. It is a matter for Member States to determine their own tax policies, and this is one of the areas of sovereignty most jealously guarded by them.

It is very rare to find a provision of national law which directly discriminates against goods form another Member State. Article 95 pulls no punches when it comes to such provisions, so has an important deterrent effect.

7.3.1   Direct discrimination

There are a couple of cases where the court has found direct discrimination:

- In Case 57/65, *Lütticke GmbH v Hauptzollamt Saarlouis* (1966) a claim for tax due levied on an importer of dried milk was challenged successfully on the ground that it would not be charged on domestic production.

- In Case 127/75, *Getränkevertrieb Bobie v Hauptzollamt Aachen-Nord* (1975) the court held that the German tax on beer, though it could operate to the advantage of imports, was nonetheless prohibited because it sometimes discriminated against imports. It was in fact designed to favour small breweries in Germany by taxing them at a rate which depended on their output: all imported beers were taxed at the same rate, so large foreign breweries were treated comparatively well.

The conditions under which a tax is payable may also amount to discrimination. In Case 55/79, *Commission v Ireland* (1980) the court held that Article 95 was breached when a tax which applied equally to imports and domestic goods was payable immediately by importers, while domestic producers got several weeks' grace.

Case 112/84, *Humblot v Directeur des Services Fiscaux* (1985) is a classic example of indirect discrimination. The French government taxed cars according to objective criteria, based on the vehicle's power output. Under 16 CV, there was a graduated scale rising to 1,100 francs per annum for the most powerful cars. Over 16 CV, there was a flat rate of 5,000 Francs. On the face of it, the system was a rational (if draconian) approach to the problem of anti-social, large cars. However, no French manufacturer produced cars over 16 CV. The court held that this was prohibited:

7.3.2   Indirect discrimination

'... the special tax reduces the amount of competition to which cars of domestic manufacture are subject and hence is contrary to the principle of neutrality with which domestic taxation must comply.'

That case also illustrates that an indirectly discriminatory tax may nevertheless have some objective justification. Had the French government adopted a less draconian approach, they may have been able to establish that the tax system for cars was justified: the proportionality rule would also have applied. In fact, France subsequently replaced the original scale with nine separate tax bands for cars over 16 CV, but still at a very much higher rate of tax than smaller cars. It had still made the system objectively justified (Case 433/85, *Feldain v Directeur des Services Fiscaux* (1985)).

7.3.3   **Similar and competing goods**

The case law is primarily concerned with whether goods can be said to be similar or to be in competition with each other. One or other is needed to bring Article 95(1) or (2) to bear. The consequences of one or other of these prohibitions applying will be different, a point which we shall explore further below.

Alcohol provides several examples. All Member States levy taxes on alcoholic drinks, which has social justifications in addition to revenue ones. Frequently, imported drinks are treated less favourably than domestically-made ones. The authorities will usually argue that the two drinks are not the same.

• Similar goods

Article 95(1) requires that similar products from different sources be accorded the same tax treatment. Taxes may be levied, but they must be *origin neutral.*

If products fall within the same classification for tax purposes, the issue of similarity is not too difficult (Case 27/67, *Fink-Frucht GmbH v Hauptzollamt München Landbergerstrasse* (1968)). The converse is not necessarily true: just because goods are not classified together for tax purposes does not mean that they are not similar.

In Case 168/78, *Commission v France* (1980) tax on grain spirits was higher than on fruit spirits. By chance, this meant that imported whisky, gin and vodka were taxed more than brandy, armagnac and calvados produced in France. The court had to determine whether the two sorts of spirits were similar, and decided that this had to be judged from the consumer's point of view. They were broadly in competition according to this test, so the legislation was discriminatory and contrary to Article 95(1).

In Case 170/78, *Commission v UK* (1980), the court was satisfied that there was a competitive relationship between domestic beer and cheap imported wine, as a result of which the duty on the wine was reduced.

In Case 243/84, *John Walker v Ministeriet for Skatter* (1986) where the question was whether liqueur fruit wine and whisky were similar, the court began with the objective features of the two products. Their alcohol content and method of manufacture were considered. Then the court turned to the manner in which the products fulfilled consumer needs. The court considered that the characteristics of the products were so different that they could not be considered similar.

However, in Case 106/84 *Commission v Denmark* (1986) the Court considered the similarity of wines made from grapes (which is in fact inherent in the term 'wine') and drinks made by a similar process from other fruits. It concluded that the products were similar and had to be taxed at a similar level.

- Competing goods

If goods are not similar, Article 95(2) may still apply if the goods are in competition with each other. If they are, then the tax system may not protect domestic products against competition from imports.

The court's approach is laid down on a series of decisions in what are known as the *Spirits* cases. The *John Walker* case referred to above is the last in the line.

There, the court had decided that there was no breach of Article 95(1). It went on to determine that the Danish system of taxing spirits was origin neutral, so whisky was not discriminated against. It was treated by the taxation system in the same way as other spirits, including domestically-produced ones.

In many of these cases, the court has failed to distinguish between the two paragraphs of Article 95. It found it unnecessary to decide whether the products were similar or competing. This approach obscures an important distinction: where the goods are similar, the correct thing for the member state to do is to equalise the tax burden, but if they are competing it is only necessary for the protective effect of the law to be removed.

This approach was rejected in the *John Walker* case, and in *Commission v UK* where the issue was whether wine and beer are in competition. There, the court was faced with the problem that the two products are clearly not similar, but arguably may be in competition: it had to treat the two legs of Article 95 as separate. After requesting further information about the competitive relationship of the products, and three years and two sets of oral arguments later, the court decided that the two did compete.

7.4 Harmonisation of taxation

7.4.1 Value added tax

The Treaty envisages harmonisation of certain taxes between Member States.

The most important indirect tax which may come in for consideration under Article 95 is value added tax. Article 99 provides for the harmonisation of various types of taxation, including VAT, to the extent that this is necessary to ensure the establishment and functioning of the common market.

Much has already been done to achieve harmonisation of various aspects of indirect taxation and to create a Community system of VAT. This involves the harmonisation of:

- the base or scope of the tax;

- the number of different rates of VAT; and

- the actual rates of tax.

VAT was identified as an area requiring action to complete the harmonisation process in the White Paper, *Completing the Internal Market* which laid the ground for the 1992 programme.

In 1991 the Member States agreed transitional arrangements for the application of VAT in intra-Community trade from the beginning of 1993. This will be replaced from 1997 by a permanent system.

In the transitional phase, transactions between persons liable to VAT in different Member States will be taxed in the state of importation. This will do away with border controls and place the burden on the taxpayers themselves to administer the tax.

The goods are invoiced without VAT, and on its VAT returns the seller will show the volume of intra-Community sales. The buyer's return will show how much it bought from other EC Member States and it will account for the tax due on them.

Member States have now agreed that there is no need for harmonisation of the precise rates of tax throughout the Community, and that broad bands will suffice. There will be a minimum rate of 15%, and no maximum. In certain cases, rates below 15% will be permitted and existing zero rates (such as that in the UK for most foods) will be retained for the time being. Provided that national rates are brought sufficiently close together, there will be no significant distortion of trade and competition.

A Community-wide VAT system is envisaged for 1997, within which there will be no discrimination between goods from different Member States. This will eliminate a significant fiscal barrier to free trade within the common market, and also an important physical barrier associated with the collection of the tax at national boundaries.

The permanent system will replace payment in the state of destination with payment in the state of origin. The supplier will account for tax in the normal way in its own Member State, and the customer will reclaim input tax on the transaction in its own Member State.

Similar work is being done on excise duties, and the Member States have accepted in principle that there should be binding minimum excise rates on petrol, tobacco and alcohol. Border controls have been eliminated by instituting a system in which goods between bonded warehouses, and the duty only bites when the goods leave bond.

7.4.2   Excise duties

The existence of duty free shops in a common market is a nonsense, but one which it would be politically difficult to do away with. As part of the 1991 agreement, the Council decided that duty free shops could remain until 1999: after that date they will operate only at the Community's external boundary.

The Common Market

The creation of a common market among the Member States is a central concern of the Treaty of Rome. This entails:

- a customs union;

- prohibition of discriminatory taxation;

- freedom of movement of goods, workers and capital, the right of establishment and the freedom to provide services;

- harmonisation and the creation of Community legal régimes to replace national systems in certain areas.

Article 2 of the Treaty refers to the creation of the common market. The objective of completing the single market is contained in Article 7c EC.

Article 9 of the Treaty provides that the Community shall be based on a customs union, involving the prohibition of customs duties on imports and exports and of charges having equivalent effect, and the adoption of a common customs tariff in the Member States' relations with third countries.

Article 3 committed the Community to the establishment of a common customs tariff, and of a common commercial policy towards third countries. Article 12 contains the provisions which achieve the abolition of customs duties.

Article 12 catches not only customs duties in the strict sense, but also measures having equivalent effect. The Court has strictly interpreted its provisions. See *Commission v Italy* and *Sociaal Fonds voor de Diamantarbeiders v SA Ch Brachfeld & Sons*.

The Court has defined the sort of charge which is caught as including any charge which is imposed unilaterally on domestic or foreign goods by reason of the fact that they cross a frontier, and which is not a customs duty.

Article 95 is concerned with other fiscal charges which may have the capacity to interfere with inter-state trade. The provisions aim is to ensure the free movement of goods between the Member States in normal conditions of competition by the elimination of all forms of protection which result from the application of internal taxation which discriminates against products from other Member States.

Creating the common market

The Customs Union

Internal taxation

Article 95 must guarantee the complete neutrality of internal taxation as regards competition between domestic products and imported products.

The taxation system may not:

- discriminate against imported products which are the same as or similar to domestic products. See *Lütticke GmbH v Hauptzollamt Saarlouis* and *Getränkevertrieb Bobie v Hauptzollamt Aachen-Nord*. The conditions under which a tax is payable may also amount to discrimination (see *Commission v Ireland*) or;

- be applied to imported products in order to protect the market position of a domestic product which, though not the same or similar, does compete in the same market (see *Humblot v Directeur des Services Fiscaux*).

The case law is primarily concerned with whether goods can be said to be similar or to be in competition with each other. Article 95(1) requires that similar products from different sources be accorded the same tax treatment. Taxes may be levied, but they must be origin neutral. Products are likely to be considered similar if they fall within the same classification for tax purposes (*Fink-Frucht GmbH v Hauptzollamt München Landbergerstrasse*, *Commission v France* and *Commission v UK*).

If goods are not similar, Article 95(2) may still apply if the goods are in competition with each other. If they are, then the tax system may not protect domestic products against competition from imports.

Tax harmonisation

Article 99 provides for the harmonisation of various types of taxation, including VAT, to the extent that this is necessary to ensure the establishment and functioning of the common market.

In 1991 the Member States agreed transitional arrangements for the application of VAT in intra-Community trade from the beginning of 1993. Similar work is being done on excise duties.

Chapter 8

Free Movement of Goods

Articles 30 to 36 of the Treaty of Rome are concerned with the free movement of goods. Of these Articles 31, 32, 33 and 35 have expired.

Articles 30 and 34 contain the basic prohibition on restrictions on free movement of goods: Article 36 contains derogations from this principle, allowing national laws to restrict free movement in certain limited circumstances.

The free movement provisions of the Treaty have been described as 'the most important of the pillars upon which the Community edifice rests' (Mancini AG in Case 238/82, *Duphar v Netherlands* (1984)).

The provisions on free movement of goods are related to the competition rules. But while the competition rules are directed at the activities of private undertakings, the provisions on free movement are directed at state measures. The line is sometimes difficult to draw: for example, Case 144/81, the *Buy Irish* case discussed below (and in Chapter 5, para 5.1.2), the promotional body was a private company but the state funded it and appointed its board.

Articles 30 to 36 should be seen as steps along the road to the creation of a fully-functioning common market. One day, in theory, they should be unnecessary. However, that day is a long way off.

National rules which can restrict the free movement of goods are only tolerated in so far as there is no Community law in the area. The whole purpose of the 1992 programme was to put in place all the necessary legislation to ensure that national laws would no longer have any role to play where they could interfere with the common market.

Article 30 states with admirable brevity that:

'Quantitative restrictions on imports and all measures having equivalent effect shall, without prejudice to the following provisions, be prohibited between Member States.'

Article 34 similarly prohibits quantitative restrictions on exports and all measures having equivalent effect.

8.1 Introduction

8.1.1 Relationship with competition rules

8.1.2 Transitional nature

8.2 Article 30

8.2.1   Quantitative restrictions

Quantitative restrictions are measures designed to prohibit or limit exports or imports of particular classes of goods by reference to their number, weight, value or other quantitative criteria. They are what are commonly referred to as quotas, and a total ban on imports or exports is a zero quota (see Case 34/79, *R v Henn and Darby* (1979)).

8.2.2   Measures having equivalent effect

Measures having equivalent effect have proved more difficult to define, and the court (encouraged by Article 2 of the Treaty) has elaborated the notion so that it is now far removed from a simple numerical restriction on trade.

Almost anything which hinders the free movement of goods can be caught. In Case 8/74 *Procureur du Roi v B & G Dassonville* (1974) the European Court of Justice held that:

'All trading rules enacted by Member States are capable of hindering, directly or indirectly, actually or potentially, intra-community trade are to be considered as measures having an effect equivalent to quantitative restrictions.'

Effect, not aim, is the important thing, so the court held in the *Buy Irish* case described below that the failure of the campaign made no difference. There is no *de minimis* rule.

However, the court indicated in the *Dassonville* case that there was a limit to how far Article 30 would go. Provided that there is no existing Community law on the subject, state action to prevent unfair practices would not be prohibited so long as it was reasonable. This has become known as the rule of reason, and has since been amplified by the court in a series of cases dealt with below.

8.2.3   Discrimination

Measures which discriminate against imports are clearly going to be prohibited by Article 30. But discrimination is not essential for Article 30 to apply: it is the effect on inter-state trade which is important.

The interpretation of Article 30 is facilitated by Directive 70/50, which on the face of it only applies to the abolition of restrictions during the transitional period (which for the original Member States ended in 1969). Nevertheless, it still provides some very useful guidance on interpretation.

The directive distinguishes measures that discriminate against imports from those which are non-discriminatory: these categories have come to be referred to as distinctly applicable and indistinctly applicable measures. Article 2 deals with distinctly applicable (ie discriminatory) measures:

'1   This directive concerns measures, other than those applicable equally to domestic or imported products, which hinder imports which could otherwise take place, including measures which make importation more difficult or costly than the disposal of domestic products.

2   In particular it covers measures which make imports or the disposal, at any marketing stage, of imported products subject to a condition – other than a formality – which is required in respect of imported products only, or a condition differing from that required for domestic products and more difficult to satisfy. Equally, it covers, in particular, measures which favour domestic products or grant them a preference, other than an aid.'

Article 3 covers indistinctly applicable measures:

'This directive also covers measures governing the marketing of products which deal, in particular, with shape, size, weight, composition, presentation, identification or putting up and which are equally applicable to domestic and imported products, where the restrictive effect of such measures on the free movement of goods exceeds the effects intrinsic to trade rules.'

This is the case, in particular, where:

- the restrictive effects on the free movement of goods are out of proportion to their purpose;

- the same objective can be achieved by other means which are less of a hindrance to trade.

Readers will recognise the familiar concepts of proportionality and alternative means in the last couple of paragraphs.

The list of matters which may constitute measures having equivalent effect is not closed, but the court has dealt with a variety of distinctly applicable measures. The following list is illustrative: since effect, not form, determines whether a measure is caught by Article 30, the value of examining the subject-matter of the prohibited measure is limited.

8.3   Distinctly applicable measures

The following types of restrictions have been held to be restricted:

- Import and export licences, customs formalities and similar requirements. (See Case 154/85, *Commission v Italy* (1987), where elaborate documentation was required before a used car could be imported into Italy: and Case 251/78 *Denkavit Futtermittel GmbH v Minister für Ernährung* (1979), concerning veterinary inspections of animal feedstuffs, intended to prevent the spread of disease.) This applies even where they are purely a formality: Case 124/81, *Commission v UK* (1983), a case concerning restrictions on the import of UHT milk.

- 'Buy National' campaigns, even where they are non-binding. (See Case 244/81, *Commission v Ireland* (1982), where the court held that Article 30 prohibited a campaign designed to provide consumers with the information needed to discriminate in favour of domestically-produced goods: cf Case 222/82, *Apple and Pear Council v Lewis* (1983), where the court held that extolling the virtues of certain fruits, even where those fruits were typical of national production, was not caught.)

- Origin marking requirements. (See Case 113/80, *Commission v Ireland (the Irish Souvenirs case)* (1981), where souvenirs of Ireland not manufactured in that country had to be marked with an indication of that fact: and Case 207/83, *Commission v United Kingdom* (1985), which concerned a requirement that all goods of certain types offered for sale in the UK had to be marked with an indication of their country of origin. It applied to imported and domestically-produced goods alike, but since it provided the consumer with the information necessary to exercise a prejudice against foreign products it was considered by the court to be indirectly discriminatory.)

- Government financial assistance provided for the purchase of domestically-produced goods. (In Case 103/84, *Commission v Italy* (1986), motor vehicles were involved.)

- Providing a legal remedy to prevent the marketing of an imported product which infringed a patent, but not where the product was domestically-produced (Case 263/85, *Allen and Hanburys v Generics* (1988)).

- Excessive roadworthiness tests on vehicles imported from other Member States (Case 50/85, *Schloh v Auto Controle Technique Sprl* (1987)).

8.4 Indistinctly applicable measures: the rule of reason

A wide variety of national measures may be prohibited because they have the effect of hindering imports, even though they apply equally to domestic and imported goods. Pending harmonisation, barriers to trade arising from the diversity of national laws may be caught by Article 30 even though there is no discrimination. As Advocate General Slynn put it in Case *Cinéthique v Fédération Nationale des Cinémas Françaises* (1985):

'discrimination ... although it may be sufficient, even conclusive, to bring a measure within Article 30, is not a necessary precondition for Article 30 to apply'.

As we saw, the principles of proportionality and alternative means will apply: thus in Case 261/81, *Walter Rau v de Smedt* (1982), the court held that the objective of enabling consumers to distinguish butter from margarine could be attained without requiring that all margarine be sold in cubic containers.

This much can be gleaned from a reading of Directive 70/50, but the importance of the concept of prohibiting indistinctly applicable measures under Article 30 was emphasised by the court in one of its most celebrated decisions.

In the *Cassis de Dijon* case, Case 120/78, *Rewe-Zentrale v Bundesmonopolverwalting für Branntwein* (1979) the German law which required certain alcoholic drinks to have a minimum alcohol level had the effect of excluding cassis from the German market.

8.4.1   The *Cassis de Dijon* case

The court was prepared to accept that the Member States had the right to make such laws:

> 'In the absence of common rules relating to the production and marketing of alcohol ... it is for the Member States to regulate all matters relating to the production of alcohol and alcoholic beverages on their own territory.'

However, the court's broad statement was qualified:

> 'Obstacles to movement within the Community resulting from disparities between the national laws relating to the marketing of the products in question must be accepted in so far as those provisions may be recognised as being necessary in order to satisfy mandatory requirements relating in particular to the effectiveness of fiscal supervision, the protection of public health, the fairness of commercial transactions and the defence of the consumer.'

This is generally referred to as the rule of reason. But in the *Cassis* case, the court did not believe that the restrictions were justified:

> 'There is ... no valid reason why, provided they have been lawfully produced and marketed in one of the Member States, alcoholic beverages should not be introduced into any other Member State; the sale of such products may not be subject to a legal prohibition on the marketing of beverages with an alcohol content lower than the limit set by the national rules.'

This introduces the important concept of *mutual recognition*. It applies as a presumption, unless national rules can be justified on the basis of mandatory requirements.

This is a major step in the direction of unhindered free trade. If goods have been put on the market in one Member State, they can only exceptionally be excluded from other national markets within the Community.

| 8.4.2 | Qualifications to the rule of reason | The rule of reason is itself qualified by the requirement – adapted by the Court of Justice from the second sentence of Article 36 – that such measures must not constitute *arbitrary discrimination* or a *disguised restriction on trade* between Member States. The rule of reason will only apply where the interest or value which is sought to be protected is analogous to the matters mentioned in Article 36. |

There must be *no Community system* covering the interest or value concerned. National measures may exceptionally be upheld despite the existence of Community measures if the Community measures are designed to supplement rather than replace national ones. Finally the measures concerned may not be disguised restrictions on intra-community trade or means of arbitrary discrimination, a requirement borrowed directly from Article 36.

Measures which are justified under the rule of reason must be *proportionate* to the end to be achieved, and the principle of alternative means will also apply. In *Cassis de Dijon* the court thought that the end which the German authorities claimed to be pursuing (the protection of the consumer, who might more easily become addicted to alcohol if he or she took it in weak beverages) than if full-strength drinks were consumed) could be attained by labelling instead, with much less of an impact on trade.

| 8.4.3 | Subsequent development | Since the *Cassis de Dijon* decision there have been many cases in the same area. Some have been very similar to the original case: |

- Case 788/79, *Gilli and Andres* (1980) concerned an Italian law which prohibited the sale of vinegar made from anything other than wine. The defendants imported German cider vinegar and were prosecuted. The Court (on an Article 177 reference) reiterated that the restrictions would only be permitted if they were necessary to satisfy mandatory requirements: there was no threat to public health, and the principles of proportionality and alternative means suggested that any problems could be overcome by labelling.

- In Case 178/84, *Commission v Germany* (1987), Germany's Reinheitsgebot, the beer purity law, was in issue. The law restricted the use of the word Bier to something produced using only the four traditional ingredients (water, hops, yeast and barley) and also prohibited the inclusion of any additives. Although it was ostensibly non-discriminatory, the law effectively excluded foreign beers from the German market. The court was not convinced that there was any possibility of consumer confusion, and in any case if there was any it could be overcome by appropriate labelling.

In the *Cassis* case, the court listed four matters which could justify the existence of national measures (see above): it has developed more 'mandatory grounds' in subsequent cases.

- In Case 240/83, *Brûleurs d'Huiles Usagées* (1985) environmental protection was accepted by the court as a mandatory requirement: in Case 302/86, *Commission v Denmark* (1988) the court was asked to consider a requirement that certain drinks be marketed only in reusable containers. It held that the approval system for containers was prohibited by Article 30 but that the deposit system for empties was permissible.

- In Case 155/80, *Oebel* (1981) the court recognised that legitimate interests of social and economic policy might be mandatory requirements, provided they were consistent with the Treaty.

- The court has also held that restrictions arising from national laws on Sunday trading might be justified by 'national or regional socio-cultural characteristics' (Case C-169/91, *Stoke-on-Trent City Council and Norwich City Council v B&Q plc* (1993)).

- In the *Cinéthique* case the court upheld a non-discriminatory French rule requiring that video cassettes of films not be sold or hired out for a year after their first cinema showing. It did restrict imports, but the court considered it to be justified.

Article 36 states that:

8.5   Article 36

'The provisions of Articles 30 to 34 shall not preclude prohibitions or restrictions on imports, exports or goods in transit justified on grounds of public morality, public policy or public security; the protection of health and life of humans, animals or plants; the protection of national treasures possessing artistic, historic or archaeological value; or the protection of industrial and commercial property. Such prohibitions or restrictions shall not, however, constitute a means of arbitrary discrimination or a disguised restriction on trade between Member States.'

This principle is subject always to the application of the proportionality test.

The Court of Justice explained the effect of Article 36 in Case 35/76, *Simmenthal SpA v Italian Minister for Finance* (1976):

'Article 36 is not designed to reserve certain matters to the exclusive jurisdiction of Member States, but permits national laws to derogate from the principle of the free movement of goods to the extent to which such derogation is and continues to be justified for the attainment of the objectives referred to in that Article.'

We shall now examine these categories in greater detail.

8.5.1   Public morality

In principle, it is for each Member State to decide what its own values in the sphere of public morality should be. See the Court of Justice decision in Case 34/79, *R v Henn and Darby* (1979), which concerned the import of pornography into the UK. This was permissible, but would constitute an instrument of arbitrary discrimination if there was a legitimate trade within the Member State in the articles the import of which was prohibited (cf Case 121/85, *Conegate v HM Customs and Excise* (1986)).

8.5.2   Public policy

This means a serious threat to one of the fundamental interests of society. It has been held to include the right to mint coinage (Case 7/78, *R v Thompson, Johnson and Woodiniss* (1978)) but is not to be used to embrace any matter about which the state may feel concerned. Specific types of welfare law will not be assumed to fall within the rubric: in Case 177/83, *Kohl v Ringelhan* (1984) the court refused to accept that measures introduced for consumer protection are legitimate measures of public policy.

8.5.3   Public security

This covers safeguarding the existence of the institutions of a Member State and its essential public services and the survival of its inhabitants. How far it goes is not clear other than that it will cover controls on explosives and firearms. In Case 72/83, *Campus Oil Ltd et al v Minister for Industry and Energy et al* (1984), the court accepted that a requirement that oil importers purchase a proportion of their requirements from Irish refineries could be justified if it was essential for guaranteeing the availability of petroleum supplies and was not disproportionate.

8.5.4   The protection of health and life of humans, animals and plants

There are several principles enunciated under this head:

(a) Member States are generally free to set such health standards as they think necessary, but any standards set will be subject to the proportionality rule. Thus, in the *Cassis de Dijon* case the court held that the German laws on alcoholic content went beyond what was required for consumer protection. In Case 104/75, *Officier van Justitie v De Peijper* (1976) the court held that measures would not fall within the Article 36 exception if the health and life of humans can be as effectively protected by measures which do not restrict intra-community trade so much. The risk to health must be a real one for the measures to be permitted.

(b) The proportionality rule will also prevent checks of foods on importation when they have already been checked on exportation, unless they might have changed in the meantime or the second checks are to ensure the first checks are being done. In Case 186/86 *Commission v Germany* (1986) the court held that systematic veterinary inspections of imported poultry meat were prohibited by Article 30. The products were covered by a harmonising Directive, so only general administrative checks would be allowed.

(c) Import bans or licences may be permitted although the court has been reluctant to accept them. In Case 40/82, *Commission v United Kingdom* (1982) (the first *Newcastle Disease* case) the court found it evident that the requirements imposed by the UK were designed to protect the British poultry industry. In Case 124/81, *Commission v United Kingdom* (1983) (the *UHT Milk* case) the court held Britain's system of specific import licences to be disproportionate as it could be done away with without impairing the protection of animals' health or increasing administrative or financial burdens.

(d) On the other hand, in the second and third *Newcastle Disease* judgments (the *Bourgoigne* cases: Case 40/82 *Commission v United Kingdom* (1984), *Commission v Ireland* (1984)) the court weighed the inconvenience caused by the financial and administrative burdens against the dangers and the risks to animals' health which would arise from a continuation of the imports and found the restrictions justified.

(e) Import bans will not be allowed if clear labelling will suffice instead as in the case of Italy's prohibition of food containing animal gelatin lawfully manufactured in another Member State. However, Member States are free (in the absence of EC legislation) to devise their own requirements in the light of climatic conditions and the dietary habits and general state of health of the population (Case 94/83, *Heijn* (1984); Case 54/85, *Ministère Public v Mirepoix* (1986); Case 247/84, *The State v Motte* (1985)).

This provision has been considered only once by the Court of Justice. In Case 7/68, *Commission v Italy* (1968) it was used to justify an export restriction on art treasures: but that restriction took the form of an export tax, and the court held that Article 36 could not be used to justify a tax. The scope of this provision therefore remains indeterminate.

8.5.5   Protection of national treasures

8.5.6	Protection of industrial and commercial property	

The protection of 'industrial and commercial property' is the last exception provided by Article 36. This wording is acknowledged to cover patents, trademarks, designs and copyright, the last somewhat reluctantly: the Court of Justice has held that copyright can also be form of industrial or commercial property because it 'includes the protection conferred by copyright, especially when exploited commercially in the form of licences capable of affecting distribution in the various Member States of goods incorporating the protected literary or artistic work' (Cases 55 and 57/80, *Membran v GEMA 2* (1981)).

National intellectual property rights are undoubtedly measures having equivalent effect to quantitative restrictions, within the meaning of the *Dassonville* decision. But Article 36 indicates that their market-partitioning effect will be tolerated, and this is reinforced by Article 222:

> 'This Treaty shall in no way prejudice the rules in Member States governing the system of property ownership.'

Articles 36 and 222 therefore conflict at the most fundamental level with the principle of economic integration which lies at the heart of the Treaty and which is the rationale for Article 30.

The case law shows that the court has addressed the incompatibility of these provisions by seeking a compromise. This is based on three principles which have their origin in Case 78/70, *Deutsche Gramophon v Metro-SB Grossmärkte* (1971):

- While the Treaty cannot affect the *existence* of intellectual property rights, there are nonetheless circumstances in which the *exercise* of such rights may be restricted by the prohibitions laid down in the Treaty.

- Article 36 permits exceptions to the free movement of goods only to the extent to which such exceptions are necessary to safeguard intellectual property. The court will only allow a derogation from the basic principle of Article 30 where it is justified for the purpose of safeguarding rights which constitute the *specific subject matter* of the property rights specified in Article 36.

- The exclusive right conferred on the owner of intellectual property is *exhausted* when products are put into circulation anywhere within the common market by the owner of the rights or with its consent.

The subsequent cases have been concerned with developing these themes, and in particular with identifying the specific subject matter of each type of intellectual property.

(a) *Exercise and existence*

Articles 36 and 222 preclude the Treaty having any effect on the existence of intellectual property rights. The ultimate solution to the dilemma posed by these rules is to replace national intellectual property rights with Community rights, or at least to harmonise national laws: these topics are dealt with elsewhere. In the meantime, the court has maintained that national rules about the existence of intellectual property rights must prevail.

In Case 144/81, *Keurkoop v Nancy Kean* (1982) the court upheld the right of the Member States to legislate to protect intellectual property as they considered necessary:

> '... in the present state of Community law and in the absence of Community standardisation or the harmonisation of laws the determination of the conditions and procedures under which protection is granted is a matter of national rules and, in this instance, for the common legislation established under regional union between Belgium, Luxembourg and the Netherlands referred to in Article 233 of the Treaty.'

This has now been confirmed in Case 35/87, *Thetford v Fiamma* (1988).

Restrictions on the ownership of intellectual property rights to nationals of a particular Member State, and requirements that the holder of the patent manufactures in that Member State, would be considered unlawful. They would amount to arbitrary discrimination, so Article 36 would not apply.

The same principle applies to national provisions which govern the transfer or extinction of intellectual property rights, including compulsory licensing (Case 435/85, *Allen and Hanburys v Generics* (1988), where the Court of Justice ruled that compulsory licences for the importation of a product may not be withheld if they are available for the same product's manufacture).

The grounds in UK patent law for granting a compulsory licence, namely that demand in the UK is being met substantially by imports, were also held unlawful by the Court in Case 30/90, *Commission v UK* (1993).

(b) *Specific subject matter*

Intellectual property rights cannot be used to create arbitrary discrimination or disguised restrictions on trade. Article 36 specifically attaches this proviso to all the rights which it preserves. The doctrine of proportionality also requires that any derogation from a basic principle of the Treaty be strictly construed and go no further than is necessary to realise the purpose of the exception.

- Patents

  In Case 15/74, *Centrafarm v Sterling Drug* (1974) the court defined the specific subject matter of patents:

  'In relation to patents the specific subject matter of the industrial property is the guarantee that the patentee, to reward the creative effort of the inventor, has the exclusive right to use an invention with a view to manufacturing industrial products and putting them into circulation for the first time, either directly or by the grant of licences for third parties, as well as to oppose infringements.'

- Trademarks

  In Case 16/74, *Centrafarm v Winthrop* (1974) the court defined the specific subject matter of trademarks as:

  '... the guarantee that the owner of the trade mark has the exclusive right to use that mark, for the purpose of putting products protected by the trade mark into circulation for the first time, and is therefore intended to protect him against competitors wishing to take advantage of the status and reputation of the trade mark by selling products illegally bearing that trade mark.'

- Copyright

  The court has had less opportunity to consider the specific subject matter of copyright. It is assumed to be similar in nature to the specific subject matter of patents and trademarks, consisting of the basic exclusive right to do the acts restricted by copyright and to restrain infringement.

  In Case 62/79, *Coditel v Cine Vog* (1980), which concerned the retransmission in Belgium by Coditel of a German television broadcast of a film. The exclusive rights to show the film in Belgium had been assigned to Cine Vog on condition that it would not be shown on television in Belgium for 40 months after its release in the cinemas.

  Cine Vog sued Coditel for infringement of its rights and the matter was referred to the Court of Justice. The court held that 'the right of the copyright owner and his assigns to require fees for any showing of a film is part of the essential function of copyright in this type of literary and artistic work'. The court concluded:

  'The exclusive assignee of the performing right in a film for the whole of a Member State may therefore rely upon his right against cable television diffusion companies which have transmitted that film on their diffusion network having received it from a television broadcasting station established in another Member State, without thereby infringing Community law.'

Copyright is, however, a bundle of rights relating to different acts. The specific subject matter of the right to restrict performance of a copyright work may well differ from the specific subject matter of other acts restricted by copyright. The court's piecemeal approach to defining specific subject matter enables it to be flexible.

In Case 402/85, *Basset v SACEM* (1987) the plaintiff was the owner of a discotheque in France. He failed to pay the agreed royalties, including a 'supplementary reproduction royalty' which is unique to France. It does not, however, make the total royalty payable necessarily any higher than in other Member State.

The court decided the case on the basis that the supplement was outside Article 30. As far as the court was concerned levying the supplementary reproduction royalties was merely a normal exploitation of copyright.

(c) *Exhaustion*

Implicit in the notion of specific subject matter is the idea that intellectual property rights are exhausted when that subject matter has been realised. The court has stressed that the specific subject matter of intellectual property rights is limited to first putting a product (meaning an individual item, not a type of product) onto the market. Once that has been accomplished, and the goods are out of the control of the right holder, intellectual property rights cannot be used to control what happens to them.

Within the common market, this is particularly important. Prices differ from one Member State to another, making it attractive to buy in one country for resale in another, an activity known as parallel importing. Intellectual property rights cannot be used to hinder this.

The doctrine of exhaustion of rights was first laid down in the *Deutsche Grammophon v Metro* case:

'If a right related to copyright is relied upon to prevent the marketing in a Member State of products distributed by the holder of the right or with his consent on the territory of another Member State on the sole ground that such distribution did not take place on the national territory, such a prohibition which would legitimise the isolation of national markets, would be repugnant to the essential purpose of the Treaty which is to unite national markets into a single market.'

Centrafarm v Sterling Drug concerned a drug marketed under the brand Negram. The price of the drug differed between the UK and the Netherlands by a factor of some 50% so Centrafarm bought it in the UK for resale in the Netherlands. The drug was patented in both countries. The patent owner, Sterling Drug, commenced proceedings in the Netherlands and the Dutch Court referred the matter to the Court of Justice which held that Sterling Drug could not use its patent rights to stop parallel imports:

> 'Whereas an obstacle to the free movement of goods ... may be justified on the grounds of protection of industrial property where such protection is invoked against a product coming from a Member State where it is not patentable and has been manufactured by third parties without the consent of the patentee and in cases where there exist patents, the original proprietors of which are legally and economically independent, a derogation from the principle of the free movement of goods is not, however, justified where the product has been put onto the market in a legal manner, by the patentee himself or with his consent, in the Member State from which it has been imported, in particular in the case of a proprietor of parallel patents.'

In *Centrafarm v Winthrop* (the facts of which are the same as the *Sterling Drug* case) the Court held that it was incompatible with the Treaty to exercise a trade mark in one Member State so as prohibit the sale there of a product which has been marketed by the trade mark owner under the same trade mark in another Member State, or which has been so marketed with the consent of the trade mark owner.

The basic principle of exhaustion has required refinement since these early cases. In particular, the question of what constitutes consent has to be addressed: and in the trademarks context, there are problems to be dealt with when products are repackaged.

- Consent

    The exhaustion principle applies even where no protection is available in the Member State where the goods are first marketed. If the owner of the rights chooses to put products on the market in a country where there is no protection, it has to live with the consequences.

    In Cases 55 and 57/80, *Musik-Vertrieb Membran v GEMA* (1981), records were put on the market in the UK and imported back into Germany. The royalty rates were lower in the UK than in Germany and GEMA, the collective licensing body, sought the difference between the two rates. The question for the court was whether exhaustion operated to stop them doing so, and the court held that it did; the owner of copyright was free to choose where to sell the product. Article 30 prevailed over national intellectual property rights.

Article 30 also prevailed in Case 187/80, *Merck v Stephar* (1981). The plaintiff was the owner of a Dutch patent for a pharmaceutical product which it also sold in Italy, where pharmaceutical products were not at that time capable of being patented. The defendant acquired the product in Italy and sold it in the Netherlands. The court held that the patent was exhausted when the goods were sold in Italy, so it could not be used to keep the products off the Dutch market. Had the product been sold in Italy without Merck's authorisation, the outcome would have been different.

However, while the rights owner will be stuck with a decision to enter a new market, they will not necessarily suffer all the consequences imposed by the law of the Member State whose market they have entered. In Case 19/84, *Pharmon v Hoechst* (1985) a compulsory licence to manufacture certain products in the UK was granted, but with a ban on exports written into it. Pharmon nevertheless exported the product to the Netherlands and Hoechst sought an injunction to stop the sale of the drug in that country. The court held that Hoechst had not consented to the manufacture of the product by the compulsory licensee, so it could enforce its Dutch patent. The product had not been made in the UK by the patentee or with its consent: right are exhausted only on consensual marketing.

The court also allowed intellectual property rights to prevail in Case 186/86, *Warner Brothers v Christiansen* (1988), which concerned the film 'Never Say Never Again'. The defendant purchased a copy of the video in the UK, where copyright law at that time did not control rental. He took it back to Denmark, where he ran a video shop, and rented it out. Rental was at the time a restricted act under Danish copyright law (as it still is) and the copyright owner in Denmark sued for infringement. The court ruled that since there was no Community law in the field, it was for Member States to determine what acts their copyright laws should restrict, and the legislation was saved by Article 36.

In Case 341/87, *EMI v Patricia Import* (1989), the court limited the notion of consent to the actual marketing of the product in question, rather than all the consequences of the decision to enter a particular market. In Denmark, certain recordings by Cliff Richard had ceased to be protected (the term under Danish law being 25 years), but they were still protected in Germany (where the term was 30 years). The defendant imported records not made by EMI from Denmark into Germany, and claimed that the rights of the copyright owner were exhausted. EMI had known that the rights would expire in Denmark, but the court held that consent by the rights owner did not extend to third parties' acts after the expiry of protection.

(d) *Repackaging*

Repackaging is an issue particularly in the pharmaceuticals field, where different prescribing practices often mean that different size packs are needed in different countries. This matter arose in a number of cases.

In Case 102/77, *Hoffman la Roche v Centrafarm* (1978) the defendant acquired valium tablets made by the plaintiff in the UK and repackaged them for the German market, affixing the plaintiffs' trade mark to them. The court held that the plaintiff was entitled to use his trade mark rights to prevent these parallel imports.

In order to answer the question whether that exclusive right involves the right to prevent the trade mark being affixed by a third person after the product has been repackaged, regard must be had to the essential function of the trade mark, which is to guarantee the identity of the origin of the trade marked product to the consumer or ultimate user, by enabling him without any possibility of confusion to distinguish that product from products which have another origin. This guarantee of origin means that the consumer or ultimate user can be certain that a trade marked product which is sold to him has not been subject at a previous stage of marketing to interference by a third person, without the authorisation of the proprietor of the trade mark, such as to affect the original condition of the product. The right attributed to the proprietor of preventing any use of the trade mark which is likely to impair the guarantee of origin so understood is therefore part of the specific subject matter of the trade mark right. The court went on to explore the circumstances in which the use of a trade mark in this way would nevertheless amount to a disguised restriction on trade. The prevention of marketing repackaged products would constitute such a disguised restriction where:

(a) it is established that the use of the trade mark right by the proprietor, having regard to the marketing system which he has adopted, will contribute to the artificial partitioning of the markets between Member States; and

(b)   it is shown that the repacking can adversely affect the original condition of the product; and

(c)   the proprietor of the mark receives prior notice of the marketing of the repackaged product; and

(d)   it is stated on the new packaging by whom the product is being re-packaged.

This proposition was reaffirmed in Case 3/78, *Centrafarm v American Home Products* (1978), and refined in Case 1/81, *Pfizer v Eurim-Pharm* (1981). That case arose from the different prescribing practices of doctors in Germany and the UK. Eurim-Pharm repackaged pharmaceuticals into different quantities more appropriate for the German market. The tablets concerned were contained in blister packs so there was no question of any tampering with the products.

The new packages into which the drugs were put had windows through which the original trade marks were clearly visible. The outside of the packaging identified the repackager. Urim-Pharm had clearly done their homework on the *Hoffman-La Roche* case and took the step of informing Pfizer of what they were doing. The court consequently found in their favour.

(e) *Similar trademarks*

The same or similar trademarks may belong to different people in different Member States. The trademarks may be connected, or they maybe totally unconnected.

Case 192/73, *van Zuylen v Hag* (1974) concerned the well-known brand of decaffeinated coffee. Using a patented process, a German company Hag AG had developed a successful business in the early part of this century: in 1927 it formed a subsidiary in Belgium (to cover Belgium and Luxembourg) and in 1934 transferred the HAG trademarks to it.

After the war, the subsidiary was sequestrated by the Belgian government and eventually passed into the hands of van Zuylen. The German company sold decaffeinated coffee bearing its (identical) trademark in Luxembourg and van Zuylen sued for infringement. The matter was referred to the court, which held that where trademarks in different Member States held by different owners had a common origin, they could not be used to partition the market. Hag AG's product could not be excluded from the Luxembourg market, notwithstanding that the German company had not consented to the use of the mark by van Zuylen.

This extreme pro-free market (and always highly contentious) case was reversed when the same trademarks came up for consideration in Case C-10/89, *CNL-Sucal v Hag* (1990). Van Zuylen had become a subsidiary of Suchard and traded as Sucal: Hag AG sought to restrain Sucal from selling its coffee in Germany. The boot was on the other foot, and having benefitted from the common origin rule in the first case the German company now hoped the court would change its mind.

In the meantime, *Pharmon v Hoechst* had changed the climate for intellectual property rights where marketing of the product is non-consensual. In *Hag II* the court stressed that there was no consent between the owners of the respective marks and the possibility of confusion on the part of consumers.

In Case 119/75, *Terrapin v Terranova* (1976) the court had made plain that the common origin doctrine would not be extended so far as to prevent the owners of national trademark rights from preventing others using confusingly similar marks even where there was no common origin or economic connection between the parties. Terrapin, a UK company which manufactured prefabricated buildings, applied to register its trademark in Germany. It was denied registration and Terranova (a manufacturer of finished plaster products) sued for infringement.

The marks had been acquired by different owners in different countries, and there was no common origin or economic relationship between them. The goods each supplied and the names were sufficiently similar for there to be a danger of confusion. The German company was therefore entitled to use its trademark in the way it had.

In Case C-317/91, *Deutsche Renault v Audi* (1993) the court held that national laws which permit numbers to be protected as trademarks are permissible. Audi had registered the mark QUATTRO for its four-wheel drive cars in Germany: Renault began selling four wheel drive versions of its Espace APV under the name QUADRA. Audi objected to this and Renault sought to have Audi's registration cancelled. Audi won at first instance and on appeal, and Renault appealed to the Federal Supreme Court (the Bundesgerichtshof) which referred the matter to the Court of Justice.

The court ruled that it was for national law to determine the conditions for protection of the mark. There was no evidence that the law operated in a discriminatory fashion, or that it was a disguised restriction on trade: German law could legally permit the registration of the mark, notwithstanding that it was merely an Italian numeral. As for the criteria for determining whether there was a likelihood of confusion, this too was properly a matter for national law, and there would be no breach of the Treaty unless the rules were applied in a discriminatory way.

In Case 9/93, *IHT Internazionale Heiztechnik GmbH v Ideal Standard GmbH* (1993) the court held that national trademark rules which allowed imports to be banned where they might be confused with domestic goods were permitted under Article 36. The mark was owned by different, totally independent, proprietors in France and Germany: the original French subsidiary of the US corporation which owned the German subsidiary too had been liquidated and its assets (including the trademark) sold.

A German subsidiary of the new owner of the French trademark imported the French company's products into Germany where it was sued for infringement. However, the goods the subject of the action were heating installations: although the plaintiff company had the Ideal Standard mark registered in Germany for such goods and for sanitary equipment, it had stopped making heating equipment in 1976.

The restriction was clearly within Article 30. The *Hag II* decision indicated that such a restriction could be justified, but there the products were identical. The court held that where there was a risk of confusion, it did not matter that the goods were not identical or even similar. The national court had decided that there was a risk of confusion, and the court could not change that finding.

Hag II differed, however, in the important respect that there the trademark rights were forcibly removed from the proprietor. Here there had been a voluntary transfer. The court did not consider that this made any difference: the crucial point was the lack of consent on the part of the owner of the trademark rights. The free movement of goods would jeopardise the essential function of the trademark as an indication of origin. The proprietor of the trademark would be held responsible for the quality of goods over which it had no control. The court considered that it would have found the same result whether the rights were transferred voluntarily or by sequestration.

The Community's response to differing national laws which have the effect of hindering the free movement of goods is two-fold. First, it prohibits the operation of national laws where they have this effect; secondly, it seeks to pre-empt national laws by replacing them with Community laws, including directives to harmonise (or 'approximate') national legislation.	**8.6 Harmonisation**

The process of harmonisation has been going on for as long as the Community has been in existence. Much technical legislation is already contained in EC directives; for example, most of the components on a motor vehicle which affect its safety are designed and manufactured to EC requirements and marked by the national authorities which issue the approvals. In another field, the Consumer Protection Act 1987 is the UK's response to the Product Liability Directive.

Harmonisation has, however, been a slow process. Achieving the necessary unanimity in the Council of Ministers frequently entailed much horse-trading, so agreement was reached on illogical grounds and only after much delay. Moreover, harmonisation usually took place on a 'lowest common denominator' basis, and often so many derogations were permitted that little in the way of harmonisation was actually achieved. The Product Liability Directive is a case in point.

Lack of progress towards harmonisation led to the reform of the legislative system in the Single European Act and the setting of a date for the completion of nearly 300 key measures. The date was, of course, 31 December 1992. Now the necessary directives may be adopted by majority voting, and much swifter progress is being made.

8.7 **Intellectual property**	National intellectual property rights have the potential for hindering trade between Member States.

Applying the provisions of Articles 30 to 36 to them is only a transitional stage. As we saw earlier, it is only appropriate if there are no Community measures in the field. The Community has taken a number of steps to deal with problems in the intellectual property area by:

- creating unitary rights which will have effect throughout the Community; and

- by harmonising or approximating the laws of the Member States in areas where differences can hinder free movement.

8.7.1 Community-wide rights

Important steps have been taken in recent years towards creating EC-wide regimes for patents, trade marks and designs. Certain aspects of patent, copyright, trademark law and design protection have been or will be harmonised; and semi-conductor chips are subject to special community rules. As IP rights become more Community-based so the possibility of national laws hindering the free movement of goods becomes smaller.

(a) *Community Trade Mark*

The Community Trade Mark Regulation (Regulation 40/94) will create a new type of trade mark, valid throughout the area of the Community. Based on registration, a Community Trade Mark will have identical effect in every Member State.

The Community trade mark system will be self-contained, with a Community Trade Mark Office running it and Boards of Appeal deciding on appeals from its decisions. Ultimately, the European Court of Justice will exercise appellate jurisdiction, with designated Community Trade Mark courts in the Member States hearing matters at first and second instance.

(b) *Patents*

European patent law consists of two conventions: the Community Patent Convention (CPC) (OJ 1989 No L 401/1) and the European Patent Convention (EPC). The two are closely related.

- The EPC

    The EPC is basically a centralised filing system, with a certain amount of harmonisation built in. It offers a simplified route to obtaining a bundle of national patents based on a single application to the European Patent Office in Munich.

    Both form and substance of the application are examined in Munich, and if the application is acceptable patents are granted in the countries specified by the applicant. All issues of infringement, and most questions of validity, are dealt with at the national level.

- The Community Patent Convention

    The EPC system is seen as a stepping stone on the way to a true Community patent. The aim of the CPC is to produce such a creature, with applications and questions of validity being handled by the EPO and national courts dealing with infringements.

    The CPC has been around since 1975, but still has been ratified only by seven Member States (the original six, plus the UK, whose 1977 Act implements the requirements of the Convention). The EPC is actually two years younger, but it embraces 13 countries – but not all EC Member States are amongst them. Ireland had a particular problem (now resolved) with the CPC, requiring a referendum before it can ratify: and Denmark required a five-sixths majority in Parliament to ratify the Convention.

Like a Community trade mark, a Community patent can only be assigned, revoked (except in exceptional circumstances) or allowed to lapse throughout the Community. Licences can, however, be restricted territorially. The exhaustion principle will apply; once a product has been placed on the market in the Community by or with the consent of the patentee, the patent cannot be relied upon again to control the resale or importation of that product.

A common appeal court, known as COPAC, will hear all appeals relating to infringements of Community patents, and their validity, whether the appeal lies from a decision of the EPO or of a national court. This should ensure a degree of uniformity in the way the law is implemented.

The CPC seems unlikely to come onto operation without at least some compromise. Some sort of 'two speed' approach may well be adopted, although Spain (which joined the EC in 1984 and undertook at that time to make certain modifications to its patent laws so it could ratify the Convention) is unwilling to sign up to a system which includes less than all 12 Member States. This is more to do with its wish to have the Community Trade Marks Office in Madrid than any substantive problem with the CPC.

(c) *Designs*

Within the European Community, design laws are the most diverse area of intellectual property law. Not all Member States even have a registered design system.

In 1994, the Commission published a proposal for a Regulation to create a Community design system, similar to the Community trademark system.

The definition of a design includes features of the appearance of a product 'capable of being perceived by the human senses as regards form and/or colour'. The product may be two dimensional or three-dimensional. Functional designs will not be excluded from protection.

Designs which meet the criteria for registration will also enjoy a short period of unregistered protection. Registered designs will be protected for up to 25 years.

8.7.2   Harmonisation of trade mark and copyright law

As well as establishing Community-level rights, the Commission has proposed to harmonise aspects of the law on trade marks and designs so Member States offer protection on the same basis as the Community systems. Additionally, it is working on a programme to harmonise areas of copyright law.

(a) *Trade Marks*

The First Directive on the approximation of the laws of the Member States relating to trade marks (Directive 89/104) sets out to ensure that Member States' laws give protection on terms which are not only the same between themselves but also the same as the Community Trade Marks Regulation.

The directive does not set out to achieve total harmonisation of trade mark law throughout the Community. It only touches on those areas where differences in national laws have an affect on trade within the Community. It aims to apply the rules developed by the Court of Justice on the 'specific subject-matter' of trade marks providing that the rights given by registration are exhausted once that essential purpose has been realised.

It will also prohibit the partitioning of markets by registering different marks for the same goods in different Member States. So the whole Community eats Snickers bars rather than having Marathon bars in the UK; but how would the English consumer react to being offered mineral water under the established French brand, Pschitt?

(b) *Copyright*

Copyright and neighbouring rights have been on the Commission's agenda since 1974, when the European Parliament called for harmonisation. The Commission's 1985 White Paper, *Completing the Internal Market*, was the catalyst for harmonisation: it was followed in 1988 by the Green Paper, *Copyright and the Challenge of Technology*, which set out an ambitious programme since supplemented. The Green Paper focused on those areas where divergencies in national laws affect 'the functioning of the common market by distorting the competitive conditions under which enterprises operate in different parts of the Community'.

- The software directive

   The first instrument of copyright harmonisation to be adopted was the software directive (Directive 91/250). Computer programs have to be protected by the laws of Member States as literary works. Originality is required for a literary work to enjoy protection, and the directive applies one simple test – a program is original if it is the author's own creation. No additional criteria will be allowed.

   The purchaser of a program enjoys the right to perform certain permitted acts. They may do what is necessary to use the program – error correction, making back up copies – and may also observe, study, and test the functioning of the program, to determine the ideas and principles underlying it, while performing any of the acts which they are entitled to perform.

The directive also had to deal with the problem of interoperability. Computer programs need to interoperate with hardware, and with other programs. The directive allows programmers first to find out what is going on at that important interface, then to design a match for it.

The directive permits users to decompile or reverse engineer programs, but only provided this is necessary to achieve interoperability between the original program and an independently created one. It therefore strikes a nice balance between the interests of the user and of the right-holder, between access and incentive.

The term of protection must be the life of the author plus 50 years. As we shall see, this is to be extended under another directive, dealing with the term of copyright protection.

- Adherence to international conventions

The Council has also adopted a Resolution on adherence by the Member States to the Berne and Rome Conventions, the two primary treaties on international copyright and neighbouring rights.

- Rental and lending rights, and neighbouring rights

The Commission's second directive in the copyright field deals with the right to control the rental and lending of copyright works, and with the protection of performers, phonogram producers and broadcasting organisations – neighbouring rights owners. It makes both rental and lending of works acts restricted by copyright.

- Neighbouring rights

The rights of performing artists, producers of phonograms and videograms and broadcasting organisations are dealt with in the second part of the same Directive. Member States must protect certain neighbouring rights, in particular the right to authorise the fixation of performances, reproduction right, and distribution right.

- The term of protection

Minimum periods of protection are laid down in international conventions, but contracting states are free to apply longer periods, and some Member States do this. Consequently, the duration of protection varies within the Community from country to country and from one type of work to another. Such disparities can create obstacles to free movement of cultural goods and services and lead to distortions of competition: a good example of this is provided by *EMI v Patricia* and *Phil Collins v IMRAT*. A work within the public domain in one country may be protected in another.

Accordingly, the Commission has adopted a directive, Directive 93/98 which will harmonise the term of copyright protection at 70 years after the death of the author. Member States must implement the directive by 1 July 1995. Works still in copyright on that date anywhere in the Community will gain an extra period of protection: and since Germany already gives life of the author plus 70 years, this means that works which have fallen into the public domain in the UK will have their protection revived.

- Satellite and cable

  To assist in creating a single market for cable and satellite transmissions (which, by their very nature, are liable to spill over from one national territory to another) legislation concerning the copyright implications of satellite transmissions is to be harmonised, and a scheme for blanket licensing of broadcasts for cable retransmission put in place.

- Databases

  Creating a single information services market requires a degree of harmonisation of the relevant law, including in particular the legal protection of databases.

  The Commission's proposed directive envisages harmonisation of the copyright rules which apply to databases, in particular concerning the originality test to be applied, and a *sui generis* type of protection against unfair extraction, lasting 15 years.

- Other areas of copyright

  Further initiatives are promised on a range of copyright issues:

  - moral rights;
  - reprography (photocopying); and
  - resale rights.

The Green Paper also addressed differences in the treatment of home copying and the difficulties involved in remunerating authors and rights owners.

The Commission intends to lay a proposal before the Council for a directive on home copying. Technical solutions, such as the serial copy management system, provide one possible solution: a levy on blank tapes is also being considered.

(c) *Semiconductor chips*

Semiconductor chips are something of a special case. The US enacted a new form of protection for chips which extended to chips originating in other countries only if that country protected US chips. The EC took advantage of this reciprocal protection by producing a directive (87/54) which lays down minimum standards of chip protection for Member States and enabled the Commission to obtain reciprocal protection under the US legislation for all 12 countries.

(d) *Plant varieties*

Plant varieties enjoy their own system for protection, similar in many ways to patents. The EC plans to introduce a single system for protecting rights in plant varieties throughout the Community.

(e) *Designs*

Alongside the introduction of a Community design right (see above), harmonisation of national design laws is the subject of a draft directive.

(f) *Biotechnological inventions*

A directive on the protection of biotechnological inventions was proposed to ensure that Member States' patent laws do not exclude matter from patentability simply because it relates to living matter. It also dealt with the deposit of micro-organisms and other biological material. The perceived danger that individuals' genetic make-up would become someone else's intellectual property was extremely controversial, and in March 1995 the Parliament used its new veto for the first time to kill this proposal.

(g) *Supplementary protection certificates*

Finally, a regulation has been adopted (Regulation EEC/1768/92) to provide for supplementary protection certificates for medicinal products. Since they take so long to come to market, because of the lengthy approval system which they must go through, such products have a dramatically shortened period of effective protection under patent law.

The supplementary protection certificate will give additional protection for up to five years after the expiry of the normal patent term.

Free Movement of Goods

Article 30 contains prohibits quantitative restrictions on imports and measures having equivalent effect. Article 36 contains derogations from this principle, allowing national laws to restrict free movement in certain limited circumstances.

Quantitative restrictions are measures designed to prohibit or limit exports or imports of particular classes of goods by reference to their number, weight, value or other quantitative criteria. The Court has defined measures having equivalent effect:

> 'All trading rules enacted by Member States are capable of hindering, directly or indirectly, actually or potentially, intra-community trade are to be considered as measures having an effect equivalent to quantitative restrictions.'

Discrimination is not required for Article 30 to apply. Directive 70/50 provides assistance in interpreting the provisions of the article, categorising measures into those which are distinctly applicable and those which are not.

Distinctly applicable measures include import and export formalities, buy national campaigns, origin marking requirements, and financial assistance to purchase domestically-produced goods.

Indistinctly applicable measures include barriers to trade arising from the diversity of national laws. The principles of proportionality and alternative means will apply (see *Walter Rau v de Smedt*).

In the *Cassis de Dijon* case, *Rewe-Zentrale v Bundesmonopolverwalting für Branntwein* the Court elaborated a rule of reason based on the notion of indistinctly applicable measures:

> 'Obstacles to movement within the Community resulting from disparities between the national laws relating to the marketing of the products in question must be accepted in so far as those provisions may be recognised as being necessary in order to satisfy mandatory requirements relating in particular to the effectiveness of fiscal supervision, the protection of public health, the fairness of commercial transactions and the defence of the consumer.'

But the Court held in that case that goods which were lawfully sold in one Member State should be allowed onto the market in other Member States.

Quantitative restrictions and measures having equivalent effect

Cassis de Dijon: **the rule of reason**

Measures permitted by the rule of reason must not constitute *arbitrary discrimination* or a *disguised restriction on trade* between Member States. They must also be proportionate.

Article 36: exceptions

Article 36 permits certain national measures which would otherwise be prohibited by Article 30. The doctrine of proportionality must be applied, and they must not amount to arbitrary discrimination or be a disguised restriction on trade between Member States.

The categories are:

- Public Morality. In *R v Henn and Darby* a restriction on the import of pornography into the UK was permissible, but would constitute an instrument of arbitrary discrimination if there was a legitimate trade within the Member State in the articles the import of which was prohibited.

- Public Policy. This means a serious threat to one of the fundamental interests of society.

- Public Security. This covers safeguarding the existence of the institutions of a Member State and its essential public services and the survival of its inhabitants.

- The Protection of Health and Life of Humans, Animals and Plants. Member States are generally free to set such health standards as they think necessary, but any standards set will be subject to the proportionality rule. The proportionality rule will also prevent checks of foods on importation when they have already been checked on exportation, unless they might have changed in the meantime or the second checks are to ensure the first checks are being done. Import bans or licences may be permitted although the Court has been reluctant to accept them. Import bans will not be allowed if clear labelling will suffice.

- Protection of National Treasures.

- Protection of Industrial and Commercial Property. The Court has developed three principles to deal with the application of Article 36 to national intellectual property laws:
  - The Treaty cannot affect the *existence* of intellectual property rights (see Article 222) but the *exercise* of such rights may be restricted by the prohibitions laid down in the Treaty.

- To satisfy the proportionality test, the Court will only allow a derogation from the basic principle of Article 30 where it helps safeguard rights which constitute the *specific subject matter* of the property rights.
- The exclusive right conferred on the owner of intellectual property is *exhausted* when products are put into circulation anywhere within the Common Market by the owner of the rights or with its consent.

Chapter 9

Free Movement of Workers

The second of the four freedoms guaranteed by the Treaty is the free movement of workers. This is governed by Articles 48 and 49, as amended by TEU.

9.1 Introduction

'1 Freedom of movement of workers shall be secured within the Community by the end of the transitional period at the latest.

9.2 Article 48

2 Such freedom of movement shall entail the abolition of any discrimination based on nationality between workers of the Member States as regards employment, remuneration and other conditions of work and employment.

3 It shall entail the right, subject to limitations based on grounds of public policy, public security or public health:

(a) to accept offers of employment actually made;

(b) to move freely within the territory of Member States for this purpose;

(c) to stay in a Member State for the purpose of employment in accordance with the provisions governing the employment of nationals of that state laid down by law, regulation or administrative action;

(d) to remain in the territory of a Member State having been employed in that State, subject to conditions which shall be embodied in implementing regulations to be drawn up by the Commission.

4 The provisions of this Article shall not apply to employment in the public service.'

'[As soon as this Treaty enters into force, the Council shall, acting in accordance with the procedure referred to in Article 189b and after consulting the Economic and Social Committee, issue directives or make regulations setting out the measures required to bring about, by progressive stages, freedom of movement for workers, as defined in Article 48, in particular:]

9.3 Article 49

1 by ensuring close co-operation between national employment services;

2 by systematically and progressively abolishing those administrative procedures and practices and those qualifying periods in respect of eligibility for available employment, whether resulting from national

legislation or from agreements previously concluded between Member States, the maintenance of which would form an obstacle to liberalisation of the movement of workers;

3 by systematically and progressively abolishing all such qualifying periods and other restrictions provided for whether under national legislation or under agreements previously concluded between Member States as imposed on workers of other Member States conditions regarding the free choice of employment other than those imposed on workers of the state involved;

4 by setting up appropriate machinery to bring offers of employment into touch with applications for employment and to facilitate the achievement of a balance between supply and demand in the employment market in such a way as to avoid serious threats to the standards of living and level of employment in the various regions and industries.'

[Words in square brackets substituted by TEU.]

9.4 Relationship with other provisions

Note that free movement of self-employed people is covered by Article 52 and Article 59, dealt with in the following chapter. Article 48 deals with employees.

The Treaty only guarantees freedom of movement to people who are economically active (and to their dependants). This follows from the fact that the purpose of the Treaty is to create an economic community. It deals with people as factors of production.

Although the relevant Treaty provisions differ, the court has tended to emphasise the common features of Articles 48, 52 and 59. In Case 48/75, Royer, the precise status of the individual concerned was not clear but the court did not consider it necessary to decide, since the basic principles of entry into and residence in the territory of Member States and the prohibition of discrimination between them on grounds of nationality were fundamental (see also case 36/74, *Walrave and Koch v Union Cycliste International* (1974)).

The basic rules laid down in these Treaty articles have been developed in the case law. In line with the basic principles of the Treaty, the court has been concerned to advance the cause of market integration, and legislative initiatives have followed. The process has now reached the logical conclusion with the Treaty on European Union granting citizenship of the Union to nationals of all Member States.

Although Article 48 deals with the free movement of workers, it does not define what a worker is. A definition has emerged from a number of judgments of the court.

In Case 53/81, *Levin* (1982), the Dutch authorities refused a British national a residence permit because they considered her income to be inadequate. The court rejected the notion that the Member States could stipulate minimum wages and minimum numbers of hours worked: the concept of a worker had to have a uniform meaning throughout the Community, otherwise different interpretations at the national level would unilaterally modify the scope of Community law. Part time workers had to be included, since this is an effective means of improving living conditions and developing economic activities within the scope of Articles 2 and 3 EC. The worker's motives in seeking employment in the Member State concerned do not enter into the equation.

The *Levin* definition was extended in Case 139/85, *Kemp* (1986), where a German national worked part time in the Netherlands as a music teacher. He supplemented his income with state benefits. The court held that, provided effective and genuine part time work is undertaken, the person is a worker notwithstanding that remuneration is below the national minimum subsistence level.

In Case 196/87, *Steymann* (1988), the court held that the definition of a worker included a member of a quasi-religious commune who did work in return for having all his material needs taken care of.

In Case 66/85, *Lawrie-Blum* (1986), a trainee teacher who taught for a few hours a week was considered to be a worker. It was argued that this was in fact part of the teacher's training and therefore did not constitute work, but the court held that: 'the essential features of an employment relationship ... is that for a certain period of time a person performs certain services for and under the direction of another person in return for which he receives remuneration.'

Article 48(2) amplifies the basic Treaty rule (Article 6 EC) which forbids discrimination on grounds of nationality. Article 48(3) elaborates further, specifying that subject to certain exceptions the worker has the right:

- to accept offers of employment actually made;

- to move freely within the territory of Member States for this purpose;

9.5   What is a worker?

9.6   Workers' rights

- to stay in a Member State for the purpose of employment in accordance with the provisions governing the employment of nationals of that state; and

- to remain in the territory of a Member State after having been employed there.

Article 48(2) has been held to prohibit:

- a requirement in French law that crews of merchant ships should comprise three French crew members for every non-French crew member (Case 167/73, *Commission v France* (1974));

- restrictions on ownership of immovable property applicable to migrants but not to nationals of the Member State concerned (Case 305/87, *Commission v Greece* (1989)).

Article 49 deals with important ancillary matters including the right for workers to bring their families with them to live in the host country and to obtain access to social benefits. While the Treaty addresses these as issues relating to market integration, they also constitute an aspect of social policy since they are concerned with conferring rights on individuals.

9.7 Secondary legislation

The various rights covered by Articles 48 and 49 are expanded on in secondary legislation. The principal secondary legislation in this area is:

- Directive 68/360/EEC on suppression of restrictions on the movement and residence of workers and their families within the Community;

- Regulation 1612/68/EEC on free movement of workers within the Community;

- Regulation 1251/70/EEC on the right of workers to remain in the territory of a Member State after having been employed in that state; and

- Directive 64/221/EEC on derogation from free movement provisions available to Member States on the grounds of public policy, public security or public health.

9.7.1 Regulation 1612/68

This regulation deals with three important aspects of the rights safeguarded by Article 48:

- Eligibility for employment

  Any national of a Member State has the right to take up and pursue activity as an employed person under the same conditions as those imposed on nationals of the host state. They must be afforded the same priority in obtaining available employment as the host state's nationals.

Discrimination is therefore prohibited, although Article 3(1) of the regulation exempts conditions of linguistic competence even though the effect of this may be to exclude non-nationals. In Case C379/87, *Groener*, the court accepted that competence in the Irish language could be a requirement for holding a lectureship. Such a requirement would, however, be subject to the proportionality test and must apply to all individuals irrespective of nationality.

- Employment and equality of treatment

Migrant workers must not be treated differently from national workers by reason of their nationality in such matters as conditions of employment and work regarding remuneration, dismissal, reinstatement and re-employment. They are also guaranteed the same social and tax advantages as national workers. This includes:

(a) separation payments for time spent away from their families (Case 152/73, *Sotgiu v Deutsches Bundespost* (1974));

(b) the right to choose the German language in court proceedings (Case 137/84, *Ministère Public v Mutsch* (1985)) the court has been prepared to accept that the social and tax advantages protected by Article 7(2) do not have to be related to a contract of employment: they may remain even after the worker dies, for the benefit of his family.

The court has applied a broad interpretation to Article 7(2) because it considered essential to bring about labour mobility, which is a fundamental Community objective. Thus it is taken to include advantages 'generally granted to national workers primarily because of their objective status as workers or by virtue of the mere fact of their residence on national territory'.

Article 7(3) allows migrant workers access to vocational training and retraining courses provided for national workers and Article 8 allows them to join trade unions and gives them attendant rights.

Article 9 develops one particular matter which could be considered to fall under the heading of Article 7(2), namely equal access to housing. Both public and private housing must be made available to migrant workers on the same terms and conditions as they are made available to nationals of the host state.

- Workers' families

These provisions of the regulation apply to the worker's spouse and their dependants under the age of 21 or dependant on them, and dependant relatives in the ascending line of the worker and spouse. These persons have the right to migrate with the worker, irrespective of their own nationality. Article 10(2) requires Member States to facilitate the admission of other family members who are dependant on the worker or lived under the same roof in the state of origin.

These rights are subject to Article 10(3), which requires the worker has suitable housing available for them.

The rights conferred by Article 10 depend on the status of the worker, not of the family member. They do not permit nationals of third countries to live with their relations who are nationals of a Member State and living in that Member State. In that situation the relatives have no right as migrant workers (Cases 35 and 36/82, *Morson and Jhanjan v Netherlands* (1982)).

The expression 'spouse' means an individual who is married to the worker: it does not include cohabitees (Case 59/85, *Netherlands v Reed* (1987)). A spouse who is separated from the worker is still entitled to remain in the Member State until the marriage is finally dissolved (Case 267/83, *Diatta v Berlin* (1985)).

Article 11 gives the right to family members who are entitled to live with a worker the right to engage in economic activities. This does not, however, carry with it an independent right of residence: that will still be derived from the spouse's rights. In Case 131/85, Gul, the Turkish Cypriot husband of an English woman working in Germany, who was a qualified doctor, was entitled to practice medicine in Germany.

The children of workers are entitled under Article 12 to non-discriminatory access to general education, apprenticeship and vocational training course. If funding is available for such courses then this must be made available to them too. Children will be allowed to remain in the Member State after their parents have returned to their state of origin in order to complete their studies (Case 389 and 390/87, *Echternach and Morritz*.

9.7.2   Regulation 1251/70

This regulation grants to workers the right to remain in the territory of a Member State after having been employed there. It also extends to their families. One of three conditions must be satisfied:

- the worker has worked in the host Member State for the last 12 months, resided there for the last 36 months, and has now retired;

- the worker has resided in the host Member State for the last 24 months and has ceased employment due to a permanent incapacity preventing work; or

- the worker takes up employment in another Member State after 36 months employment and residence in the host Member State, while continuing to reside in that Member State.

If at the time of death the worker has acquired the right to reside under any of these provisions, the family can continue reside in the host Member State. They may also stay on if:

- the worker had resided there continuously for 24 months prior to death;

- the worker died as a result of an occupational illness or accident; or

- the surviving spouse is, or prior to marrying the worker was, a national of the host Member State.

Continuity of residence is not broken by absences of less than three months or absences due to obligatory military service. Periods of involuntary unemployment and absences due to illness or accident do not count against continuity of employment.

This directive is concerned with the control of Member States' administrative procedures under Article 48. The privilege status given to workers under the Treaty must be capable of being proved, and the directive specifies what documentation the host state may demand.

9.7.3   Directive 68/360

Penalties can be imposed for failure to obtain the relevant documents, but must not be disproportionate. However, failure to adhere to the rules relating to proof of status cannot be punished by denial of the status itself: a worker incapable of producing the necessary documents may be fined but may not be deported.

Article 3 requires that workers and family members covered by Regulation 1612/68 must be admitted to the host Member State on production of a valid identity card or passport. Further documentation may be required from family members of the worker who are not nationals of a Member State.

The worker must be given the right of residence on production of the ID card or passport which secured entry to the territory plus confirmation of engagement from the employer or a certificate of employment. For family members, the right must be given on production of the ID or passport (with visa where they are from outside the community) together with a document from their state of origin or the state from which they have come proving their relationship and a further document testifying to their dependence (Article 4).

The host state is compelled to grant the right of residence on production of these documents and it must issue a residence permit. This must be valid for at least five years from the date of issue, automatically renewable and valid throughout the territory of the issuing state.

Several practices adopted by Member States have been scrutinised by the European Court of Justice under the Directive:

- Requirements for migrant workers to register with police are compatible with community law provided the time limits are reasonable (Case 118/75, *The State v Watson and Belman* (1976) and Case C-165/88, *Messner* (1989)).

Correct classification as an employee or self-employed is irrelevant to the entitlement of a residence permit (Case C-363/89, *Roux*) freedom of movement would be guaranteed under Article 48, 52 or 59.

9.7.4	Exceptions	The basic rights given by Article 48 are subject to exceptions concerning public policy, public security and public health (Article 48(3) and Directive 64/221) and concerning employment in the public service (Article 48(4)). As with other exceptions to basic principles of the Treaty, there provisions have been interpreted very narrowly.
9.7.5	Article 48(3) and Directive 64/221	Article 48(3) permits a Member State in certain circumstances to exclude an individual from its territories. The exceptions cannot be used once the individual has lawfully gained entry to discriminate against them (Case 15/69, *Sudmilch v Uglia* (1969)).

The host state is also prohibited from imposing restrictions on the movement of a migrant worker (Case 36/75, *Rutili* (1975)). It may, however be possible for a Member State to impose such restrictions if it has the power to impose them on its own nationals.

The directive elaborates on the basic principles of Article 48(3) and applies equally to workers and their families. It also covers the self-employed.

Article 48(3) covers public policy, public security and public health, and the directive puts flesh on these bare bones.

It also provides that they may not be invoked for economic purposes.

The directive also provides that measures may only be taken against an individual on the basis of the personal conduct of that individual (Article 3(1)). The fact that an individual has passed criminal convictions is not in itself enough to justify exclusion.

The directive lists those diseases and disabilities which would justify exclusion on the ground of public health. It also provides that if an individual contracts a disease or suffers disability while resident in the host Member State, this will not justify non-renewal of a residents permit or expulsion.

The directive further provides that an individual has to be informed of the reasons on which the decision to bar him from entry was taken, subject to an exception where this would threaten state security. The individual is entitled to at least 15 days' notice of the refusal to issue or renew a resident's permit, or of a decision to expel him, subject to an exception where the situation is urgent.

In Case 41/74, *Van Duyn v Home Office* (1974), a Dutch national was refused entry into the UK to work at the headquarters of the Church of Scientology. The UK government considered scientology to be socially harmful. It argued that this was a ground of public policy within Article 48(3): but the Church of Scientology was not banned in the UK so a UK national would be allowed to take up the job. However, the European Court ruled that the UK could exclude the migrant on the grounds that their association with a socially harmful institution was current personal conduct.

By contrast, in Case 30/77, *R v Bouchereau* (1977), the court held that while a previous criminal record can only be taken into account as providing evidence of future personal conduct which could justify public policy arguments, it could also imply the propensity to act in the same way in the future and may therefore constitute a threat to the requirements of public policy. (In the event, the London magistrate who referred the matter to the European Court decided that the offence was not sufficiently grave to justify a recommendation of deportation.)

Two cases decided in the UK also require consideration: in *Proll v Entry Clearance Officer Düsseldorf* a former member of the Bader Meinhoff terrorist group, who the German courts accepted was reformed and would probably not commit any more crimes, successfully appealed to the Immigration Appeal Tribunal against the refusal to give her leave to enter the UK. In this instance, the decision turned on the Aliens Rules.

In *Marchon*, a doctor who was a national of another Member State but established in Britain was convicted of importing 4.5 kg of heroin and sentenced to 14 years' imprisonment, later reduced to 11 years. Subsequently he was given notice that a deportation order would be made: he appealed against that decision and the court held that the European Court's construction of Article 3 in *Bouchereau* should apply. A defendant's past conduct leading to the conviction could meet the requirements of Article 3 if it were sufficiently serious. Here the court considered the conduct to be very serious indeed.

9.8 **The Schengen Agreement and Article 7a**	The powers of Member States to exclude nationals of other Member States from their territories are, as we have seen, extremely limited. There is therefore little justification for border controls, and Article 7a EC foresees an internal market comprising an area without internal frontiers. This implies unrestricted free movement of persons between Member States, and under the Schengen Agreement a group of Member States (initially the Benelux Countries, France and Germany, and now also Italy, Spain and Portugal) the gradual abolition of all checks at common borders is under way.

9.8   The Schengen Agreement and Article 7a

The powers of Member States to exclude nationals of other Member States from their territories are, as we have seen, extremely limited. There is therefore little justification for border controls, and Article 7a EC foresees an internal market comprising an area without internal frontiers. This implies unrestricted free movement of persons between Member States, and under the Schengen Agreement a group of Member States (initially the Benelux Countries, France and Germany, and now also Italy, Spain and Portugal) the gradual abolition of all checks at common borders is under way.

9.9   Public service – Article 48(4)

Employment in the public service is excluded from the provisions of Article 48. In addition to the natural disinclination of the court to apply a generous interpretation to exceptions to general rules in the Treaty, the fact that the definition of 'public service' varies widely between Member States has also limited the scope of the exception.

The reason for including the provision in the Treaty was to protect certain key positions within the public service of the Member States. It does not apply to all public service positions: it is restricted to certain activities connected with the exercise of official authority, and only allows Member States to exclude nationals of Member States from those activities (Case 152/73, *Sotgiu*).

In Case 149/79, *Commission v Belgium* (1980), the Member State asserted that the exception covered a vast range of positions including nurses, plumbers, electricians and architects. The court held that the concept was a Community concept, not one for the Member States to make up, and Article 48(4) referred only to those positions which involved safeguarding the interests of the state.

9.10   Social security entitlements

The objective of the free circulation of workers would be frustrated if a migrant was not entitled to social security benefits. This principal has been stated by the court in a number of cases (see for example Case 100/63, *Kalsbeck* (1964), Case 24/75, *Petroni* (1975) and Case C-186/90, *Durighello v INPS*. However, social security provisions in the Member States vary widely. A degree of harmonisation is necessary not only to promote worker mobility but also to avoid benefit tourism.

Article 51 gives the council the power to adopt measures in the field of social security to secure free movement for workers.

The Council has adopted Regulation 1408/71, which has subsequently been amended many times. It deals with the application of social security schemes to workers and self-employed people and members of their families moving within the community. It provides that the legislation of the state where the worker of self-employed individual is engages in their economic activity will be applicable, regardless of the state in which they are resident. It covers a wide variety of social security benefits, and because Member States' laws change fairly frequently in this area so it needs to be amended on an annual basis.

The regulation is a very small amount of intervention in a field which remains the province of the Member States. Huge variations in the amount of social security protection given still remain. The Council has made a recommendation, number 92/441/EEC on common criteria concerning sufficient resources and social assistance in the national social protection systems, which sets out some general principles designed to guarantee citizens' rights to resources. It proposes a number of ways of implementing the recommendation, specifying the means of calculating and revising aid, and it provides guidelines to Member States which have already recognised the right to resources on how they might develop or improve their national provision. It is designed to complement existing national systems without changing their general form, and it takes into account financial constraints on Member States. It suggests that the aim of Member States should be to guarantee a decent minimum standard of living and medical care for all people residing legally within the EC territory; to contribute to the social integration of all people who are able to exercise a remunerated activity; and to ensure that the standard of living of workers is not significantly affected in the case of illness, accident, maternity leave, disability, unemployment or retirement.

In addition to the rights described in this chapter, workers have other entitlements under the Treaty of Rome. Article 119 provides for equal pay for equal work, and the Treaty contains

9.11   Other rights

other provisions in the social field which go beyond those necessary to protect workers as productive resources. These developments are described in Chapter 14, below.

Free Movement of Workers

Free movement of workers is governed by Articles 48 and 49. Free movement of self-employed people is covered by Article 52 and Article 59: see Chapter 10.

Free movement of persons

Article 48 requires that Member States secure freedom of movement for workers. This entails the abolition of any discrimination based on nationality between workers of the Member States as regards employment, remuneration and other conditions of work and employment.

The Treaty does not define what a worker is. A definition has emerged from a number of judgments of the Court: in *Levin*, the court rejected the notion that the Member States could stipulate minimum wages and minimum numbers of hours worked: in *Kempf* the Court held that, provided effective and genuine part time work is undertaken, the person is a worker not withstanding that remuneration is below the national minimum subsistence level: in *Steymann*, the Court held that the definition of a worker included a member of a quasi-religious commune who did work in return for having all his material needs taken care of: in *Lawrie-Blum*, a trainee teacher who taught for a few hours a week was considered to be a worker.

Workers

Article 48(2) amplifies the basic Treaty rule (Article 6 EC) which forbids discrimination on grounds of nationality. Article 48(3) elaborates further, specifying that subject to certain exceptions the worker has the right:

Discrimination

- to accept offers of employment actually made;

- to move freely within the territory of Member States for this purpose;

- to stay in a Member State for the purpose of employment in accordance with the provisions governing the employment of nationals of that state; and

- to remain in the territory of a Member State after having been employed there.

Article 49 deals with important ancillary matters including the right for workers to bring their families with them to live in the host country and to obtain access to social benefits. While the Treaty addresses these as issues relating to market integration,

Ancillary rights

they also constitute an aspect of social policy since they are concerned with conferring rights on individuals.

Secondary legislation

The various rights covered by Articles 48 and 49 are expanded on in secondary legislation, including:

- Regulation 1612/68/EEC on Free Movement of workers within the Community;
- Regulation 1251/70/EEC on the right of workers to remain in the territory of a Member State after having been employed in that state; and
- Directive 64/221/EEC on derogation from free movement provisions available to Member States on the grounds of public policy, public security or public health.

Exceptions

Article 48(3) permits a Member State in certain circumstances to exclude an individual from its territories. The exceptions cannot be used once the individual has lawfully gained entry to discriminate against them (*Sudmilch v Uglia*).

Directive 64/221 also provides that measures may only be taken against an individual on the basis of the personal conduct of that individual. It lists those diseases and disabilities which would justify exclusion on the ground of public health.

Abolition of border controls

Under the Schengen Agreement a group of Member States (initially the Benelux Countries, France and Germany, and now also Italy, Spain and Portugal) the gradual abolition of all checks at common borders is under way.

Public service

Employment in the public service is excluded from the provisions of Article 48. The Court construes exceptions to general rules in the Treaty narrowly, and the fact that the definition of 'public service' varies widely between Member States has also limited the scope of the exception.

It is designed to preserve certain positions in public service for nationals of the Member State, and therefore does not apply to all public service positions (see *Sotgiu*).

Social security

Article 51 gives the council the power to adopt measures in the field of social security to secure free movement for workers. The Council has adopted Regulation 1408/71, which has subsequently been amended many times. It deals with the application of social security schemes to workers and self-employed people and members of their families moving within the Community.

Chapter 10

Right of Establishment and Freedom to Provide Services

This chapter is primarily concerned with the right of establishment: but the freedom to provide services is so closely related to that right, and the related case law so often applicable to both sets of provisions, that they have to be treated together.

Additionally, the two principles often touch and overlap: there is little practical difference between the right of a French construction company to provide services in England and its right to establish an operation in this country.

The freedoms guaranteed under the treaty are essentially transitional. Once the laws of the Member States have been harmonised in line with EC directives, or Community wide rights have been created, there will be nothing left for the Treaty provisions to do in this area. However, that day is a long way off, and indeed may never come: we shall see below what progress has been made towards the goal of a perfect common market in this area.

Article 52 of the Treaty of Rome lays down the basic principle governing the right of establishment.

Within the framework of the provisions set out below, restrictions on the free movement of nationals of a Member State in the territory of another Member State shall be abolished in progressive stages in the course of the transition period. Such progressive abolition shall also apply to restrictions on the setting up of agencies, branches or subsidiaries by nationals of any Member State established in the territory of any Member State.

Freedom of establishment shall include the right to take up and pursue activities as self-employed persons and to set up and manage undertakings, in particular companies or firms within the meaning of the second paragraph of Article 58, under the conditions laid down for its own nationals by the law of the country where such establishment is effected, subject to the provisions of the chapter relating to capital.

Member States may not introduce any new restrictions on the right of establishment in their territories of nationals of other Member States, save as otherwise provided in this Treaty.

10.1 Introduction

10.2 Right of establishment

10.2.1 Article 52

Article 54 provides for the creation of a general programme for the abolition of existing barriers to the right of establishment, and empowers the institutions of the Community to adopt directives to attain this goal for particular activities. Article 57 deals with the adoption of directives relating to the mutual recognition of diplomas, certificates and other evidence of formal qualifications.

10.3	**Freedom to provide services**	Article 59 mirrors Article 52, requiring the abolition of restrictions on the freedom to provide services, and Article 63 deals with the setting up of a general programme for this.

10.3 Freedom to provide services

Article 59 mirrors Article 52, requiring the abolition of restrictions on the freedom to provide services, and Article 63 deals with the setting up of a general programme for this.

10.4 Discrimination

Articles 52 and 59 are both based on the rule against discrimination, which is expressly included in the Treaty in Article 7 (which as a result of the Maastricht amendments is now Article 6). Nationals of other Member States must be treated in the same way as nationals of the 'host' Member State: this principle is of fundamental importance for market integration.

Articles 52 and 59 must be seen as a specific implementation of the basic principle. The Treaty provides for secondary legislation to be adopted, but the basic rule is enforceable independently of any directives.

In Case 2/74, *Reyners v Belgium* (1974) a Dutch national was resident in Belgium. He held a Belgian legal qualification, and sought admission as an avocat in Belgium: but the rules provided that only Belgian nationals could be admitted. He argued that Article 52 allowed him to establish himself in Belgium: the counter-argument, that specific secondary legislation under Articles 54 and 57 was needed to apply these provisions to the professions, was rejected.

Readers will not be surprised to find that most of the cases in this area concern lawyers!

Provided the qualification of the migrant is recognised by the host country as equivalent with its own qualifications, the right not to be discriminated against can be enforced. If the host does not recognise the migrant's qualification, that is a different matter which has to be dealt with separately.

The principle applies equally to companies as to individuals (or, as the Treaty refers to them, to natural and legal persons). However, Article 58 (which expressly extends the principle to companies and firms) excludes non-profit-making bodies.

In Case C-246/89, *Commission v UK* (1991), the Merchant Shipping Act 1988 required that the legal and beneficial owners of British-registered fishing vessels had to be British. Where a company was the owner, 75% of the shares had to be in the hands of British shareholders. This was held to be in breach of the Treaty.

Companies are entitled to set up branches or subsidiaries in other Member States on the same terms as apply to nationals of that Member State. Company law remains mostly national (though there is a sizeable body of Community law in this area: see below), and the Court of Justice has therefore exercised greater caution in applying the rules in favour of legal persons than in favour of natural persons.

In Case 81/87, *R v HM Treasury, ex p Daily Mail* (1988) the newspaper wanted to shift its legal residence to the Netherlands. This would have tax advantages. UK tax law required it to have the consent of the Treasury, which was not forthcoming, and it submitted that under Article 52 it had the right to do so without permission. The Court of Justice held (on a reference from the UK court) that Community law has not yet touched upon transfers of this type, so the company remained subject to the UK laws.

10.5 Derogations

There are derogations from the basic principles, set out in Articles 55 and 56, and applied to the provisions relating to the freedom to provide services by 66. These cover:

- activities connected with the exercise of official authority; and

- measures providing for the special treatment of foreign nationals on grounds of public policy, public security or public health.

As with any derogations from the fundamental principles of the Treaty, they have to be construed strictly and are subject to overriding principles of Community law, such as the doctrine of *proportionality* which holds that the rules permitted under a derogation may be no more restrictive than is necessary to achieve the end which the derogation is designed to protect, and the related doctrine of alternative means.

In the *Reyners* case, the court considered Article 55, which excludes activities concerned with the exercise of official authority. It held that the legal profession would not be covered by this derogation simply because it is concerned with the state's administration of justice: to hold otherwise would go further than necessary for the purposes of the Article 55 derogation.

Note that the principle of non-discrimination is limited by the permissible extent of the operation of Community law.

The Treaty of Rome does not affect non-economic activities, and it has been held that the principle of non-discrimination therefore has no application in the field of sport, where selection for national teams is legitimately restricted (Case 36/74, *Walgrave and Koch v Union Cycliste Internationale* (1974)).

10.6	Non-discrimination

While the abolition of discrimination is an important goal along the road to the creation of a common market, it is not sufficient to complete the job. Freedom of establishment and to provide services can also be hindered by non-discriminatory measures.

Market integration is still hindered if the professional qualification of an individual is not recognised in other Member States. Article 52 envisages that this will be the case: the right of establishment is subject to the conditions laid down by the Member State for its own nationals. Market regulation is left in the hands of the national authorities.

In other areas of the law, the Court of Justice has held that even non-discriminatory national requirements that restrict free movement may be prohibited. In a celebrated decision on free movement of goods, Case 136/78, *Rewe Zentrale v Bundesmonopolverwaltung für Branntwein* (1979) (the *Cassis de Dijon* case) the court held that national technical and administrative rules that constitute barriers to trade between Member States due to different national characteristics must be justified under Community law. In that case, German law set a minimum alcohol content for certain drinks: *Cassis* did not meet it. The German government argued that it was necessary to protect consumers against weak alcoholic drinks, but the court declined to accept this as a justification. Although German and imported drinks had to comply, it effectively excluded some imported drinks from the German market.

National regulatory rules which affect the right of establishment or the freedom to provide service may be subject to a similar analysis. National rules which have such restrictive effects must be justified by the general good, and the objective of the national rules must not be attainable by other methods which would have less effect on trade – the doctrines of proportionality and alternative means.

In Case 33/74, *van Binsbergen v Bestuur van de Bedrijsvereniging voor de Metaalnijverheid* (1974) the Court of Justice held that a requirement that there is a link between where a person is permanently established and where they provide services is not permitted. Dutch law provided that only persons established in the Netherlands could act as legal advisers or representatives before the social service courts. The objective of the rule could be realised by requiring that the lawyer merely have an address for service in the Netherlands.

National regulations that impede the provision of services across national frontiers will depend on the state being able to show that there are overriding public interest considerations, and that they cannot be met by less restrictive means.

The court has been less liberal with the right of establishment. Clearly, there is a qualitative difference between the situation where a service provider, subject to the laws of the Member State in which they are established, provides services in another Member State, and that where the service provider (or other undertaking) seeks to become established in that other Member State. In the latter case, it is going to be more often appropriate for national rules to govern their conduct.

The regulation imposed must nevertheless be proportionate to the objective. Foreign lawyers may with justification be required to register with the Bar of the host country, but tighter restrictions may be unlawful. The court will have regard to the nature of the activities involved: a higher degree of control is likely to be tolerated in the medical profession.

In Case 107/83, *Ordre des Avocats au Barreau de Paris v Klopp* (1984) the Paris Bar rules permitted a member to have only one chambers, and that within the jurisdiction of the court with which they were registered. Klopp was a member of the Düsseldorf Bar and practised there, but wished to set up in Paris too. The Court of Justice held that Article 52 envisaged that persons might have more than one establishment in the Community, and that availability to courts and clients could be achieved by other means (aeroplanes, telecommunications) than permanent and exclusive establishment.

The market-partitioning effects of Articles 52 and 59 are also diluted by the application of the general principle laid down in Article 5 of the Treaty, which requires Member States to apply national law and practice in accordance with the objectives of the Treaty.

10.7 Legislation

Where national requirements remain lawful under the rules described above, market integration can only be achieved by legislative action. This takes two forms under the relevant provisions of the Treaty: *general programmes*, and *specific directives*.

10.7.1	The general programme

Articles 53 and 63, para 1, envisage general programmes, or policy statements, being created. They are not legislation but do assist with interpretation.

The general programme in this area was adopted in 1961.

10.7.2	Directives

- Specific professions

  Directives are binding on the Member States as to the result to be achieved, but leave it to the national legislature to enact the necessary measures to do so. If the Member State fails to pass the necessary legislation, the directive may have direct effect.

  The regulation of several professions has been liberalised following the adoption of directives. Where this has happened, the directive displaces national law and the migrant may rely on it to secure access to the market. The Member States may not then fix stricter rules than those permitted by the directive.

- Mutual recognition

  Adopting directives for every profession in the Community would take forever. An alternative, more general, approach has been adopted instead, based on mutual recognition of national qualifications. Being unspecific in its application, all professions can be dealt with at once this way.

  Directive 89/48 provides that where an individual has acquired a higher education qualification (taking at least three years to obtain) in their home Member State, they are in principle entitled to pursue the profession covered by that qualification in another Member State. In certain circumstances, the host state can require the production of evidence of professional experience or the completion of an adaptation period: as an alternative to the adaptation period, the individual concerned may choose to sit an aptitude test.

  There is one important exception to this general rule, and that concerns lawyers. The basic principles apply, but where the profession requires precise knowledge of the law of the host Member State, that state may choose whether to require an aptitude test or adaptation period.

  Lawyers qualified in other EC Member States may qualify as solicitors on completion of the aptitude test set by the Law Society. In form, this is less a test of aptitude as of detailed knowledge of English law. Other Member States impose similar requirements: the German requirements are particularly onerous, but since it is difficult for Germans to qualify as lawyers there this is neither surprising nor disproportionate.

- Other regulatory regimes

Apart from the professions, there are many other areas of economic activity where divergent national regulations may create barriers to the right of establishment and the freedom to provide services. Just as the so-called 1992 programme addressed different technical standards applicable to goods, so it also deals with the regulation of service industries.

- Company law

Many provisions of UK company law have their origin in the EC's company law harmonisation programme. Divergent national company laws inhibit the exercise of the freedom of establishment, and the result has been a concerted attempt on the part of the Community to narrow the gaps between the Member States.

The Community is active at another level, too. The first steps have been taken towards the introduction of a body of Community company law. This encompasses two elements:

(a) European Economic Interest Grouping

EEIGs are bodies set up by parties in two or more Member States. Its purposes must be ancillary to the business of the parties: it can assist them in the co-ordination and development of their activities but cannot carry on those activities itself.

The EEIG cannot make profits for itself: anything it does make is taxed in the hands of the parties. It facilitates cross-border co-operation for small and medium-sized enterprises (SMEs), partly by ensuring that there is no need to operate under unfamiliar foreign legal systems.

(b) The European company

The pursuit of business activity across national boundaries within the Community will also be facilitated by the introduction of the European Company Statute, though this is still only a proposal. It will allow a European company to be established, independently of national laws, and will remove the problem of incorporating under several different national laws.

Summary of Chapter 10

Right of Establishment and Freedom to Provide Services

Article 52 of the Treaty of Rome lays down the basic principle governing the right of establishment. Article 59 deals with the abolition of restrictions on the freedom to provide services.

The basic principle

Articles 52 and 59 are both based on the rule against discrimination. The Treaty provides for secondary legislation to be adopted, but the basic rule is enforceable independently of any directives (*Reyners v Belgium*).

Provided the qualification of the migrant is recognised by the host country as equivalent with its own qualifications, the right not to be discriminated against can be enforced. If the host does not recognise the migrant's qualification, that is a different matter which has to be dealt with separately.

In *R v HM Treasury, ex parte Daily Mail* (1988) the Court held that Community law has not yet touched upon transfers of this type, so the company remained subject to the UK laws.

Exceptions

There are derogations from the basic principle of freedom of establishment:

- Activities connected with the exercise of official authority (Article 55); and

- Measures providing for the special treatment of foreign nationals on grounds of public policy, public security or public health (Article 56).

These are applied to the provisions relating to the freedom to provide services by Article 66.

In the *Reyners* case, the Court held that Article 55 did not cover the legal profession simply because it is concerned with the state's administration of justice.

The principle of non-discrimination has no application in the field of sport, where selection for national teams is legitimately restricted (*Walgrave and Koch v Union Cycliste Internationale*).

Non-discriminatory measures

Freedom of establishment and to provide services can also be hindered by non-discriminatory measures. A person may not be able to become established in another Member State because that state does not recognise her qualifications. The Court held in the *Cassis de Dijon* case that even non-discriminatory national requirements that restrict free movement may be prohibited.

In *van Binsbergen v Bestuur van de Bedrijsvereniging voor de Metaalnijverheid* the Court held that a requirement that there is a link between where a person is permanently established and where they provide services is not permitted. It is disproportionate.

Foreign lawyers may with justification be required to register with the Bar of the host country, but tighter restrictions may be unlawful. In *Ordre des Avocats au Barreau de Paris v Klopp* the Court of Justice held that Article 52 envisaged that persons might have more than one establishment in the Community.

The Commission's programme

Articles 53 and 63, paragraph 1, envisage general programmes, or policy statements, being created. They are not legislation but do assist with interpretation. The general programme in this area was adopted in 1961.

The regulation of several professions has been liberalised following the adoption of directives. Where this has happened, the directive displaces national law and the migrant may rely on it to secure access to the market. The Member States may not then fix stricter rules than those permitted by the directive.

An alternative, more general, approach has also been adopted, based on mutual recognition of national qualifications. Being unspecific in its application, all professions can be dealt with at once this way. Directive 89/48 provides that where an individual has acquired a higher education qualification (taking at least three years to obtain) in their home Member State, they are in principle entitled to pursue the profession covered by that qualification in another Member State.

In certain circumstances, the host state can require the production of evidence of professional experience or the completion of an adaptation period: as an alternative to the adaptation period, the individual concerned may choose to sit an aptitude test. In the case of lawyers, the state may choose whether to require an aptitude test or adaptation period. Lawyers qualified in other EC Member States may now qualify as solicitors on completion of the aptitude test set by the Law Society.

Company law

Divergent national company laws inhibit the exercise of the freedom of establishment, and the result has been a concerted attempt on the part of the Community to narrow the gaps between the Member States. The Community is also developing a body of company law alongside national laws.

Chapter 11

Free Movement of Capital and Economic and Monetary Union

The final freedom which is preserved under the Treaty is the free movement of capital. This is governed by Articles 67 to 73 EC. Article 67 sets the scene:

- During the transitional period and to the extent necessary to ensure the proper functioning of the common market, Member States shall progressively abolish among themselves all restrictions on the free movement of capital belonging to persons resident in Member States and any discrimination based on the nationality or on the place of residence of the parties or on the place where such capital is invested.

- These provisions differ somewhat from those that govern the freedom of movement of other factors of production. The continued existence of national currencies limits the extent to which there can be completely free movement of capital, and these limitations are reflected in the Treaty provisions.

To begin with, Article 67 requires only that capital movement be freed 'to the extent necessary to ensure the proper functioning of the common market'. This deprives Article 67 of direct effect. The Council is given the power to implement Article 67 by acting under the provisions of Article 69.

Article 69 allows the Council to issue the necessary directives for the progressive implementation of the provisions of Article 67. During the first two stages it acts unanimously and thereafter by qualified majority. The Council made very slow progress in this field until fairly recently, and as a result several Member States maintain strict exchange controls.

There is relatively little case law on this area of the Treaty. The court has drawn a distinction between free movement of payments and free movement of capital in general. Payments are treated in a manner similar to goods, persons and services, while capital in itself is much more subject to restrictions. In Case 203/80, Cassati, an Italian national resident in Germany was charged with attempting to export German currency from Italy. He claimed he had brought the money into Italy to buy machinery but had found the factory closed for its holidays and therefore had to take the money back again. At the time, the Council had introduced very little legislation in this area, mainly the first Council directive of 11 May 1960. This still permitted Member States to forbid the movement of financial assets, including banknotes. The court observed that currency may be transferred either to invest the funds themselves or to make a specific purchase. The freedom to transfer funds to make a specific purchases is a precondition for the exercise of the other freedoms guaranteed by the Treaty. Community law did not on the face of it protect the re-export of money previously imported for such a purpose, and the court also observed that the freedom to transfer currency to ensure the free movement of goods would not normally include the right to move banknotes as these were not the normal way of paying for commercial transactions.

Cases 286/82 and 26/83, Luisi and Carbone, confirmed the distinction. Here foreign currencies for use abroad had been purchased in Italy but in amounts exceeding those permitted by Italian law. The defendants contended that they needed to export the money to be able to travel in France and Germany and, in the case of Luisi, to have medical treatment in Germany. In these activities the applicants would be migrants in receipt of services and therefore protected by Articles 50 and 60; the court said that to make this freedom a reality they had to be able to take with them the means to pay for the services. Such transactions were not movements of capital even where they were performed by the physical movement of banknotes.

11.2 Economic policy

The Treaty of Rome contains provisions relating to the economic policy of the Member States. This is dealt with under three headings:

11.2.1 Conjunctural policy

This is governed by Article 103 which declares that:

'Member States shall regard their conjunctural policies as a matter of common concern. They shall consult each other and the Commission on the measures to be taken on the light of the prevailing circumstances.'

11.2.2 Balance of payments

Article 104 provides that:

'Each Member State shall pursue the economic policy needed to ensure the equilibrium of its overall balance of payments and maintain confidence in its currency, while taking care to ensure a high level of employment and a stable level of prices.'

Articles 105 to 109 further promote common action between the Member States in the field of economic policy-making. Article 105 says that Member States shall co-ordinate their economic policies and Article 106 requires Member States to liberalise cross-frontier payments in line with the movement of goods, persons and services. (This provision was referred to in the cases mentioned above.) Article 107 states:

> 'Each Member State shall treat its policy with regard to rates of exchange as a matter of common concern.'

In Luisi and Carbone the court considered that Articles 104 and 107 gave Member States a responsibility relating to monetary matters. The Treaty recognised that uncontrolled cross-border capital flows would undo domestic economic policy, so the Member States had included provisions in the Treaty securing protection against the automatic creation of a principle of the free movement of capital. This freedom must be conditional upon a substantial alignment of economic policies.

While the provisions in the economic policy title are clearly aimed at aligning economic policies, they are extremely imprecise and envisage nothing more than co-ordination. A great deal more would need to be done before free movement of capital became reality.

Articles 110 to 116 deal with the Community's commercial policy. Article 110 sets the scene, stating that:

> 'By establishing a customs union between themselves, Member States aim to contribute, in the common interest, to the harmonious development of world trade, the progressive abolition of restrictions on international trade, and the lowering of customs barriers.'

11.3   Commercial policy

These provisions are concerned with external trade. Relations in the trade field between the Member States and third countries will become the responsibility of the Community by the end of the transitional period. Thus, the Community negotiates on behalf of its members on the General Agreement on Tariffs and Trade (GATT) and also has responsibility for taking measures to prevent dumping by countries outside the Community.

The Single European Act added a further provision, Article 102a, to the title of the Treaty dealing with economic policy. This provision states that:

11.4   Co-operation in economic and monetary policies

> 'In order to ensure the convergence of economic and monetary policies which is necessary for the further development of the Community, Member States shall co-operate in accordance with the objectives of Article 104. In so doing, they shall take account of the experience acquired in co-operation within the framework of the European Monetary System (EMS) and in developing the ECU and shall respect existing powers in this field.'

This is the first reference in the Treaty to the European Monetary System, which was established in 1979 with the purpose of developing closer co-operation in monetary policy, which in turn should lead to capital liberalisation.

The EMS established the Exchange Rate Mechanism (ERM) and also created a European currency unit (ecu) the value of which is calculated by reference to a 'basket' of national currencies. The ERM sets an exchange rate for each national currency against the ecu.

The idea of the ERM is that members will maintain the value of their currency within a band around the central ecu rate, which will minimise the effect of fluctuations in exchange rates. Member States must intervene in the foreign exchange markets, buying or selling currency as appropriate, or altering their interest rates, to keep the value within the permitted band.

The aim of the provisions is to move forward from the co-ordinating provisions of the Treaty as originally drafted towards the eventual liberalisation of capital markets. The UK joined the ERM at the outset but did not enter the exchange rate mechanism. This was largely due to the concerns of the Thatcher government about the loss of sovereignty in domestic economic management which would follow. Eventually, late in 1990, the UK did join, but in 1992, following a series of crises brought about by massive speculation in a variety of currencies, the UK government found it impossible to maintain sterling's parity and left the mechanism again.

11.5   Directive 88/361

Directive 88/361 was designed to implement Article 87, abolishing the remaining restrictions on movements of capital between persons resident in Member States. Exceptionally, Member States are permitted to take safeguard measures where short-term capital movements of exceptional size impose severe strains on the foreign exchange markets (such as happened in September 1992). Member States are also permitted to rely on existing derogations in the Treaty (such as Article 108).

The fact that, notwithstanding the directive, it remains possible for Member States to impose restrictions on capital movements, further illustrates how differences between Member States' economic policies prevent the completion of an internal market for capital. Market integration in this field can only be achieved if the Community assumes competence in economic policy-making, which is the aim of the provisions on economic and monetary union introduced in the Maastricht Treaty.

The Maastricht Treaty has replaced Articles 67 to 73 with new provisions entailing a total liberalisation of capital movements between Member States and between the Community and third countries. (The possibility of restrictions regarding third countries is retained, though a unanimous decision of the Council will be required to invoke it.) The possibility of temporary safeguard measures by the Council is also preserved.

The new provisions restate the need for Member States to regard their economic policies as a matter of common concern and to co-ordinate these through the Council. The Council is given powers to draft proposals for guidelines on economic policy for the Member States and for the Community, which then have to be submitted to the European Council. The Council can then, by a qualified majority, direct a recommendation to the Member States.

If a Member State faces severe economic difficulties, the Council may unanimously grant it financial assistance. In the case of difficulties arising from a natural disaster, a qualified majority will suffice.

Member States are advised to avoid excessive budget deficits. The Commission has the responsibility for monitoring government debt and examining budgetary discipline, and if it sees a risk of an excessive budget deficit it has to inform the Council which may then make recommendations to the state concerned aimed at bringing the situation under control. Articles 169 and 170 cannot be used to make Member States toe the line, but persistent failure to heed recommendations may lead to a fine imposed by the Council.

Monetary policy will be dealt with by the European System of Central Banks (ESCB), which the Maastricht Treaty will set up. This consists of the European Central Bank (ECB) and the national central banks of the Member States, and the responsibility of the system is to maintain price stability. The ESCB is charged with:

- defining and implementing the monetary policy of the Community;

- conducting foreign exchange operations;

- holding and managing the foreign reserves of the Member States; and

- promoting the smooth operation of payments systems.

The ECB is given the exclusive right to authorise the issue of ECU banknotes in the Community. These may be issued by the ECB and by national central banks. These notes alone will

11.6 Economic and Monetary Union

be legal tender within the Community, although Member States will still be able to issue coins subject to ECB approval.

The Treaty envisages the replacement of national currencies by a common Community currency.

11.7   Institutional framework

The European Council has the central role in the EMU structure. Thus the important decisions will be taken by the heads of government, assisted by finance ministers. Underneath the European Council, the other institutions have roles to play:

- The Commission proposes policies to the Council, and assists in the surveillance of economic activities and monitors implementation of EMU measures. It participates in an advisory capacity in the Monetary Committee and one of the Commissioners will attend (but not vote at) meetings of the governing body of the ECB.

- The European Parliament must be informed and consulted on economic policy surveillance, and certain aspects of monetary policy. Institutional adjustments require its assent.

- The Council is the chief executive body, reporting to the European Council on major issues and informing the Parliament as required. With the Commission, it enforces the obligations imposed by the system. The President of the Council will be a non-voting participant in the governing body of the ECB.

- The ESCB is similar to the German central bank system, where the state banks form part of the Bundesbank. The statutes of the ESCB and the ECB are laid down in a protocol to the Treaty and their respective functions are defined.

The ECB is independent of the Community institutions and must not seek or take instructions from them. Nor may it take instructions from any government of a Member State or any other body. The same principle of independence applies to the national central banks.

The governing council of the ECB, comprising the members of the Executive Board and the governors of the national central banks, will take decisions by a simple majority. The President will have a casting vote in the event of a tie, and each member has one vote unless the statute provides otherwise. A quorum of two-thirds is required.

The Governing Council is responsible for formulating the monetary policy of the Community, including decisions on intermediate monetary objectives, key interest rates and the supply of reserves in the ESCB. The Executive Board, which is responsible for the day to day conduct of the business of the ECB, consists of the President, the Vice-President and four other members. They are all full-time employees of the ECB, appointed by the European Council for a non-renewable eight year term of office. They must be nationals of Member States and be of recognised standing and professional experience in monetary and banking matters. The Executive Board is responsible for implementing monetary policy, following the guidelines and decisions laid down by the Governing Council, and for giving the necessary instructions to the national central banks.

The Member States are responsible for making sure that the legislation governing their national central bank is compatible with the Treaty and the Protocol. The governor of the national bank may be appointed for no more than five years and may be relieved from office only on very limited grounds.

As integral parts of the ESCB, the national central banks are obliged to act in accordance with the guidelines and instructions of the ESCB. The Governing Council is responsible for making sure that they comply.

The Protocol governs the operations of the ESCB, including:

- provisions on the accounts with the EC and national central banks;

- open market and credit operations;

- minimum reserves;

- instruments on monetary control;

- operations with public entities;

- clearing and payment systems; and

- external operations.

For this last purpose, the ECB and the national central banks may establish relations with equivalent institutions in other countries and with international organisations. They may also:

- acquire and sell all kinds of foreign exchange assets and precious metals;

- hold and manage foreign exchange assets, including securities and all other assets in the currency of any country or in units of account; and

- conduct all kinds of banking transactions in relations with third countries and international organisations.

The national central banks will provide the operational capital of the ECB, which shall be at least 5,000 million ECU. The relative contributions will depend on a variety of factors and will determine the voting power of the national central banks.

The national central banks will also provide the ECB with foreign reserve assets.

The ECB is given power to issue recommendations and opinions, to take decisions and to adopt regulations. These have the same application as similar acts issued by the other institutions of the Community. It can also be given the power to impose fines and periodic penalties on undertakings which fail to comply with its regulations and decisions.

- A Monetary Committee, consisting of two members from each Member State and from the Commission, will advise the Commission and the Council. It will keep under review the monetary and financial situation of the Member States and the Community and will report to the Commission and the Council. It will also deliver opinions on request and will help to prepare the Council's decisions.

When the third stage of EMU is reached, the Monetary Committee will be replaced by the Economic and Financial Committee. The ECB will then also be represented on it.

- A European Monetary Institute will be established at the beginning of the second stage. It will have a Council by which it will be directed and managed, and which will consist of a President and the governors of the central banks of the Member States. The EMI will have the job of developing EMU through its second stage, in particular by strengthening the co-ordination of monetary policies, by preparing for the institution of a single currency, by monitoring the EMS and by facilitating the use of ECU. It will also have an advisory role.

The EMI will have operational and technical functions including the multilateralisation of positions resulting from positions by the national central banks in Community currencies, and the multilateralisation of intra-Community settlements; the administration of the short-term financing mechanism agreed in 1979 between the central banks and the short-term monetary mechanism agreed in 1970; and the co-operation in the provision of financial assistance for Member States' balance of payments.

The EMI is a transitional stage, and when the third stage arrives and the ECB is established it will be wound up.

- The Court of Justice is given responsibility for ensuring that the European Monetary Union conforms with the Treaty. This amounts to exercising judicial control over its implementation. The ECB's and EMI's acts or omissions will be subject to review by the Court of Justice just like those of other Community institutions. They will also be allowed to institute proceedings under Articles 173 to 178 and 184, although only within their own fields of competence.

The ECB will also be able to enforce the duties of national central banks in a manner similar to the enforcement actions the Commission can take under Article 169.

A timetable was agreed at Maastricht for the implementation of the EMU. The first stage ran until the Treaty on European Union came into force, and the third stage will commence on 31 December 1996 provided that the majority if the Member States have met four convergence criteria. These are:

11.8   Implementation

- price stability (a rate of inflation no more than 1.5% above the average of the three best-performing countries);

- government deficit not exceeding 3% of GDP and public debt not exceeding 60% of GDP;

- stable exchange rates within the Member State; and

- interest rates not more than 2% above the average of the three best-performing countries over the previous 12 months.

If no date has been fixed by the end of 1997, the ESCB must be established by 1 July 1998. The Council will determine by qualified majority which Member States are qualified to participate. At that point, the participating Member States will agree the conversion rates at which their currencies will be irrevocably fixed and exchanged for ECUs, and the ECU will then become the single currency.

The UK has negotiated the right to opt out of stage 3 without a positive decision of the government and Parliament. It must notify the European Council by 31 December 1996 whether it intends to move to stage 3, or, if no decision has been taken by the Council at that time, by 1 January 1998.

11.9   The UK

If it does not join stage 3, the UK will retain control of monetary and exchange rate policy and will not be subject to

EC disciplines. However, under stage 2 it is bound not to run up excessive public deficits.

The weighted vote of the UK will be inapplicable when computing the majority for the EMU decisions so long as it is absent from the system. Nor shall the UK participate in the appointment of the executive board of the ECB. The ECB statutes will not apply to the UK and it, and the Bank of England, will be effectively excluded from the relevant provisions. The UK remains free to decide to move to stage 3 if it satisfies the convergence criteria.

Free Movement of Capital and Economic and Monetary Union

The free movement of capital is governed by Articles 67 to 73 EC. Article 67 requires the Member States progressively to abolish restrictions on the free movement of capital during the transitional period *'to the extent necessary to ensure the proper functioning of the common market'*. The fact that national currencies continued to exist made it impossible to deal with this freedom on the same basis as the others: and the words in italics deprive the Article of direct effect.

The principle

Article 67 also requires that all restrictions on payments be removed. The Court has drawn a distinction between free movement of payments and free movement of capital in general, treating payments in a manner similar to goods, persons and services, while capital in itself is much more subject to restrictions. In *Cassati*, the Court had to consider the reimportation of banknotes taken from Germany to Italy to finance the purchase of industrial machinery: the Court held that although the freedom to move capital to make a specific purchase was essential to the exercise of other freedoms protected by the Treaty, this did not extend to permitting the reimportation of currency. This distinction was confirmed in *Luisi and Carbone*.

Directives may be adopted by the Council under Article 69, though until recently very little progress was made on this front.

The Treaty contains provisions concerning the economic policy of the Member States, which are dealt with under three headings:

Economic policy under the Treaty

- Conjunctural policy. This is governed by Article 103 which requires Member States to regard their conjunctural policies as a matter of common concern and to consult each other and the Commission on the measures to be taken in the light of the prevailing circumstances.

- Balance of Payments. Article 104 provides that Member States shall pursue the economic policy needed to ensure the equilibrium of its overall balance of payments and maintain confidence in its currency, while taking care to ensure a high level of employment and a stable level of prices.

Articles 105 to 109 further promote common action between the Member States in the field of economic policy-making.

In *Luisi and Carbone* the Court considered that Articles 104 and 107 gave Member States a responsibility relating to monetary matters. While the provisions in the economic policy title are clearly aimed at aligning economic policies, they are extremely imprecise and envisage nothing more than co-ordination. A great deal more would need to be done before free movement of capital became reality.

Articles 110 to 116 deal with the Community's commercial policy. Member States aim to contribute to the harmonious development of world trade, the progressive abolition of restrictions on international trade, and the lowering of customs barriers, starting with a customs union.

Relations in the trade field between the Member States and third countries are the responsibility of the Community.

Co-operation

The Single European Act added a further provision, Article 102a, to the title of the Treaty dealing with economic policy.

This requires co-operation between the Member States in the light of the experience gained by them in the context of the European Monetary System, which was established in 1979 and sets up the Exchange Rate Mechanism and the European Currency Unit (ECU).

The ERM envisages Member States keeping the value of their currency within a band around its ECU parity. The effect of currency fluctuations would therefore be minimised. However, the UK is no longer part of the ERM.

Directive 88/361 abolished the remaining restrictions on movements of capital between persons resident in Member States. Member States were permitted to take safeguard measures where short-term capital movements of exceptional size impose severe strains on the foreign exchange markets.

The Maastricht Treaty has replaced Articles 67 to 73 with new provisions entailing a total liberalisation of capital movements between Member States and between the Community and third countries.

The new provisions require Member States to avoid excessive budget deficits, though there is no legal obligation on them. The Maastricht Treaty sets up a system of European Central Banks which includes the European Central Bank, also set up by the TEU. This system is designed to ensure price stability.

The ECB is permitted to authorise the issue of ECU banknotes in the Community. This common currency is designed to replace the national currencies of the Member States.

The Council has the central role in the EMS, with the Commission responsible for making proposals to it. The Parliament has the right to be consulted on certain aspects.

The ECB is totally independent of the Member States. It is modelled on the German Bundesbank. Its Governing Council, comprising the members of the Executive Board and the governors of the national central banks, will formulate the monetary policy of the Community, including decisions on intermediate monetary objectives, key interest rates and the supply of reserves in the ESCB. The Constitution and functions of the ECB are set out in a separate Protocol.

There will also be a Monetary Committee, comprising two members from each Member State and from the Commission. It keeps the Member States' economic and monetary situations under review and advises the Council and the Commission. It will be replaced in the third stage of EMU by the Economic and Financial Committee, on which the ECB will also be represented. At the beginning of the second stage, a European Monetary Institute will be set up. A transitional body, it will see the process through the second stage. The Court of Justice has powers over the entire process.

A timetable for implementation was agreed at Maastricht. The important third stage will commence on 31 December 1996 provided that most Member States meet 'convergence criteria'. If no date is fixed by the end of 1997, the ESCB must be established by 1 July 1998. The participating Member States will agree the conversion rates at which their currencies will be irrevocably fixed and exchanged for ecus, and the ecu will then become the single currency.

The UK has negotiated the right to opt out of stage 3 without a positive decision of the government and Parliament.

Chapter 12

The Common Policies

In this chapter we bring together some disparate areas, united in the fact that the Community has a common policy concerning them. In each case there is a vast amount of detailed secondary legislation, which it would be far outside the scope of a work like this to explore. The following is therefore the briefest of outlines of the common agricultural, fisheries and transport policies.

At least one author has suggested that an understanding of the book of Genesis is the best preparation for studying the Common Agricultural Policy (CAP). David Medhurst, in his *A Brief and Practical Guide to EC Law* (Oxford, Blackwell Law, 1990), wrote:

> 'Pharaoh, having had serious differences with the food processing industry, arrested the Head Baker and the Chief Butler. While they were on remand, Joseph, their cell-mate, demonstrated a talent for the prediction of dreams, predicting that the Chief Baker would be hanged.

> The Head Butler, happily, was acquitted and reinstated. One day he heard that Pharaoh had had a bad night dreaming about food shortages, and put in a word for Joseph. The latter, having foreseen seven years of plenty and seven years of famine, was asked to formulate a plan to deal with the problem.

> Joseph proposed that commissioners should be appointed to buy up the corn of Egypt during the years of plenty. This meant that the price of grain would be maintained in times of surplus. When there were shortages Pharaoh would be able to guarantee supplies. So impressed was Pharaoh that he took up the idea, discovered that it enabled him to finance structural reforms, and bought up all the land in Egypt.'

The Common Agricultural Policy is based on the same principles, though (fortunately) the Commission has not been able to buy up all the land in the Community. The Common Fisheries Policy (CFP) is based on similar principles, and legally it is based on the same Treaty provisions as the CAP. Indeed, agriculture is defined to include fisheries. We shall examine the CAP first, then turn to the CFP: but before we do, there are some matters common to both.

12.1   Introduction

12.2   Common Agricultural Policy

12.2.1	Basic principles	Provisions on agriculture had to be included in the Rome Treaty alongside those dealing with industry and commerce: it was – and is – an essential sector of the economy. The provisions in question rest on two principles set out in Article 38:

- the rules governing agriculture derogate form the rules establishing the common market; and

- the operation and development of the common market for agricultural products must be accompanied by a common agricultural policy.

12.2.2	Competition	Article 42 of the Treaty disapplies the rules on competition to production of and trade in agricultural products, to the extent determined by the Council. The Council has adopted a regulation (Council Regulation 26/62) which exempts agreements essential to an agricultural marketing organisation or the production and sale of and trade in agricultural products from the operation of Articles 85 and 86. The provisions on state aids (Articles 92 to 94) do not apply to agriculture, although specific regulations provide that these provisions are not derogated from unless that is specifically stipulated.

12.2.3	Structure	Article 39 sets out the objectives of the CAP:

'(a) to increase agricultural productivity by promoting technical progress and by ensuring the rational development of agricultural production and the optimum utilisation of all factors of production, in particular labour;

(b) thus to ensure a fair standard of living for the agricultural community, in particular by increasing the individual earnings of persons engaged in agriculture;

(c)   to stabilise markets;

(d)   to provide certainty of supplies; and

(e)   to ensure supplies to consumers at reasonable prices.'

To attain these, the Treaty requires Member States to develop a common organisation of agricultural markets (Article 40). One or more agricultural guidance and guarantee funds are provided for in Article 40(4), and under this power the European Agricultural Guidance and Guarantee Fund (EAGGF, or FEOGA from its French name) is established. Agriculture accounts for a large proportion of the Community budget – (61% in 1986).

FEOGA has two sections:

- a Guidance Section, which finances structural policy; and

- a Guarantee Section, which deals with expenditure relating to refunds on exports and intervention measures.

- the common organisation of agricultural markets is achieved by one of three methods (Article 43(2)):

- common rules on competition;

- compulsory co-ordination of the various national marketing organisations; or

- the creation of a Community market organisation.

In practice, the latter is invariably the option chosen. National marketing arrangements are replaced by a single, Community-wide marketing structure. This is based on a series of Council Regulations, one for each product affected. Fisheries are treated as a product for this purpose. In addition, there are numerous ancillary and implementing regulations.

Responsibility for intervening in the market, operating the system of import and export certificates, collecting levies and paying out refunds lies with the Member States. In the UK the body responsible is the Intervention Board for Agricultural Produce.

Some of the regulations underlying the CAP are common to all regimes – milk, wine, cereals and the rest. These are referred to as horizontal regulations. They are themselves amended frequently but not consolidated, so reference to them is difficult.

12.2.4   Horizontal regulations

Although the system for each regime is different, they do share certain features:

12.2.5   The system

- The *target price* is set annually, before 1 August. The Council acts on a proposal from the Commission and after consulting the Parliament. The target price reflects what the price of the product should be during the following year, and enables producers to make their plans. It is also intended to discourage trade in the product from surplus areas to deficit areas.

- An *intervention price* (sometimes called the floor price or purchase price) is set by the same method. Intervention agencies in the Member States are required to buy in the products at this price, which ensures that producers receive a proper price for their crops.

- A *threshold price* is also set. Above this price, goods can be imported from outside the Community. This protects the internal market by excluding cheap imports.

- *Export refunds and levies* are used to encourage and discourage exports, depending on the conditions on world markets.

The regimes for different products display different features. The cereals regime is the most comprehensive, while the fruits and vegetables regime concentrates on quality, setting common standards for products and a withdrawal price below which producers' organisations will not offer products for sale.

| 12.2.6 | The cereals market |

Council Regulation 2727/75 sets out the system of prices for cereals. A target price is fixed each year for Duisberg, the place in the Community with the greatest cereals deficit. The intervention price is fixed for the place with the greatest surplus, Ormes, and the intervention agencies purchase cereals at slightly less than the intervention price.

| 12.2.7 | Intervention |

Intervention is at the heart of the CAP, but the existence of an intervention price has meant that farmers produce for intervention rather than for consumption. After all, the whole point was to distort the operation of the market, which left alone would produce alternating gluts and shortages – seven years of plenty followed by seven years of famine.

However, the CAP was to an extent the victim of its own success. The geography of the Community came to consist largely of butter and beef mountains and wine and oil lakes. This led to the Community taking a variety of measures to curb overproduction.

A battery of measures to address this problem has been developed. These include co-responsibility levies, schemes for turning wine into industrial alcohol and quotas. In the cereals market, for example, there is a co-responsibility levy for cereals undergoing processing, intervention buying or export.

The introduction of milk quotas is one of the most visible and controversial elements of attempts to deal with this problem. They amount to a quasi-interest in land, and broadly speaking they cannot be dealt in separately from the land to which they are attached.

The basis of milk quotas is Council Regulation 856/84, which amended the basic Council Regulation 804/68. The basic regulation set up an intervention system with a target price for milk, intervention prices for butter, skimmed milk and cheese, and a guarantee threshold price for milk. The amendment raised a levy, payable by the producer, on quantities of milk sold for direct consumption in excess of a certain reference quantity.

Case 120/86, *Mulder v Minister van Landbouw en Visserij* (1989) (discussed in Chapter 3, para 3.4.4) illustrates the importance of milk quotas. In addition, Advocate-General Slynn's opinion gives a good description of the development of the system.

In the UK, the body responsible for intervention in the market is the Intervention Board for Agriculture, which was created under s 6 of the European Communities Act 1972. It usually delegates its powers to other agencies in the appropriate sectors.

12.2.8   Intervention bodies

The second leg of the Common Agricultural Policy is structural reorganisation. In 1968 the Commission submitted a memorandum on the reform of agriculture to the Council, which in 1971 adopted a resolution on the subject. The Commission then proceeded to make recommendations, focusing particularly on the problem of the number of people engaged in agriculture, the size of farms and production methods.

12.2.9   Structural reorganisation

Fewer people would be needed as agriculture became more mechanised: the consequential social problems had to be addressed, with help for those wishing to leave the land, assistance for farmers over 55 who wished to give it up, and training and placement schemes for others.

Farms in the Community were considered too small so the Commission recommended a policy of increasing their size, depending on the type of production in which they were engaged.

Finally, production methods needed modernising and there had to be greater adaptability to market needs and better marketing.

These proposals led to a further Council resolution and new Commission proposals, resulting on 17 April 1972 in the issue of a draft of directives covering:

- modernisation of the farming industry;

- assistance to farmers leaving the land; and

- professional training and advice.

In 1975 a directive on farming in less favourable areas was adopted. But the CAP faced all sorts of problems which slowed implementation: steps were taken to secure a greater share of the available funds for the Mediterranean and the west of Ireland in 1981, and in 1985 there was a major initiative to improve the efficiency of agricultural structures. Existing provisions were replaced by a new regulation, Regulation

797/85, which enables Member States to give financial aid to full-time skilled farmers and amounts almost to a social policy for rural areas.

| 12.2.10 | A victim of its own success |

The CAP has raised the living standards of farmers (at the expense of dearer food), resulted in massively increased production, made the Community self-sufficient and allowed it to help poorer countries with famine relief. However, this success has led in turn to problems of surpluses and storage.

The CAP is contentious within the Community because it benefits the agricultural countries at the expense of the non-agricultural ones, and consumes a large part of the budget which might otherwise be available for other projects.

It is also contentious in a wider context. The GATT world trade talks stalled for some time over the impact on free trade of the CAP.

| 12.2.11 | Reform of the CAP |

Having succeeded in its original goals, the CAP is in need of reform. The process actually started in 1988, with increases in farm spending being capped at 74% of Community GNP growth. Guarantee limits were also introduced for all sectors which did not already have them: support payments to farmers would be reduced if production in the sector exceeded its maximum guaranteed quantity. Set-aside schemes were also introduced for the first time, designed to remove land from agricultural production. Co-responsibility levies were also introduced in some sectors.

However, the Commission does not consider that these reforms have been entirely successful. The enlargement of the Community with the addition of Scandinavian countries, whose farmers (especially the northern ones) face special problems, creates further difficulties for the CAP: the prospect of eastern European countries joining too will further exacerbate the problems surrounding the CAP. However, reform cannot be fundamental: it can only be detailed. The political consequences of trying to replace the whole system would be too great.

In 1992 a further reform package was adopted and introduced for three years from 1993. It aims to cut costs and alleviate the surplus problem, directing assistance more selectively to those sectors which need it. It comprises:

- reductions in prices for certain products – 30% in the case of cereals, 15% for beef, over three years;

- a compulsory annual set-aside scheme for farmers wishing to claim the permanent compensatory payments offered to alleviate the decline in income resulting from reduced prices for cereals;

- aid programmes covering environmental protection, afforestation and early retirement;

- alterations to the market organisations for certain products;

- new regulations dealing with milk and livestock products, poultry and eggs; and

- harmonisation of legislation on animal health, public health, feeding stuffs, plant health products and seeds and propagating material.

Monetary compensation amounts, part of the financial arrangements surrounding the CAP, have been replaced by new 'agrimonetary' arrangements based on the ECU.

12.3   Common Fisheries Policy

The Common Fisheries Policy (CFP) is dealt with in the Treaty of Rome within the framework of the CAP. In the early days, the CFP (such as it was) consisted of two Council regulations covering a common structural policy for the fishing industry (Regulation 2140/71) and the common organisation of the market for fisheries products (Regulation 2142/70).

The establishment of the CFP was delayed because of conflicts of interest between the Member States. It began to take shape in the first Act of Accession, when the UK, Ireland and Denmark joined the Community: transitional arrangements gave concessions to the new members, and gave the Council the power to legislate on the management of the industry and the conservation of resources. Meanwhile, the Member States retained the power to regulate fisheries.

The regulations which make up the CFP as it now stands were adopted from 1983. The present CFP is a very recent creation, based on monitoring arrangements, licensing and a structure fund scheme.

The CFP is based on four elements.

12.3.1   Equal access

The CFP gives Community fishermen equal access to the Community 'pond', which is defined by the 200 nautical mile limit of the Member States, or a median line where appropriate. Within the Member States' 12-mile limit, licensing arrangements for certain species are permitted, and specifications for vessels may be laid down by the Member States.

Conservation and management of stocks is achieved by fixing total allowable catches (TACs) annually. The annual quotas are allocated between the Member States, which may exchange them among themselves.

Council Regulation 3690/93 set up a Community fishing licence system, as envisaged by Regulation 3760/92. Decision 94/15 contains detailed rules for restructuring the industry. Council Regulation 2847/93 set up monitoring and control arrangements covering fishing activities in Community waters and Community vessels wherever they might be.

The Commission is responsible for monitoring TACs and the quotas and for enforcing conservation measures.

12.3.2	Structural reform	Regulation 2141/70 and subsidies from the EAGGF provide the means of dealing with over-production by the Community fishing industry. Council Regulation 2080/93 established a financial instrument for fisheries guidance, bringing together all the various financial resources allocated to structural measures in the fisheries sector under the CAP or CAP. Council Regulation 3690/93 provides structural assistance in the fisheries and aquaculture sector.

12.3.3	Marketing organisation	Regulation 2142/70 set up a common organisation for fisheries markets consisting of producers' associations, common marketing standards and a price support system. The latter is financed by the EAGGF. A Council decision in 1992 brought new products within the system and common market standards were laid down for them.

Protective measures were taken on in 1993 as a result of the crisis regarding certain white fish species.

12.3.4	Conservation and policing	Regulation 2527/80 seeks to conserve diminishing resources by imposing technical restrictions, including mesh sizes for nets. Regulation 753/80 required reporting of catches.

12.4　Common Transport Policy

In a common market, an integrated transport system is essential. Article 3(c) EC envisages a common transport policy, but it has proved difficult in practice to realise.

Article 75(1) EC (amended by the TEU) provides:

'... the Council shall, acting in accordance with the procedure referred to in Article 189c and after consulting the Economic and Social Committee, lay down:

(a) common rules applicable to international transport to or from the territory of a Member State or passing across the territory of one or more Member States;

(b) the conditions under which non-resident carriers may operate transport services within a Member State;

(c) measures to improve transport safety;

(d) any other appropriate measures.'

The Treaty spoke only (Article 84) of transport by rail, road and inland waterway: the Council had the power to extend the policy to air and sea transport. In *Commission v France* (1974) the ECJ held that job discrimination on the basis of nationality on board merchant ships was prohibited, notwithstanding that sea transport was not included by the Treaty.

The Maastricht amendments also stipulate that provisions concerning the regulatory system for transport which would be able to have a serious effect on the standard of living and on employment in certain areas and on the operation of transport facilities they must be enacted unanimously by the Council, on a proposal from the Commission and after consulting the Parliament and the Economic and Social Committee.

The Commission made proposals to establish a Common Transport Policy (CTP) as long ago as 1961: but progress was so slow that in 1983 the Parliament took the matter to the Court of Justice (Case 13/83, *European Parliament v Council* (1985)). In 1985 the Commission's white paper 'Completing the Internal Market' highlighted the areas where action was needed: matters such as delays to truck drivers at national borders arising from the need to provide copious paperwork were an important element in giving momentum to the completion of the single market.

12.4.1 Implementation of the Common Transport Policy

The first steps towards the CTP sought to regulate three areas:

12.4.2 Initial moves

- Operational

  Harmonisation in this area covered tariff measures, comprising bilaterally agreed maximum and minimum charges, and non-tariff measures, including rules of competition and various conditions for the operation of transport services. Linked with this area are insurance against civil liability arising from the use of a motor vehicle on the road, and the exercise of the profession of transport operator. Both these areas are dealt with in directives.

- Technical

  Standards of equipment, safety and comfort and the control of pollution are dealt with in harmonising directives. For example, Directive 70/156 governs the approximation of the laws of the Member States on the type approval of motor vehicles and trailers. Detailed directives made under it govern the technical standards to be attained by a number of different systems in a vehicle, eg lighting, brakes, seat belt anchorages, etc.

- Social

  Council regulations set out common standards for working conditions in internal and inter-state transport. Rest periods are mandatory for drivers and the number of hours which can be driven are prescribed. The Member States are required to ensure that prescribed recording equipment – the tachograph – is used.

12.4.3   Completion of the CTP

The Commission produced a white paper on the future development of the CTP in 1992 (Bull EC Supp 3-93). This has been endorsed by the Parliament, the Economic and Social Committee, and the Council.

The Maastricht Treaty committed the Community to the creation of trans-European networks in several fields, including transport (Article 129b EC). Even before the Maastricht Treaty was finalised, the Council had approved the high speed rail network master plan and had adopted three decisions on combined transport. The Commission is working on a strategy which combines master plans for the networks of ports, airports and conventional (non-high speed) railways.

In specific areas, the Community has developed a number of policy initiatives:

- Road transport

  Here there are already numerous Community instruments, covering matters such as the Community driving licence, border inspections and administrative formalities, motor vehicle insurance, and many others. Additionally, there are several further provisions in the pipeline.

- Railways

  There is little Community legislation in the field of rail transport. What there is concerns the financial relations between railway undertakings and Member States: uniform costing principles: rates for international carriage: and the commercial independence of railways. Directive 91/440 concerns the right of access to railway infrastructure: further directives deal with licensing of railway undertakings and the allocation of capacity and fees.

- Maritime transport

  There is Community legislation on freedom to provide services to maritime transport between Member States and third countries: the application of Articles 85 and 86 EC to this area; unfair pricing practices; free access to cargoes; and minimum requirements for dangerous or polluting goods. A Community shipping register is on the cards, as is a Community flag for sea-going vessels. A common definition of Community ship-owner will be adopted, and another proposal will apply the principle of freedom to provide services to maritime transport between Member States.

• Air transport

The Community got round to dealing with air transport very late in the day. Two Decisions of 1980 set up consultation procedures on relations between Member States and third countries, and co-operation on investigating air accidents. Since then there have been several additional measures, including Council Regulation 3975/87, applying the competition rules of the Treaty of Rome to this sector, and Commission Regulation 2671/88 which exempts certain restrictive agreements in the area from Article 85(1). The Commission has also recently adopted controversial decisions regarding the access of non-French operators to Orly airport. A raft of additional proposals awaits adoption.

The Common Policies

Provisions on agriculture had to be included in the Rome Treaty alongside those dealing with industry and commerce: it was – and is – an essential sector of the economy. The provisions in question rest on two principles set out in Article 38:

- the rules governing agriculture derogate form the rules establishing the common market; and

- the operation and development of the common market for agricultural products must be accompanied by a common agricultural policy.

Article 42 disapplies the rules on competition to production of and trade in agricultural products, to the extent determined by the Council. Council Regulation 26/62 exempts agreements essential to an agricultural marketing organisation or the production and sale of and trade in agricultural products from the operation of Articles 85 and 86. The provisions on state aids (Articles 92 to 94) do not apply to agriculture.

The objectives of the CAP are:

- to increase agricultural productivity;

- to ensure a fair standard of living for the agricultural community;

- to stabilise markets;

- to provide certainty of supplies; and

- to ensure supplies to consumers at reasonable prices.

The Treaty requires Member States to develop a common organisation of agricultural markets.

The European Agricultural Guidance and Guarantee Fund (FEOGA) has a Guidance Section, which finances structural policy; and a Guarantee Section, which deals with expenditure relating to refunds on exports and intervention measures.

The common organisation of agricultural markets is achieved by the creation of Community market organisations, whereby national marketing arrangements are replaced by a single, Community-wide marketing structure.

Common Agricultural Policy

Responsibility for intervening in the market, operating the system of import and export certificates, collecting levies and paying out refunds lies with the Member States.

Horizontal regulations are common to all regimes. Although the system for each regime is different, they each have:

- A *target price*, which reflects what the price of the product should be during the following year.

- An *intervention price* at which intervention agencies in the Member States are required to buy in the products.

- A *threshold price* above which goods can be imported from outside the Community.

- *Export refunds and levies* are used to encourage and discourage exports, depending on the conditions on world markets.

Intervention has led to overproduction, and the Community has developed a variety of methods of dealing with this. One of these is milk quotas.

Structural reorganisation is made necessary by developments in agricultural measures. The Commission has adopted directives covering:

- modernisation of the farming industry;

- assistance to farmers leaving the land; and

- professional training and advice.

In 1975 a directive on farming in less favourable areas was adopted.

Reform of the CAP has been an issue for some time, due to the large proportion of the Community budget dedicated to it. Increases in spending in this area were capped in 1988, guarantee limits were introduced, set-aside schemes were introduced and co-responsibility levies were also introduced in some sectors.

A further reform package was introduced for three years from 1993 to cut costs and alleviate the surplus problem, directing assistance more selectively to those sectors which need it. It comprises:

- reductions in prices for certain products;

- a compulsory annual set-aside scheme for farmers wishing to claim permanent compensatory payments;

- aid programmes covering environmental protection, afforestation and early retirement;

- alterations to the market organisations for certain products;

- new regulations dealing with milk and livestock products, poultry and eggs; and

- harmonisation of legislation on animal health, public health, feeding stuffs, plant health products and seeds and propagating material.

Monetary compensation amounts, part of the financial arrangements surrounding the CAP, have been replaced by new 'agrimonetary' arrangements based on the ECU.

The Common Fisheries Policy (CFP) is based on four elements: **Common Fisheries Policy**

- Equal access;

- Structural reform;

- Marketing organisation;

- Conservation and policing.

The Common Transport Policy has been difficult to realise. **Common Transport Policy** The original Treaty provisions have developed through the decisions of the Court (*Commission v France*) and amendment of the Treaty. The first steps towards the CTP sought to regulate three areas:

- *Operational* – tariff measures, comprising bilaterally agreed maximum and minimum charges, and non-tariff measures, including rules of competition and various conditions for the operation of transport services; insurance against civil liability arising from the use of a motor vehicle on the road, and the exercise of the profession of transport operator.

- *Technical* – standards of equipment, safety and comfort and the control of pollution.

- *Social* – Council regulations set out common standards for working conditions in internal and inter-state transport.

The Commission produced a white paper on the future development of the CTP in 1992. The Maastricht Treaty committed the Community to the creation of trans-European networks in several fields, including transport.

In specific areas, the Community has developed a number of policy initiatives in the fields of road, rail, maritime and air transport.

Chapter 13

Competition Policy

13.1   Introduction

The EC's competition policy is found in two articles of the Treaty of Rome: Article 85 deals with restrictive practices, and Article 86 with abuses of dominant positions. Mergers are subject to control under a specific Regulation. In addition, there are provisions which deal with competition in particular sectors (such as transport) and with state aids. Since just the two main Articles could easily fill a year-long course, we do not propose to go beyond them in this book.

The institution of a competition policy is provided for in Article 3 EC, which states that this (and other activities of the Community) are for the purposes set out in Article 2. Thus, a competition policy has to be viewed first and foremost as a tool of single market integration.

Article 85 reads:

13.2   Article 85

'1   The following shall be prohibited as incompatible with the common market: all agreements between undertakings, decisions by associations of undertakings and concerted practices which may affect trade between Member States and which have as their object or effect the prevention, restriction or distortion of competition within the common market, and in particular those which:

(a)   directly or indirectly fix purchase or selling-prices or any other trading conditions;

(b)   limit or control production, markets, technical development, or investment;

(c)   share markets or sources of supply;

(d)   apply dissimilar conditions to equivalent transactions with other trading parties, thereby placing them at a competitive disadvantage;

(e)   make the conclusion of contracts subject to acceptance by the other parties of supplementary obligations which, by their nature, or according to commercial usage, have no connection with the subject of such contracts.

2   Any agreements or decisions prohibited pursuant to this Article shall be automatically void.

3   The provisions of paragraph 1 may, however, be declared inapplicable in the case of:

• any agreement or category of agreements between undertakings;

- any decision or category of decisions by associations of undertakings;

- any concerted practice or category of concerted practices;

which contributes to improving the production or distribution of the goods or to promoting technical or economic progress, while allowing consumers a fair share of the resulting benefit, and which does not:

(a)   impose on the undertakings concerned restrictions which are not indispensable to the attainment of those objectives;

(b)   afford such undertakings the possibility of eliminating competition in respect of a substantial part of the products in question.'

13.2.1   The prohibition

Article 85(1) prohibits:

'all agreements between undertakings, decisions of associations and concerted practices' where:

(a)   there is collusion;

(b)   competition is, or is intended to be, prevented, restricted or distorted; and

(c)   there is an effect (or a potential effect) on trade between Member States.'

Article 85(2) makes such agreements automatically void. It does not matter if the agreement, etc, has some justification: it will not escape the prohibition. It may be eligible for exemption – described below – but the application of Article 85 is automatic and not (despite pleas from some commentators) subject to a 'rule of reason'.

A licence which gives the licensee the right to do something which formerly they could not might appear to raise no competition issues under Article 85. This is the nearest thing to a 'rule of reason' approach in EC competition law, and was applied in *Nungesser v Commission* (the *Maize Seed* case (1982). Indeed the European Court of Justice held there that exclusive rights for a national territory within the Community could be granted without infringing Article 85, because without such protection no licensee would be prepared to take on the risk of investing in an unknown product. But attempts to partition the common market, by hindering parallel imports, would not be permitted.

However, additional ancillary restrictions might bring the agreement within Article 85. In *Windsurfing International v Commission* (1986) clauses governing quality control and other matters were caught by Article 85(1). Exemption under Article

85(3) was unavailable because the agreement had not been notified, although the Commission doubted that it would have been given anyway.

Article 85 does not seek to create perfect competition. It acknowledges that this is unattainable, so mechanisms are put in place to exempt certain agreements from the rules. The aim is what the European Court of Justice has described as 'workable competition' (*Metro v Commission* (1977)). This approach is less dogmatic than the American system, on which the EC rules were originally based.

- 'Agreements'

  The expression 'agreements' includes much more than just legally enforceable contracts. In Case 41/69, *ACF Centrafarmie v Commission* (1970), the ECJ held that a 'gentlemen's agreement' was caught. It:

  '... amounted to the faithful expression of the joint intention of the parties to the agreement with regard to their conduct in the Common Market.'

  There has to be a binding character to the agreement for Article 85 to apply to it.

  The concept of an agreement has come to bear an extended meaning. In *Polypropolene* (1986), affirmed by CFI: Case T-7/89, SA *Hercules v Commission* (1992) the Commission found that there was an agreement despite the fact that it was oral, was not legally binding, had no specific sanctions, and had not been universally observed.

- 'Undertakings'

  The concept of an undertaking is very broad, encompassing almost any economically active unit (whether profit-making or not: see Joined Cases 209-15 and 218/78, *van Landewyck v Commission* (1980). Legal personality or form is not important: what matters is whether the undertaking exercises an economic activity.

  In *Polypropolene* (1986), the Commission said an undertaking could be:

  '... any entity engaged in commercial activities and in the case of corporate bodies may refer to a parent or subsidiary or the unit formed by the parent and the subsidiaries together.'

  The definition does not, however, embrace public undertakings acting in their capacity as public authorities: Case 30/87, *Bodsen v Pompes Funèbres des Regions Libérées* (1985).

A successor to the business of an undertaking may be considered to be the same undertaking: Joined Cases 29 and 30/83, *Compagnie Royale Asturienne des Mines SA v Commission* (1984).

- 'Concerted practices'

Parallel behaviour by parties to an arrangement leads to market conditions other than those that would have existed normally. The leading case on this sort of practice is Case 48/69, *ICI v Commission* (1972), known by the name of the product involved, *Dyestuffs*. The court stated that a concerted practice:

'... without going so far as to amount to an agreement properly so called, knowingly substitutes a practical co-operation for the risks of competition.'

Determining whether a concerted practice exists requires examination of the market as well as of the parties. The normal behaviour of competitors in an oligopolitic market looks remarkably similar.

In *Dyestuffs*, there was no oligopoly because the parties were independent and there was no transparency of prices. The parties only knew about each others' prices because of the arrangements between them.

Non-independent economic conduct is the key to a finding that there is a concerted practice – as in Joined Cases 40–48/73, etc, *Suiker Unie v Commission* (1975).

Selective distribution systems are an interesting case. Refusal to supply dealers outside the system could be considered a unilateral act, putting it outside the reach of Article 85. But in (107/82) *AEG Telefunken v Commission* (1983) the ECJ rejected this argument: the refusal would be part of the contractual arrangements between the parties.

- 'Decisions'

The breadth of the concepts of agreements and concerted practices has squeezed out the importance of decisions of associations. The inclusion of this category has however permitted the Commission to hold an association liable for the activities of its members (*AROW v BNIC* (1982)).

The constitution of a trade association may also be considered to be a decision (*National Sulphuric Acid Association* (1980)), and so too may an association's regulations (*Net Book Agreement* (1989), affirmed by the CFI as Case T-66/89, *Publishers' Association v Commission* (1992), under appeal to the ECJ as Case C-360 92P).

In Joined Cases 96-102, 104, 105, 108 and 110/82, *IAZ International v Commission* (1983), it was held that an agreement within a trade association may be a decision of the agreements actually influence the conduct of the members.

- 'Object or effect'

Note that Article 85 either requires that the object of the agreement, etc, be prohibited (Case 56/65, *Société Technique Minière v Maschinenbau Ulm* (1966)) or looks for a prohibited effect. Only if there is no prohibited object will the authorities have to look to the effects of the arrangement.

The law looks for an effect on competition and on trade between Member States, whereas the UK law is form-based and considers only whether there is a restriction of a particular type in an agreement.

The form and content of a restriction on competition is immaterial to Article 85. While the Article contains an illustrative list of prohibited practices it is not exhaustive. In *Consten/Grundig v Commission* (1966) the court held that Article 85 prohibited an arrangement that perpetuated national boundaries as barriers to the free circulation of goods.

Nor does Article 85 distinguish between horizontal restraints (which are normally much more damaging to competition) and vertical restraints (which are usually benign and generally recognised as such in US law). However, it can be difficult to distinguish agreements on this basis as both types of effects are frequently present. Because of the underlying policy of market integration in EC competition law, a general acceptance of vertical restraints would not be appropriate.

- Collusion

Unilateral action by an undertaking is outside the scope of Article 85 (though if the undertaking is dominant, Article 86 may well prohibit whatever it is doing). However, an agreement of some sort is frequently found to exist: in *AEG v Commission* (1983) the court held that a refusal to admit a dealer to a manufacturer's network is not unilateral. It had to be considered as part of a contractual system, involving agreements with the existing dealers. In *Sandoz* (1983) the inclusion of a notice saying 'not to be exported' on invoices for goods was held to be an agreed export ban rather than a unilateral declaration.

- Effect on trade

  The requirement that there is an effect on trade between Member States is a jurisdictional threshold which the authorities must get over. It differentiates purely national concerns from Community ones.

  The requirement has been interpreted in such a way as to ensure that it does not constitute a serious obstacle. The author of one leading textbook, Professor Whish, even suggests that:

  '... it would be reasonable to start with a presumption that agreements that restrict competition will fall within Article 85 unless a clear case can be made to the contrary.'

  In the *Société Technique Minière* case the court looked for a foreseeable influence, direct or indirect, actual or potential, on the pattern of trade between Member States.

  In *Consten/Grundig* the court held that the necessary effect included an increase in trade as well as a decrease.

  In *Windsurfing v Commission* the court held that the agreement had to be looked at as a whole: it was not just a question of whether individual restrictions run outside the national territory.

  Even if the arrangements concern only one Member State an effect on trade may be found: in *Cementhandeleren* (1972) an agreement limited to Dutch cement companies was found to have 'inevitable' implications for other markets. Dutch price fixing affected the ability of German or Belgian producers to enter the market. See also *Carlsberg* (1983) and the *Net Book Agreement* case, where the CFI found that the domestic agreement had an effect on trade between Member States as a result of the impact of the agreement on the Irish market.

- Extra-territorial application

  Any agreement having the prohibited effect in the common market is caught. It does not matter if the agreement is made wholly outside the Community, by foreign companies. In Joined Cases 89 etc *Ahlström Oy v Commission* – the *Wood Pulp* case (1988) the court upheld the Commission's approach, holding that if a contract made by non-nationals outside the common market is implemented within it the Commission is competent. (Investigating such conduct may not, however, be easy.)

- Prevention, distortion or restriction

  This three-part list shows quite clearly that anything anti-competitive will be caught. Decisions and judgments do not seek to distinguish between the three: the list is treated as expressing a single concept.

The necessary effect (or intended effect) is often perfectly clear from the agreement. Many such agreements (if not all of them) are entered into because they are expected to have these effects. For example, in *Zanussi* (1978) the manufacturer's warranty scheme prescribed that warranty claims be made in the country of purchase, which would not wash with the Commission.

Certain situations are outside the scope of Article 85(1).

13.2.2   Exceptions

- Some commercial agency agreements and agreements between companies in the same group will not be caught, where the parties do not constitute separate undertakings. In *Christiani v Neilsen* (1969) the Commission decided that the Dutch subsidiary of a Danish company was incapable of entering into a prohibited agreement with its parent. It was already effectively controlled by the parent and had no economic independence.

  The court has several times upheld this view where the parties constituted a single economic unit. By the same token, a parent company outside the EC can be liable for its subsidiaries' acts in the Community (Case 15/74, *Centrafarm v Sterling Drug Inc* (1974)).

- Further exclusions cover the coal and steel sectors which are subject to special regimes. Transport is something of a special case, which we will not go into here.

- Article 85 catches even a potential effect on trade between Member States: but if the effect is not significant the prohibition will not apply. In Case 5/69, *Völk v Verwaeke* (1969), a German washing machine manufacturer appointed an exclusive distributor in the Netherlands. The agreement contained a ban on parallel imports, normally a complete 'no-no' under Article 85. But the manufacturer's share of the relevant market was a mere 1%, so the restriction was considered by the ECJ to have no appreciable effect.

- The Commission formalised this *de minimis* rule in 1968, updating it in 1986. The Notice on Minor Agreements applies if:

  - the parties' market share is less than 5%; and

  - their turnover less than 200 million ECU

  so that there is no (or no significant) distortive effect on competition. Where one of the parties is part of a larger group the whole of the group's market share and turnover may have to be included.

- Where several manufacturers set up networks, the cumulative effect of what might otherwise be minor agreements will exclude the application of the Notice (Article 16, and see Case 38/79, *Brasserie de Haecht v Wilkin* (1980)).

For some types of agreement or practice the Commission has issued a notice delineating the scope of the prohibition. Co-operation agreements, subcontracting agreements and certain joint ventures are currently covered.

Negative clearance (a statement that Article 85(1) does not apply) may be applied for (Regulation 17/62, Article 2). The procedure for doing so is described below (s 7).

The court's practice is whenever possible to sever provisions in an agreement which are prohibited.

13.2.3   Exemption

An agreement which is within the scope of Article 85(1) is prohibited and automatically void (Article 85(2)) unless it is exempted by Article 85(3).

Article 85(3) sets out two positive and two negative conditions. The negative conditions specifically import the notion of proportionality found elsewhere in EC law.

Exemption is granted to agreements or practices which:

- contribute to an improvement in production or distribution, or to economic progress;

- give a fair share of the benefits to consumers (including trade customers);

- impose no restrictions which are not indispensable to realising the benefits; and

- do not afford the parties the possibility of eliminating competition in respect of a substantial part of the products in question.

Only the Commission has the power to declare Article 85(1) inapplicable, which it may do either in the course of an investigation or following notification of the agreement by the parties.

Article 85(3) seeks to balance the costs of the restrictive practice against its benefits. The restrictions may go no further than is necessary to achieve the benefits of collaboration. Unnecessary ancillary restrictions may not be included.

In the *Net Book Agreement* case, the CFI did not accept that certain restrictions which were convenient for the parties were indispensable for the operation of the agreement.

The Commission must first look at the broad economic context of the collaboration. If the market would have realised the claimed benefits itself the justification for the restriction is undermined. The market must be examined without the restriction in operation so the benefits unavailable without it can be seen. For example, in an exclusive distribution agreement the parties' freedom of action is restricted, but it may mean that a manufacturer is able to enter a new market which without the help of a distributor remained closed to him.

The possibility of third party competition must remain. The economic benefits of an agreement are only likely to continue if the parties remain exposed to competition from other undertakings. In Van Landewyck the agreement in question covered the suppliers of 80% of the Belgian cigarette market. The agreement could not be justified under Article 85(3).

Crisis cartels will be permitted under Article 85(3) if they permit restructuring (and therefore preserve jobs) which would otherwise be impossible (*Synthetic Fibres* (1984)).

The need to notify an agreement is removed if it can be brought within the terms of a block exemption regulation.

Council Regulation 17/62 Article 9.1 lays down conditions for automatic exemption under Article 85(3). The Commission has delegated powers to exempt categories of agreements, thereby clearing some of the logjams of notified agreements which had built up. Powers are delegated under:

- Regulation 19/65 (exclusive dealing and intellectual property licensing);

- Regulation 2821/71 (standardisation, research and development, specialisation);

- Regulation 1534/91 (insurance);

- Regulation 39/76 (transport).

In adopting a block exemption regulation, it is crucial for the Commission to use the right power. For example, when Regulation 123/85 was first mooted, the Commission's powers to adopt it under Regulation 19/65 were queried by the motor industry. The House of Lords Select Committee on the European Communities recommended that the Commission obtain new powers from the Council before proceeding with it. The Commission did not do so, and no challenge to the legality of the regulation has ever been made.

Block exemption regulations express in concrete form for particular categories of agreements the requirements of Article 85(3).

The following main block exemption regulations have been made under this power.

- exclusive distribution agreements (Regulation 1983/83);
- exclusive purchasing agreements (including special rules for beer and service station agreements) (Regulation 1984/83);
- patent licensing agreements (Regulation 2349/84);
- motor vehicle distribution and servicing agreements (Regulation 123/85);
- specialisation agreements (Regulation 417/85);
- research and development agreements (Regulation 418/85);
- know-how licensing (Regulation 556/89);
- franchising (Regulation 4087/88).

Block exemption regulations follow a set form:

- a list of permitted restrictions;
- a list of prohibited restrictions; and
- a list of restrictions which might not be prohibited at all but which, being permissible under Article 85(3), are exempted 'just in case'.

These are often (but potentially offensively) referred to as a 'white list', a 'black list' and a 'grey list'. The terminology is used here only to enable the reader to understand it when he or she encounters it elsewhere.

The empowering Council regulations require that a block exemption also contains a provision setting an expiry date (since an exemption cannot be open-ended, as market conditions may make it obsolete) and a provision permitting its benefit to be withdrawn if an agreement which complies with its requirements nevertheless is incompatible with Article 85(3).

It is important to identify the right block exemption for any particular agreement. In *Delta Chemie/DDD* (1989) the Commission decided that the agreement should have been brought within the R&D block exemption, not the specialisation one.

It is not compulsory for agreements to be within the terms of a block exemption: individual exemption is available, if the necessary conditions are met. In Case 10/86, *VAG France SA v Etablissements Magne SA* (1988) the court held that motor vehicle distribution agreements did not have to comply with

Regulation 123/85: the dealer in that case argued that it was entitled to an agreement with a duration within the provisions of the block exemption, but the court said that the manufacturer could keep the old agreement going and seek exemption for it.

In some of the block exemption regulations (patent licensing, know-how licensing, research and development, specialisation) there is an opposition procedure. This enables agreements which in some respect (usually minor) do not comply with the relevant block exemption to be sent to the Commission: if the Commission does not object within six months they are deemed exempted. The Commission's power to adopt such provisions in a regulation were doubted at the time, but now that it has been successfully done the precedent has been set.

An agreement which is not inside one of these regulations may still benefit from individual exemption.

Negative clearance can only be given if application has been made for it, and the Commission can only give individual exemption to an agreement which has been notified. In practice the two are normally done together, with exemption being sought as an alternative to negative clearance (Regulation 17/62, Articles 2 and 4.1).

Notification must be made on Form A/B. In fact the form itself is very brief: the important information has to be provided in an extensive annex. The questions to be addressed are set out in the explanatory note to the form, which is prescribed by Commission Regulation 2526/85.

Notification does not have to be made by all the parties to an agreement, but the notifier must be a party.

Failure to submit accurate, complete and truthful information (whether intentionally or negligently) is punishable by a fine of up to 5,000 ECU (Regulation 17/62 Article 15.1).

Certain agreements do not have to be registered. If needed, retrospective exemption can be given for these agreements. Included are:

- purely domestic agreements (no affect on trade between Member States);

- certain unilateral restrictions in bilateral agreements;

- bilateral agreements concerning standards;

- joint R&D and specialisation agreements where the parties' market share is less than 15% and their turnover less than 200m ECU.

Notification secures immunity from fines from the date of notification. (See below.) There is no fee.

13.3   Abuse of a dominant position

An undertaking which enjoys a dominant position must not abuse its economic power in any way. Any such abuse is prohibited. Article 86 provides:

> 'Any abuse by one or more undertakings of a dominant position within the common market or in a substantial part of it shall be prohibited as incompatible with the common market in so far as it may affect trade between Member States. Such abuse may, in particular, consist of:
>
> (a)   directly or indirectly imposing unfair purchase or selling prices or other unfair trading conditions;
>
> (b)   limiting production, markets or technical development to the prejudice of consumers;
>
> (c)   applying dissimilar conditions to equivalent transactions with other trading parties, thereby placing them at a competitive disadvantage;
>
> (d)   making the conclusion of contracts subject to acceptance by the other parties of supplementary obligations which, by their nature, or according to commercial usage, have no connection with the subject matter of such contracts.'

13.3.1   Dominance

This controls firms whose economic strength makes them immune from the normal pressures of a competitive market. Market share is the best indication of dominance – 40 to 45%, according to the Commission's Tenth Annual Report on Competition Policy – but other factors may be equally or even more important. It is at best only evidence of dominance, and other factors will be taken into account. In particular, the existence of barriers to entry to new competitors will be considered important. The ownership of intellectual property rights may also put a firm in a dominant position.

Monopolies created by national laws will be caught, though Article 90(2) may allow such dominant positions.

In Case 27/76, *United Brands v Commission* (1978) the court said that Article 86 'relates to a position of economic strength enjoyed by an undertaking which enables it to prevent effective competition being maintained in the relevant market by giving it the power to behave to an appreciable extent independently of its competitors, customers and ultimately ... consumers'.

Access to raw materials or capital may enable a firm to act regardless of its competitors, suppliers and purchasers.

Market-independent behaviour, which goes to show the existence of a dominant position, is often demonstrated by abusive conduct. This raises important 'chicken and egg' type questions. Such evidence was admitted in *United Brands*: but in *Michelin* the applicant argued that it was impermissible to show dominance by first demonstrating an abuse. And in *AKZO* the court upheld the Commission's finding that AKZO's ability to eliminate competition was evidence of its dominance.

Article 86 refers to dominance by 'one or more' undertakings. It clearly envisages the possibility of collective dominance, which might also be caught by Article 85. The undertakings concerned may well also fall to be considered as a single economic unit (see, for example, Commercial Solvents). The cases suggest that Article 86 will apply in such a case, and Article 85 where there is parallel behaviour.

(a) *Geographical market*

The dominant position must be in the Common Market or a substantial part of it. What constitutes a substantial part is a question of fact and will vary according to the nature of the product. A distinct geographical market partitioned from the rest of the common market will be treated as a distinct market in itself. A definition of the geographical market under consideration is needed so as to enable the authorities to understand which undertakings may be in competition. In the Single European Market, there should in theory be no need to look at anything smaller than the whole market: but differences in national laws may serve to prevent free movement of goods, and there may also be practical considerations which require the geographical market to be limited.

In the *Magill* cases (Case T-69/89, *RTE v Commission* (1991), Case T-70/89, *BBC v Commission* (1991), and Case T-76/89, *ITP v Commission*, (1991), the market for TV programme guides was limited to the area in which the TV programmes could be received.

In *United Brands*, France and Britain bought bananas from former colonies: other EC countries, particularly Germany, bought elsewhere. France and Britain had to be excluded from the geographical market under consideration.

(b) *Temporal market*

It is also necessary to know what period of time is under consideration. Defining the temporal market is less problematical than defining the geographical market, but it is still necessary in the case of seasonal foods. (The banana market, as it happens, does not vary much.) A crisis, such as the oil crisis of the late 1970s, might also create a distinct market in time (*ABG* (1977)).

(c) *Product market*

The product market in which dominance must be judged is an important consideration, and the most difficult aspect to define.

In *United Brands*, where the company supplied bananas, consideration had to be given to whether the market for fresh fruit should be considered. Some fruits are not available all the year round so could not compete effectively with bananas, which are. United Brands argued that other fruits were readily substitutable for bananas, but the Commission and the court both disagreed. Bananas had certain features (soft texture, etc) which made them particularly suitable for the very young, the elderly and the sick. There was no substitute for them to these classes of consumers, so the market in which dominance had to be tested was that for bananas alone.

In *United Brands*, and also in Case 6/72, *Europemballage and Continental Can v Commission* (1973), interchangeability was the key criterion: this mirrors the use of the substitutability criterion in Article 95 cases. In *Continental Can*, the Commission's failure to identify the product market correctly was the basis of the parties' successful appeal.

Substitutability will therefore be a major consideration: others will be price, physical characteristics and intended use. The latter makes for a very narrow definition where spare parts are concerned: often only the manufacturer of the 'complex product' will be able to supply spares – especially where (as in *Volvo v Veng* and *Renault v Maxicar*) it owns intellectual property rights.

Substitutability is usually assessed in terms of demand. Occasionally supply-side interchangeability is relevant: in Case T-51/89, *Tetra Pak Rausing SA v Commission* (1991) the CFI upheld the Commission's decision that producers of milk-packaging machines could not readily change to making aseptic packaging machines and cartons. This meant that the market for aseptic packaging was a separate one.

13.3.2   Abuse

A dominant position is abused if advantage is taken of it so as to cause injury to third parties. Examples include charging unfair prices, price discrimination, refusal to supply, fidelity rebates. There is no provision for exemption to be granted under Article 86, but it would not be necessary anyway. The concept of abuse is flexible: if the conditions for exemption existed in that the practice complained of has beneficial effects, it would not be considered abusive.

The owner of intellectual property rights has to beware of Article 86. Since intellectual property rights are concerned with granting monopolies, they can easily put (or help put) their owner in a dominant position which must not be abused.

In *Ministère Public v Tournier* (1989) the French national copyright management society was accused of charging excessively high and arbitrary rates to discotheques which wanted to use the recordings in which it owned copyright. The court agreed that this was possible and suggested that a comparison of rates in other Member States might show that there was an abuse. However, the point was also made that the differences might turn out to have objectively valid reasons.

In *Volvo v Veng* (1988) the right owners refused to licence third parties to manufacture replacement panels for motor cars which were protected by UK registered designs. The court held that this was part of the 'substance of the exclusive right' granted by the legislation and there was no abuse. However, the court observed that there could be an abuse of, for example, the right owner refusing to supply independent repairers, charging excessively high prices or stopping supplying parts for which there was still demand.

In *RTE, BBC and ITP v Commission* (1991) the Court of First Instance confirmed that a dominant right owner may not have the luxury of choosing with whom to do business. A publisher of a television guide, who wished to produce a single comprehensive guide to all the programmes shown in Ireland, was thwarted by the refusal of the owners of copyright in the listings (protected under copyright law as compilations) to licence their reproduction even for a fee.

The Commission, responding to a complaint from the independent publisher, decided that the rights owners were preventing the creation of a new market (for a single programme guide) which consumers would find attractive. This was an abuse, and the Court of First Instance upheld this decision.

The court held that marketing weekly listings constituted a distinct market from the daily listings available in the newspapers. It considered the geographical market which it had to consider to be the whole of the island of Ireland, and that within that market the exercise of copyright secured dominance on the part of the three television companies' publishing arms. Preventing the production and marketing of a new product for which there is potential consumer demand went beyond the essential function of copyright protection and therefore amounted to an abuse.

Tetra Pak Rausing v Commission (1990) provides an illustration of the way the extension of economic strength by a dominant company may be an abuse. In a merger, the dominant firm gained an exclusive licence to exploit intellectual property. The Court of First Instance held this to be a violation of Article 86. The fact that the exclusive licence the benefit of which was acquired was within the block exemption made no difference: the court was concerned with the anti-competitive implications of the acquisition in the dominated market.

13.4 The Commission's powers

The Commission, as the institution responsible for enforcing the competition rules, has extensive powers.

13.4.1 Own initiative investigations

The Commission may investigate matters of which it learns through the media, questions in the European Parliament, etc, but is under no obligation to do so. The Commission tends to resist requests to use its own resources to fight other peoples' battles, unless there is a matter of general importance involved. Complainants will be encouraged to seek redress in their national courts.

It is also empowered to conduct general enquiries into economic sectors where it thinks competition may be restricted (Regulation 17/62 Article 12).

13.4.2 Fact finding

The Commission has far-reaching powers to get to the bottom of a suspected infringement. It may request information and may carry out an investigation (Regulation 17/62 Articles 11 and 14).

(a) *Requests for information (Article 11)*

Article 11 empowers the Commission to obtain 'all necessary information'. There is a privilege against self-incrimination.

Requests for information are made in writing to suspected infringers or to third parties who may be able to provide information. Initially, such requests are informal, but supplying incorrect or incomplete information can result in a 5,000 ECU fine (Article 15.1).

If a request is ignored or refused or the reply is incomplete a formal decision may be made by the Commission ordering the information to be supplied (Article 16.1). Daily default fines of up to 1,000 ECU can be imposed if this is ignored.

(b) *Investigations (Article 14)*

Investigations also come in varying degrees of formality, though there is no two-tier system: the Commission may choose to be informal first, or it may go straight in with a formal investigation. An inspection visit is like a request for information; officials may examine business records, take copies, request explanations, and enter property. Incomplete production of records, etc, carries a penalty of up to 5,000 ECU (Articles 14.2, 15.1).

Commission inspectors must show their authorisation and prove their identity by means of their staff card.

A firm may refuse to submit to an investigation. If so this is recorded and the firm may have a copy of the minute. If it voluntarily submits it accepts all the ensuing obligations.

Investigation may also be ordered by decision of the Commission (Article 14(3)). This procedure is followed if the firm refuses to submit to investigation, if the infringement is serious and the Commission fears that evidence may disappear if the firm is forewarned, or if the firm has a bad record for co-operating in the past.

A visit by decision need not be announced. The firm is required to submit to the investigation and fines and periodic penalties may be imposed in default. The decision may be annulled on application to the European Court of Justice.

Firms which receive a visit may insist on having a legal adviser present provided this does not unduly delay the inspection.

The Commission's final decision can be:

- to grant negative clearance; or

- to grant exemption; or

- to order the termination of an infringement.

13.4.3   Final decision

Negative clearance or exemption must be preceded by publication of details of the case in the Official Journal, giving interested parties an opportunity to comment. Member states' authorities must also be consulted, through the Advisory Committee on restrictive practices and dominant positions.

A decision to grant negative clearance states that the Commission finds no infringement on the facts before it. New facts may arise causing it to reconsider whether an agreement or concerted practice violates Article 85(1) and what its saving graces are for the purposes of Article 85(3).

A decision to grant exemption indicates why the agreement violates Article 85(1) and what its saving graces are for the purposes of Article 85(3) (Regulation 17/62, Article 8). Exemption lasts for a set time but may be extended. Sometimes modifications are required to the agreement before exemption is given.

Before reaching a decision that an infringement has occurred the Commission gives the parties a statement of objections with a copy of its file attached. A time limit – usually one or two months – is specified for a written response to the objections (Commission Regulation 99/63 Article 2).

Parties can request an oral procedure before the Hearing Officer, a Commission Official charged with ensuring that due account is taken of all the facts. Following the hearing, if there is one, the Advisory Committee must be consulted.

Where it finds an infringement the Commission will issue a cease and desist order. If the infringement has already been terminated the decision will state that it was an infringement.

Positive actions may also be required – eg to restore supplies to a customer from whom they have been withheld.

Fines can also be imposed for infringements of Article 85(1) or 86, up to 1 million ECU or 10% of the worldwide turnover of the firm concerned in the previous business year – which may include the turnover in all products of the whole group (Regulation 17/62 Article 15.2). Fines of 3 million ECU are regularly imposed; 10 million is not unknown: in Tetrapak, an Article 86 case, the fine was 75 million. The level of the fine depends on the seriousness of the conduct, its duration, whether deliberate or negligent, the firm's past record, and whether the Commission has previously gone for such practices (in which case the offender should have known better).

Interim measures may be taken to preserve the status quo; a final decision may take years and immense damage could be done if protective measures were not available. For example, in *Peugeot* (1990), the Commission ordered the manufacturer to recommence supplies to the parallel trader whom it had ordered its Belgian and Luxembourg dealers to stop supplying.

Provisional decisions, which terminate immunity from fines, amount to a warning that the Commission reckons that Article 85(1) has been infringed and exemption is not justified. Since fines can be imposed again, such warnings should not lightly be ignored.

Administrative (or 'comfort') letters inform the parties that the Commission does not intend to take action. They do not have the legal status of decisions but such a letter could be useful evidence in the UK courts; if it says the agreement is outside the scope of Article 85(1) that would rebut a challenge to the validity of the agreement but if it says the agreement may be exempted that merely proves that it infringes Article 85 and the court must regard it as void because only the Commission can grant exemption.

Informal settlements may be reached by negotiation; the firms involved agree to modify the agreement or change their behaviour to the satisfaction of the Commission.

Decisions must be published in the Official Journal, except for procedural decisions publication of which is optional. Press releases are issued publicising decisions, and also informal settlements where a point of general interest is covered (see, for example, *Re Alfa Romeo* (1985)).

The Commission also takes action on complaints received from interested parties. When a complaint is received the Commission examines whether a violation is taking place. If it finds no infringement it will inform the complainant who then has an opportunity to make comments, following which the Commission will either continue its investigation or reject the complaint.

13.4.4   Complaints

A complaint may be made using Form C (available from the Commission or its information offices) but a simple letter will suffice.

Articles 85 and 86 form part of the law of the UK and can be used in legal actions in the British courts (eg for a declaration that an agreement is void under Article 85(2) or that a dominant position is being abused, or as a defence in an intellectual property infringement action). The courts, unlike the Commission, can award damages but they lack the Commission's powers of investigation. Very few such actions have been brought.

13.4.5   EC competition law in the English Courts

An appeal against a decision of the Commission in a competition matter lies in the first place to the Court of First Instance. From there, an appeal lies to the full European Court of Justice.

13.4.6   Appeals

The court may confirm, reduce, cancel or increase fines or periodic penalties imposed by the Commission. It can also review and if necessary annul all formal decisions of the Commission. Appeals can also be brought against the Commission's failure to act.

13.5	**The Merger Control Regulation**	In the past, mergers have been controlled under Article 86 (*Continental Can v Commission* (1983)) and Article 85 (*BAT and Reynolds v Commission* (1987)). Neither has proved particularly well-suited to the task. The Merger Control Regulation (4064/89) now requires pre-notification of certain mergers, and aims to achieve predictability through 'one stop shopping'. The criteria are designed to ensure that only mergers with a Community dimension are caught, so the Community regime should not in theory overlap with national ones.
13.5.1	Scope	The Regulation controls 'concentrations'. This includes the situation where two or more previously independent undertakings merge, and where control of another undertaking is acquired. The second is difficult to apply precisely: control depends on the ability to exercise decisive influence, which could be achieved by acquiring a minority interest. In *Arjimori Prioux/Wiggins Teape* (1990) acquisition of 39% of the shares, where the remaining shares were widely dispersed, gave the buyer control: on the other hand, in Renault/Volvo where 25% of the companies' car manufacturing and 45% of their truck manufacturing operations were merged the trucks but not the cars deal was caught.

The thresholds prescribed by the regulation are:

- the parties' aggregate worldwide turnover exceeds 5,000 million ECU; and

- the aggregate Community-wide turnover of each of at least two of the undertakings concerned exceeds 250 million ECU; unless

- each of the undertakings concerned achieves more than two-thirds of its aggregate Community-wide turnover within one and the same Member State.

Mergers which are caught have to be notified no more than a week after the agreement, announcement of public bid or acquisition of a controlling interest. The procedure for notification is set out in Regulation 2367/90 and form CO is prescribed. The merger may not be put into effect before, or for three weeks after, notification. Failure to observe these procedural requirements may result in fines and periodical penalty payments.

Note that a joint venture may be regarded as a 'concentration' to which the regulation applies (as does the Fair Trading Act). The question is whether the joint venture performs, on a lasting basis, all the functions of an autonomous economic entity. If it gives rise to co-ordination of the parties, or between them and the joint venture, Article 85 will still apply. The question is whether the joint venture is collaborative (ie within Article 85) or concentrative (ie within the Merger Control Regulation) and the Commission produced guidelines to help tell the difference in 1990.

Whether the merger is permitted depends on its effect on competition in the EC. If it creates or strengthens a dominant position as a result of which effective competition would be significantly impeded in the Common Market or in a substantial part of it, it will not be permitted or conditions may be attached by the Commission. The notion of dominance requires consideration of what the market is: in *Aerospatiale/MBB* (1991) the parties had more than 50% of the European helicopter market, but the entire world market was open to them. They were not dominant at the global level so the merger was allowed.

The 'one stop' principle does not apply in two situations:

- Where there is dominance in a distinct national market, national law may be applied if the Commission authorises this (Article 9).

- Article 21/93 enables a Member State to protect interests affected by a merger other than those specifically covered by the regulation. This permits intervention on grounds of public security, plurality of the media, 'prudential rules', and 'other legitimate interests'.

A merger which does not satisfy the Community dimension criteria may nevertheless be subject to Community control if a Member State requests it. The merger must significantly affect competition within that Member State's territory.

Perfect one stop shopping has therefore not been achieved, and indeed would be impossible. There will always be situations where it is not possible to work out if the thresholds have been reached (in a contested takeover, for example, where the parties do not have full information). In such cases national and Community requirements will still have to be followed. Nor does the regulation exclude Articles 85 and 86 from the field, although by prohibiting overlap between itself and Regulation 17/62 (the instrument which gives the Commission the power to apply Articles 85 and 86) the Merger Regulation does oust a large part of the jurisdiction of those provisions.

13.5.2   Exceptions to the 'one stop' principle

Competition Policy

Article 85 controls restrictive agreements and concerted practices. There must be an effect on trade between Member States and the object or effect of the agreement must be to prevent, restrict or distort competition within the common market.

Such agreements are prohibited (Article 85(1)) and automatically void (Article 85(2)).

The concept of an agreement is wide, and so-called 'gentlemen's agreements' which are not legally binding may be caught. In *Polypropolene* the Commission found that there was an agreement despite the fact that it was oral, was not legally binding, had no specific sanctions, and had not been universally observed.

The concept of an undertaking is also broad. Any economically active unit may be considered an undertaking and therefore subject to the competition rules, but this also means that arrangements between a parent company and its subsidiary are not caught, nor are those between agents and principals.

A concerted practice was defined in *Dyestuffs* as:

'... without going so far as to amount to an agreement properly so called, knowingly substitutes a practical co-operation for the risks of competition.'

The object of an agreement, etc, will be prohibited: if there is no prohibited object will the authorities have to look to the effects of the arrangement. The form and content of a restriction on competition is immaterial to Article 85.

Unilateral action by an undertaking is outside the scope of Article 85 (though if the undertaking is dominant Article 86 may well prohibit whatever it is doing).

The requirement that there is an effect on trade between Member States is a jurisdictional threshold which the authorities must get over. In the *Société Technique Minière* case the Court looked for a foreseeable influence, direct or indirect, actual or potential, on the pattern of trade between Member States. It is rarely a significant problem.

Any agreement having the prohibited effect in the common market is caught: *Ahlström Oy v Commission* – the *Wood Pulp* case.

Decisions and judgments do not seek to distinguish between prevention, distortion or restriction: the list is treated as expressing a single concept.

Minor agreements

If the effect on trade between Member States is not *significant* the prohibition will not apply (*Völk v Verwaek*). The Notice on Minor Agreements applies if the parties' market share is less than 5% and their turnover less than 200 million ECU so that there is no (or no significant) distortive effect on competition.

Co-operation agreements, subcontracting agreements and certain joint ventures are covered by Commission guidelines, indicating where the limits of the prohibition might lie.

Exemption

Article 85(3) permits agreements to be exempted. It sets out two positive and two negative conditions, which import the notion of proportionality found elsewhere in EC law. Agreements or practices which:

- contribute to an improvement in production or distribution, or to economic progress;

- give a fair share of the benefits to consumers (including trade customers);

- impose no restrictions which are not indispensable to realising the benefits; and

- do not afford the parties the possibility of eliminating competition in respect of a substantial part of the products in question.

Only the Commission has the power to grant an exemption.

The Commission has delegated powers to exempt categories of agreements, thereby clearing some of the logjams of notified agreements which had built up. Such regulations cover:

- exclusive distribution agreements (Regulation 1983/83);

- exclusive purchasing agreements (including special rules for beer and service station agreements) (Regulation 1984/83);

- patent licensing agreements (Regulation 2349/84);

- motor vehicle distribution and servicing agreements (Regulation 123/85);

- specialisation agreements (Regulation 417/85);

- research and development agreements (Regulation 418/85);

- know-how licensing (Regulation 556/89);

- franchising (Regulation 4087/88).

An agreement which is not inside one of these regulations may still benefit from individual exemption.

Article 86 provides that an undertaking which enjoys a dominant position must not abuse its economic power in any way. Any such abuse is prohibited.

Abuse of dominant position

Market share of 40 to 45% is the best indication of dominance but other factors may be equally or even more important:

- the existence of barriers to entry to new competitors;

- the ownership of intellectual property rights;

- monopolies created by national laws; and

- access to raw materials or capital.

The dominant position must be in the Common Market or a substantial part of it. What constitutes a substantial part is a question of fact and will vary according to the nature of the product.

The product market in which dominance must be judged is important. In *United Brands*, the Commission and the Court held that there was no substitute for bananas for certain consumers, so the market in which dominance had to be tested was that for bananas alone.

A dominant position is abused if advantage is taken of it so as to cause injury to third parties. Examples include

- charging unfair prices;

- price discrimination;

- refusal to supply;

- fidelity rebates.

The Merger Control regulation (4064/89) now requires pre-notification of certain mergers, and aims to achieve predictability through 'one stop shopping'. The thresholds prescribed by the regulation are:

Merger control

- the parties' aggregate worldwide turnover exceeds 5,000 million ECU; and

- the aggregate Community-wide turnover of each of at least two of the undertakings concerned exceeds 250 million ECU; unless

- each of the undertakings concerned achieves more than two-thirds of its aggregate Community-wide turnover within one and the same Member State.

Mergers which are caught have to be notified no more than a week after the agreement, announcement of public bid or acquisition of a controlling interest.

Whether the merger is permitted depends on its effect on competition in the EC.

The 'one stop' principle does not apply where there is dominance in a distinct national market (national law may be applied if the Commission authorises this) or where interests other than those specifically covered by the Regulation are affected by a merger. This permits intervention on grounds of public security, plurality of the media, 'prudential rules', and 'other legitimate interests'.

The Commission has extensive powers of investigation, mostly set out in Regulation 17/62.

Chapter 14

Social Policy

Social policy is an area of Community competence which is now rapidly developing following a slow start, due to the limited scope for action provided for in the original treaty. It embraces equality of opportunity, health and safety, employment and labour law, social protection and social security, poverty and the role of the disabled.

Legislation on social security rights for migrant workers is an important factor in guaranteeing fee movement for such people, and is dealt with above. There is also important legislation on equal treatment for men and women (dealt with below), health and safety at work, protection of workers and labour law.

The basic treaty provisions were supplemented by the Social Charter in 1989, and the Maastricht Treaty formalised the commitment to social policy of all the Member States except the UK in its Social Chapter. The European Social Fund has given financial support to training and employment measures: the Commission has developed programmes and exchanges concentrating on long-term unemployment, integration of the disabled, research and awareness campaigns and information on national situations and policies.

Article 117 sets the scene:

'Member States agree upon the need to provide improved working conditions and an improved standard of living for workers, so as to make possible their harmonisation while the improvement is being maintained.'

They believe that such a development will ensue not only from the functioning of the common market, which will favour the harmonisation of social systems, but also from the procedures provided for in this Treaty and from the approximation of provisions laid down by law, regulation or administrative decision.

Article 118a deals with health and safety, Article 119 (the only directly effective provision on social policy) with sex discrimination, Article 118b with the development of 'social dialogue between the social partners' (industry and trade unions), and Article 123 with the European Social Fund.

The Treaty on European Union made significant amendments in this area of the Community's competence.

14.1   Introduction

14.2   Social policy and the Treaty

Article 2 (as amended) now sets out a much more ambitious agenda: it speaks of the Community's task as being to promote '... a harmonious and balanced development of economic activities, sustainable and non-inflationary growth respecting the environment, a high degree of convergence of economic performance, a high level of employment and of social protection, the raising of the standard of living and quality of life, and economic and social cohesion and solidarity among Member States.'

This chapter examines the effect of these Treaty provisions. However, before turning to them, there are a couple of other major developments to mention.

14.2.1   The Social Charter and the Social Chapter

The Charter on Fundamental Social Rights for Workers was adopted by the Strasbourg European Council meeting in December 1989. It is a solemn declaration which has no binding force but is backed up with an action programme which includes 47 initiatives, 29 of which required legislative action. All the Member States except the UK adopted the Charter.

The Social Chapter, otherwise known as the Agreement on Social Policy, is a protocol to the Maastricht Treaty. It gives a legal basis to the Social Charter. The Maastricht Treaty also includes a Protocol on Social Policy. The UK is not a party to these accords either, although it has implemented most of the proposals brought forward under the Charter. It reserves the right to opt out of matters within the scope of the Chapter, and in September 1994 it used this right for the first time in Council deliberations on the proposed directive on paternity leave.

14.2.2   Implementation of the Social Charter

The Commission has now presented to the Council all the 47 proposals mentioned in the Charter. Fifteen had been adopted at the time of the Commission's second report on progress (1 November 1992), and the majority were in place by the end of 1993. These include:

- Measures to improve the employment situation in the Community. Regulation EEC 4253/88 allows the Commission to set up initiatives, which it has in the fields of equal opportunities for women and for handicapped persons and certain other disadvantaged groups, and of new qualifications, skills and employment opportunities. The Commission has also taken steps to improve the communication of information about job opportunities between Member States.

- In the fields of employment and pay, the Commission has proposed legislation:

(a) to improve the functioning of the internal market and it make the labour market more transparent (under Article 100a);

(b) to improve living and working conditions for workers (Article 100);

(c) to protect the health and safety of workers at work (Article 118a), which was adopted on 25 June 1991.

The Commission has presented a draft opinion on basic principles for equitable pay, on which the Parliament has called for a directive.

• The Commission proposed a directive on the organisation of working time in 1990 and amended it in 1991. It provides for minimum daily and weekly rest periods, and minimum conditions for shift work, night work and health and safety protection. (A common position was reached in June 1993. The UK abstained, intending to question the validity of using Article 118a as the legal basis for this proposal).

• A directive on the provision of a form of proof of an employment relationship was adopted in 1991 (Directive 91/553/EEC). It is designed to improve transparency in the labour market by balancing the needs of workers to know the nature of their employment and of employers to develop new and more flexible relationships, necessary in view of the development of distance work, work experience schemes and mixed employment/training contracts.

Article 118a EC provides that:

'Member States shall pay particular attention to encouraging improvements, especially in the working environment, as regards the health and safety of workers and shall set as their objective the harmonisation of conditions in this area, while maintaining the improvements made.'

It permits the Council by qualified majority to adopt directives setting out minimum requirements.

The UK has never been comfortable with the use of this provision to regulate matters other than physical hazards: problems arise from the fact that the Nordic countries have long used the expression 'working environment' to include also social aspects. The UK has made its stand on the working time directive, which Article 118a allows the other Member States to pass in the face of the UK's opposition. The UK wants

14.3   The working environment

to see Article 100 used as the basis for such legislation, since this would require unanimity.

Prior to the Single European Act, which introduced Article 118a, the Community had adopted some health and safety measures in the form of recommendations. It had also promulgated two Action Programmes, which had led to a few directives addressed to particular types of hazard in specific types of work, and established an Advisory Committee on health and safety.

The introduction of Article 118a gave new powers to regulate workplace health and safety. The pace of legislation increased substantially. In 1987 a new action programme was instituted, leading to many additional initiatives under Article 118a.

14.3.1 **The framework directive**	Directive 89/391/EEC establishes a framework for health and safety legislation. Several 'daughter' directive have been adopted under it. It is aimed at:

'... the prevention of occupational risks, the protection of health and safety, the elimination of risk and accident factors, the informing, consultation and balanced participation in accordance with national laws and/or practices and training of workers and their representatives.' (Article 1(2))

It imposes specific obligations on employers in a variety of fields, and generally requires the dangerous to be replaced by the non-dangerous. Training of workers is fundamental to the directive's approach.

The Council is empowered to adopt directives under the framework directive by Article 16. Twelve directives have been passed so far. It is beyond the scope of this work to detail them all: see Charlesworth and Cullen, *European Community Law* (London: Pitman, 1994) p 395, for a full list.

14.3.2 **Other health and safety legislation**

Other health and safety legislation has been passed under the Social Charter action programme. Again, a full list will be found in Charlesworth and Cullen.

The working time directive requires mention as part of this programme, though as we have already seen the UK maintains that it rightly forms part of the general harmonisation programme and should not have been made under Article 118a. Unlike measures adopted under the Protocol on social policy to the Maastricht Treaty (the Social Chapter) it will be binding on the UK, which is seeking to have it annulled by the Court of Justice.

Again, a detailed description of the measure is not appropriate here: the reader should consult Charlesworth and Cullen or some other textbook.

The UK is also challenging the basis of a draft directive on the protection of young workers. Again, it is proposed under Article 118a, and the UK argues that Article 100 would be the right enabling power. What will happen will probably depend on the fate of the working time directive.

14.4 Preservation of employment rights

Article 100 was used to implement several of the measures proposed under the 1974–76 Action Programme. These provide protection for workers in the event of fundamental changes in the structure of their employment. These include:

- Directive 75/129/EEC on collective redundancies;

- Directive 77/187/EEC on the transfer of undertakings (implemented in the UK in the infamous Transfer of Undertakings (Protection of Employment) Regulations 1979 (the TUPE Regulations). The directive is currently under review;

- Directive 80/987/EEC on insolvencies (the directive in issue in Cases C-6 and 9/90, *Francovich*).

14.5 Employee consultation

Requiring employees to be consulted on a variety of matters is central to the Community's social policy. It appears as a principle in several of the directives already mentioned.

In addition, there are three proposals which specifically seek to advance the principle of employee consultation, or participation. These are:

- The so-called Vredeling directive, named for the Dutch social affairs commissioner who was originally responsible for it. It required certain undertakings, in particular multinational companies, to inform and consult their employees in a variety of matters. The companies viewed this as an undesirable interference with their right to manage, and opposition to the draft caused it eventually to be quietly dropped.

- The draft fifth company law directive. This is concerned with harmonising the structure of public limited companies and their equivalents. It adopted initially the German and Dutch models of supervisory boards and executive boards, the supervisory boards being comprised (*inter alia*) of worker representatives. The possibility of a works council was added later, and also an alternative sufficiently wide to allow collective bargaining to provide the necessary degree of consultation. Harmonisation had just about disappeared entirely by this stage, but still it was resisted in the UK. It remains a draft.

- The European Company (*Sociaetas Europaea*) would provide a way for companies to be registered as creatures of Community, rather than national, law. There would be worker representation on the management boards of such companies. The regulation establishing the statute for such a creature and there is a draft directive which would complement it.

- The draft directive on the information and consultation of workers within European-scale undertakings, part of the Social Charter action programme, will apply to all companies which have over 1,000 employees in two or more Member States. They will be required to set up works councils, for purposes to be agreed between the company and the workers but including a list of mandatory matters. The UK does not support this proposal.

14.6	**Contracts of employment**	Directive 91/533/EEC requires Member States to adopt legislation obliging employers to provide all employees either with a written employment contract or a statement of the terms under which they are employed.
14.7	**Equal pay: Article 119**	Article 119 seeks to prohibit sex discrimination at work:

'Each Member State shall during the first stage ensure and subsequently maintain the application of the principle that men and women should receive equal pay for equal work.

For the purpose of this Article, "pay" means the ordinary basic or minimum wage or salary and any other consideration, whether in cash or kind, which the worker receives, directly or indirectly, in respect of his employment from his employer.

Equal pay without discrimination based on sex means:

(a) that pay for the same work at piece rates shall be calculated on the basis of the same unit of measurement;

(b) that pay for work at time rates shall be the same for the same job.'

The Article was inserted at the insistence of the French government. France had national equal pay legislation at the time of the Treaty, and was concerned to ensure that other countries within the Community did not secure a competitive advantage by not treating workers equally. The motive was therefore at least as much economic as social.

There have been three action programmes in this area, and a considerable amount of important legislation. These developments will be considered below.

The Court of Justice had its first opportunity to get its teeth into equal pay in Case 147/77, *Defrenne v SABENA*. Prior to that the Commission had been rather less than diligent in dealing with Member States' failures to apply the principles of Article 119, so there had been no infringement actions for the court to consider.

14.7.1   The application of Article 119

In *Defrenne* an air hostess was required to retire earlier than male colleagues, was paid less and received a smaller state pension. This latter point was held by the court in Case 80/70 to be outside the scope of the Treaty, but the employee brought actions against her employer instead. The complaint based on retirement age was considered by the court to be a matter of working conditions, not equal pay, so it too failed: now, it would be covered by the equal treatment directive (76/207/EEC), on which see below, para 14.9.

On the equal pay point, the court held that the Member States were obliged to implement the requirements of Article 119 by the end of the transitional period and that failure to comply in time gave individuals the right to rely on the direct effect of the Treaty provision. However, the Court added:

'For the purposes of the implementation of these provisions, a distinction must be drawn within the whole area of application of Article 119 between, firstly, *direct and overt discrimination*, which may be identified solely with the aid of the criteria based on equal pay referred to by the article in question, and, secondly, *indirect and disguised discrimination*, which can only be identified by reference to more explicit implementing provisions of a Community or national character.'

Direct and overt discrimination could be found in legislation, collective agreements, and particular work situations: in the national courts, an applicant would have to be able to show such discrimination to succeed in an Article 119 claim. (See also Case 129/79, *McCarthys v Smith* (1980)).

Article 119 defines pay widely. The court has adopted a generous view of the meaning of the expression in the Treaty, thus enhancing its direct effect (horizontal as well as vertical, since it is a Treaty provision) and minimising the possibilities for evasion by using disguised forms of remuneration.

14.7.2   'Pay'

• In Case 19/81, *Burton v British Railways Board* Advocate General Verloren van Themaat suggested that the wider meaning of the words used in the original language versions of the Treaty should be preferred to the English version, which said 'in respect of' employment. The French and Italian translated more accurately as 'by reason of'.

- In Case 32/71, *Sabbatini v European Parliament* (1972) expatriation allowances were made subject to this general principle.

- Any contributions made by the employer to secure a higher level of state benefits for the employee will also count as pay (Case 69/80, *Worringham v Lloyds Bank* (1982)).

- In Case 12/81, *Garland v British Rail* (1982) the court held that perks (there, reduced rail fares for the employee and their family) was 'pay', and that it did not have to arise from the contract of employment itself.

The court has summarised matters neatly in its judgment in Case 360/90, *Arbeitwohlfahrt der Stadt Berlin v Botel* (1992). It includes:

> '... all consideration, whether in cash or kind, whether immediate or future, provided that the worker receives it, albeit indirectly, in respect of his employment from his employer, whether under a contract of employment, by virtue of legislation or on a voluntary basis.'

14.7.3   Pensions

The problem with pensions is to know whether they fall to be considered as a species of pay, in which case Article 119 would apply, or as a form of social security. If pension entitlements arise under contract, it is fairly clear that they are pay: if under statute, they are social security and outside the scope of Article 119, which does not control benefits governed directly by legislation which are compulsory for general categories of workers and which are not based on agreement. The question is whether a pension is received 'directly or indirectly, in respect of [the employee's] employment from [her] employer'.

- Purely private pension arrangements clearly constitute pay.

- State pensions are outside Article 119.

- Pension schemes established by the employer *may* be pay.

The court has had to grapple with how to treat top-up pensions which supplement the state pension, and 'contracted out' pensions schemes which replace state provision.

- State pensions

  Directive 79/7/EEC, the state social security directive, deals specifically with state pensions, requiring equal treatment and therefore making it unnecessary to import equal treatment provisions from elsewhere in Community law. This directive is discussed further.

Even before that directive was adopted, the court had decided in the first *Defrenne* case that state pension entitlement was not a matter for Article 119: and in Case 19/91, *Burton v British Rail* (1982) the court considered that conditions governing eligibility for early retirement pensions under a voluntary redundancy scheme concerned working conditions, not pay, and therefore Article 119 had no application.

- Occupational pensions

The status of non-state pensions depends on whether they constitute pay or not. They may be supplementary to state pensions, or may replace them completely: that now appears to make no difference to their treatment in EC law.

The problem was first dealt with in Case 170/84, *Bilka-Kaufhaus GmbH v Weber von Hartz* (1986). There, the scheme (which concerned only top-up pensions) was established partly under contract of employment, and was partly funded by the employer. Advocate General Darmon was of the opinion that this brought it within the scope of Article 119, and the court agreed.

The distinction drawn in that case between pensions as pay and pensions as social security has been developed in later cases. The fact that the court had been considering only top-up pensions and not contracted-out schemes suggested to many that if a scheme replaces state provision it falls to be considered under the Directive, not Article 119.

Advocate General Warner suggested in Case 69/80, *Worringham v Lloyds Bank* (1982) that this approach was the correct one: the court managed to avoid the issue then, but returned to it in Case C-262/88, *Barber v Guardian Royal Exchange Assurance Group* (1990), where it took the different view.

There, the court held that pension schemes were to be treated as pay and therefore subject to the non-discrimination requirements of Article 119 if certain requirements were satisfied:

(a) The scheme results from agreement between the employee and the employer, or a unilateral act of the employer, and there is no contribution from any public authority;

(b) The scheme is not compulsory for general categories of worker, but entitlement arises from working for a particular employer, and the scheme is governed by its own rules (notwithstanding that it operates within a general statutory framework);

(c) The fact that the scheme substitutes for a general statutory one does not render Article 119 inapplicable.

The court took the view that since this decision was unexpected, it was justified in limiting its effects as it had done in *Defrenne*. Unless proceedings had already been started, no claim for benefits due prior to the date of the decision (17 May 1990) could be made. This would minimise the commercial disruption which the decision could have caused.

In *Ten Oever* the court clarified the scope and the effect in time of the *Barber* decision. Except for prior claims, the equal pay principle applied only to benefits payable for employment periods served after the date of the *Barber* judgment. The court also clarified that survivors' rights under pension schemes were also within the scope of the judgment.

In *Morroni* the court applied the principles of *Barber* to occupational pension schemes outside the social security system and not benefitting from public finance.

In *Neath* it ruled that the use of actuarial factors in funded defined-benefit schemes, which factors differed according to sex, was not covered by the equal pay rule.

The scheme in *Barber* was financed entirely by the employer's contributions. What of schemes where the employee also makes a contribution? In Case C-200 *Coloroll Pension Trustees Ltd v Russell* (not yet reported) Advocate General van Gerven suggested that Article 119 would apply regardless of whether the scheme was contracted out or not, and whether the employee contributed to it, voluntarily or compulsorily, was immaterial. The court appears to have followed this reasoning.

The *Coloroll* case was one of a group of six decided on 28 September 1994. In it, the court also held that the trustees of a pension fund are obliged to have regard to the requirements of Article 119 just as much as the employer – important here, since the employer had been wound up. It defined the duty of the trustees when using a lump sum to purchase an annuity for the employee to pay equal contributions: it was not necessary to seek to secure equal benefits for employees.

In Case C-408/92, *Smith v Advel Systems* (not yet reported) the court held that in equalising pension provisions it was legitimate for the employer to worsen the provision made for women, whose retirement age had been increased to 65 as a result of *Barber*. And in Case C-28/93, *van den Akker v Shell* (not yet reported) the court held that it was unlawful for the employer to protect women's pension rights by allowing them to keep a pensionable age of 60 while equalising retirement ages after *Barber*.

Two other cases concern the rights of access of married women and part-time workers (most of whom are women) to occupational pension schemes. In Case C-57/93 *Vroege* and Case C-128/93 *Fisscher* (not yet reported) the court confirmed its earlier decisions and established that the limitation in time of the *Barber* decision does not affect the rights of employees to enforce the equal pay rules to secure access to pensions. However, limitation rules in national laws may apply, and in the case of a contributory pension scheme the employee must make back-dated contributions.

In *Rinner Kuhn* the court determined that sick pay, although required to be paid by law, was available by virtue of the contract of employment as amounted to a form of pay.

14.7.4   Sick pay

Where men and women do different work, or the same work at different times, or there are other differences which make the situation less than straightforward discrimination, the application of Article 119 is more complicated.

14.7.5   'Equal work'

In Case 129/79, *Macarthys v Smith* (1980) the applicant was being paid less than the man she replaced. The court held that the nature of the services being provided was all that mattered: when they were provided was immaterial. The applicant was entitled to equal pay for her work.

In *Defrenne* the court stated that equal value claims would have to be dealt with by secondary legislation. But in Case 96/80, *Jenkins v Kingsgate (Clothing Productions) Ltd* (1981) the court accepted that Article 119 would permit a claim based on equal value, not just identical work. It held that the equal pay directive facilitated the implementation of Article 119 rather than creating new rights or altering its scope.

14.7.6   Equal value

In *Worringham* the court decided that Article 1 of the directive explains that the concept of 'same work' in Article 119 includes cases of 'work to which equal value is attributed'.

Article 119 only requires that women be paid as much as men (Case 157/86, *Murphy v Bord Eireann Telecom* (1988)). The law does not require that there should be proportionality between services and pay. However, the fact that the work of the different employees was not of the same value did not stop the comparison being made at all. If Article 119 required that employees be paid the same for work of equal value, it required also that they be paid the same where the work was of more than equal value. However, a woman cannot claim for greater pay than a man doing a lesser job.

14.7.7   Indirect discrimination

Indirect discrimination occurs where different classes of employee are treated differently, and due to a preponderance of one gender in the less well-treated class, there is sex discrimination. Part-time workers are more often women than men, and cases of discrimination against part-timers constitute most of the body of caselaw here.

In *Jenkins v Kingsgate* the hourly rates paid to part time and full time employees differed. The part timers were mostly female. The court found that this was potentially a violation, but it could be explained away by some objective justification. There would be no violation 'in so far as the difference in pay is attributable to factors which are objectively justified and are in no way related to any discrimination based on sex'.

The court has largely left the national courts to elaborate on these basic principles. In Danfoss the court held that quality may be rewarded, but the assessment of quality may not be tainted by discrimination: '[I]t is inconceivable that the quality of work done by women should be less good.'

In *Bilka* part time workers could only enter the pension scheme if they did enough hours. It was more difficult for women to achieve the threshold level. The court held that a three-part test had to be applied:

- Do the measures correspond to a real need on the part of the undertaking?

- Are they appropriate as a means of achieving the end?

- Are they necessary to achieve the end?

In *Rinner*, sick pay was only available for employees who were contracted for a minimum number of hours. This amounted to an exclusion of part timers from sick pay. The court held that this amounted to indirect discrimination, which could be justified by the employer: however, it was not sufficient to argue that part timers were not so well integrated into the employer's organisation as full timers.

In Case C184/89, *Nimz v Frei- und Hansestadt Hamburg* (1992), the House of Lords has applied the same reasoning. In *R v Secretary of State for Employment, ex parte Equal Opportunities Commission* (1994), the Employment Protection (Consolidation) Act 1978 was held to discriminate. It wanted the right to claim for unfair dismissal and redundancy to employees working a minimum number of hours per week: part-timers were largely excluded.

Although Article 119 is directly effective, the prohibition of indirect discrimination may not always meet the requirements. Assessing the complaint and the objective justifications put forward by the employer may be so complicated that direct effect is precluded.

This problem is partly dealt within Directive 75/117. In addition, the court has decided that the burden of proof can be shifted by the applicant to the employer.

In *Danfoss*, women employees ended up earning less than men in the same wage group. The reasons for this were complicated, but the court overcame the problem to a great extent by holding that once inequality had been shown in this way it was for the employer to explain why it had happened.

In other words, if the employer's system is non-transparent, so it is impossible to tell why the apparently discriminatory result is arising, it is up to the employer to make it transparent. This derives from the principle of *effective remedies* – a lack of clarity must not be allowed to frustrate claimants.

In *Barber* the employer was not allowed to seek to show equality by a broad, general comparison. (See also the House of Lords' decision in *Hayward v Cammell Laird*.)

In fact, in this matter the court has gone further than the other institutions have been prepared to go: a proposed directive on the burden of proof was blocked in the Council in 1988.

In Case C 184/89, *Nimz v Freie- und Hansestadt Hamburg* (1992) the Court of Justice held that Article 119 is violated if there is discrimination against part-time workers where either they or full-timers are predominantly of one gender, unless the discrimination can be justified on the basis of 'objectively justified factirs'. The House of Lords followed this approach in *R v Secretary of State for Employment, ex parte Equal Opportunities Commission* (1994).

There, the applicants sought judicial review of the Employment Protection (Consolidation) Act 1978, which granted rights to claim compensation for unfair dismissal and redundancy only to employees who worked a certain number of hours per week. Part-timers were therefore excluded from protection, and the majority of them were women. Lord Keith of Kinkel opined that any differential in pay had to be objectively justified by factors unrelated to gender. The Government's contention that it was merely trying to strike a fair balance between employers and employees could not be

14.7.8 Proving discrimination

14.7.9 Defences and justifications

14.7.10 Temporal effect

objectively justified, and the Act therefore breached Article 119.

14.8 The Equal Pay Directive (75/117)

Directive 75/117 harmonises the laws of the Member States on equal pay, and by elaborating on some of the principles involved in identifying indirect discrimination (see above, paras 14.7.7 and 14.7.8) enables national courts to deal with that problem. It restates the basic principle of Article 119 of the Treaty, adding the notion of 'work to which equal value is attributed', or work of equal value for short.

The directive requires that if a job classification system is used, it is based on the same criteria for both genders. It must be drawn up in such a way that the possibility of discrimination on grounds of sex is excluded.

In Case 58/81, *Commission v Luxembourg* (1982) the Court rejected the argument that the directive merely repeated Article 119 and that a Member State could not be in breach by failing to implement it (Article 119 being directly effective). In *Defrenne* the Court acknowledged that the Directive did not affect Article 119, but provided 'further details regarding certain aspects of the material scope of Article 119.'

14.8.1 'Equal value'

The Equal Pay Act 1970 (amended by the Sex Discrimination Act 1975) provided that only one way could be used to ascertain whether work was of equal value, and that was a job classification system which could only be introduced with the consent of the employer. In Case 61/81, *Commission v UK (Re Equal Pay Directive) (No 1)* (1982) the UK asserted that the concept of work to which equal value is attributed was too vague for the courts to enforce. The ECJ rejected this argument, stating that the UK had failed in its obligation to provide a means for employees to obtain recognition of equivalence if there was no job classification system in place.

14.9 Equal Treatment Directive (76/207)

Directive 76/207 requires equality of treatment in a number of additional areas relating to employment. These cover access to employment, vocational training and promotion, and working conditions. No discrimination on grounds of sex, direct or indirect, is permitted.

14.9.1 Access to employment

Discrimination in selection criteria for jobs is outlawed, and Member States are required to ensure that any incompatible laws or provisions in collective agreements or individual contracts are abolished, annulled or amended. In Case 165/82, *Commission v UK (Re Equal Pay Directive) (No 2)* (1983) the UK government argued that collective agreements were not legally binding, and anyway any such agreements which contained prohibited provisions would be rendered void under the Sex Discrimination Act. The Court was not impressed and held the UK in breach of its obligations under the directive.

The UK was also in breach for exempting employment in private households and employers of fewer than five people. This the government argued was done out of respect for family life: the Court rejected this, too.

Similar obligations are imposed relating to training and retraining.

14.9.2   Vocational training

Again, similar obligations are applied to working conditions, including those concerning dismissal.

14.9.3   Conditions of work and dismissal

Member States are required to introduce such measures as may be necessary to facilitate claims by employees who consider themselves wronged. They are also obliged to ensure that employees are aware of the provisions adopted under the directive.

14.9.4   Remedies

Member States may derogate from the basic principle where 'by [the nature of the duties] or the context in which they are carried out, the sex of the worker constitutes a determining factor.' In Case 165/82, *Commission v UK (Re Equal Pay Directive) (No 2)* (1983) the Court held the UK in breach for allowing discrimination in the access to the occupation of midwife, and to training for that profession: the government argued that personal sensitivities were important in this area, but the Court rejected this suggestion.

14.9.5   Exceptions

Directive 79/7, as we observed above (para 14.7.3) provides for equal treatment in social security matters. The principle of equal treatment is to be progressively implemented.

14.10   State social security directive (79/7)

The scope of the directive embraces statutory schemes which provide protection against sickness, invalidity, old age, accidents at work, occupational diseases and unemployment.

14.10.1 Scope

The directive does not extend to survivors' benefits or family benefits. Pensionable age remains a matter for the Member States to determine.

14.10.2 Exceptions

Directive 86/378 provides for equal treatment in occupational social security schemes.

14.11   Occupational social security directive

Directive 86/613 extends the principles of the equal treatment directive to the self-employed.

14.12   Equal treatment for the self employed directive

14.13 Green Paper on European Social Policy

With the entry into force of the Treaty on European Union new possibilities for action in the social field have opened up: also, increasing unemployment and other economic factors make it necessary to reconsider the links between economic and social policy. The Commission therefore launched a Green Paper on European Social Policy Options for the Union (COM (93) 551) in late 1993.

The Green Paper stresses that economic and social progress go together, and that promoting economic competitiveness must not be achieved at the expense of social progress. On the basis of the responses received to the Green Paper, the Commission will produce a White Paper in the autumn of 1994.

Social Policy

The provisions of the Treaty of Rome on social policy, which were very few, have been significantly augmented by recent initiatives and amendments. The 1989 Social Charter and the Social Chapter of TEU have changed the face of EC social policy.

Article 117 sets out the aim of the Community to enhance people's working conditions and standard of living. The only directly effective provision in the area was Article 119, on sex discrimination.

Following the TEU, Article 2 EC contains a much more ambitious agenda. Before then, the Social Charter declared (without legislative force) the Member States' intentions in the field, and spawned a number of directives. The Social Chapter, a Protocol to TEU, gives a legal basis to the Charter: the UK is not a party to it.

Article 118a concerns the working environment, and protects health and safety at work. It was introduced by SEA, and has resulted in a considerable increase in the rate of legislation in this area. The UK has resisted eg the working time directive, introduced under this provision, arguing that Article 100 is the proper basis for such a measure and that Article 118a should be restricted to health and safety issues.

In this field, Directive 89/391/EEC is an important provision. A so-called 'framework' directive, it has spawned several 'daughter' directives introducing detailed regulation.

Article 100 has been used as the basis for several directives concerned with the preservation of employment rights, including those on collective redundancies and on acquired rights. In this area, the Commission has also promoted measures designed to require employee consultation and participation.

The most important area of social policy remains that of equal treatment. Article 119 establishes the principle of equal pay for equal work, the basis of the claim in *Defrenne*. The Court held that failure of the Member State to implement the directive in time gave the employee a direct right of action.

Pay is widely defined, to include perks enjoyed by the worker's family (*Garland v British Rail*), expatriation allowances (*Sabbatini*) and additional contributions made by

The basis of social policy

Equal pay

the employer to secure a higher level of pension for the employee (*Worringham v Lloyds Bank*).

Pensions may be pay or they may be a social security benefit. If they are provided by the state, they are governed not by Article 119 but by Directive 79/7/EEC, which also requires equal treatment.

In *Bilka-Kaufhaus GmbH v Weber von Hartz* the Court defined widely the sort of pension provision which has to be considered a type of pay. A top-up scheme was considered to fall within the definition.

In *Barber v Guardian Royal Exchange Assurance Group* the Court extended the scope of Article 119 to embrace contracted-out pension schemes. Three criteria for a scheme to be within Article 119 were expounded:

- It results from agreement between the employee and the employer, or a unilateral act of the employer, and there is no contribution from any public authority.

- It is not compulsory for general categories of worker, but entitlement arises from working for a particular employer, and the scheme is governed by its own rules (notwithstanding that it operates within a general statutory framework).

- The fact that it substitutes for a general statutory one does not render Article 119 inapplicable.

The use of actuarial principles, possibly giving rise to discrimination, is not prohibited.

In *Coloroll* the Court also held that the trustees of a pension fund are obliged to have regard to the requirements of Article 119. The duty of the trustees when using a lump sum to purchase an annuity for the employee to pay equal contributions.

Objectively justified factors may be pleaded to allow what would otherwise be prohibited discrimination. In *Nimz v Hamburg* the Court accepted that discrimination against part-time workers (mainly female) could be subject to such justification: and in *R v Secretary of State for Employment, ex parte Equal Opportunities Commission* the House of Lords endorsed this approach, while nevertheless finding against the government.

Directive 75/117 harmonises the laws of the Member States on equal pay. It elaborates on Article 119, thus giving direct effect to some of its provisions (concerning indirect discrimination) and reiterates the basic principle of equal pay while adding the concept of equal pay for work of equal value.

Job classification systems, if used, must not be discriminatory: in the UK, such systems were the only method for assessing equality of pay for work of equal value, and the Court held that the UK was in breach of its obligations for failing to protect workers not covered by such systems (which could only be introduced with the consent of the employer).

Directive 76/207 requires equality of treatment in a number of additional areas relating to employment. Directive 86/378 provides for equal treatment in occupational social security schemes. Directive 86/613 extends the principles of the equal treatment directive to the self-employed.

Equal treatment

The Commission launched a Green Paper on European Social Policy Options for the Union in late 1993, based on the new scope of social policy under the TEU.

The Green Paper

Recommended Reading List

There are numerous good student textbooks on EC law available. This list contains some more specialised texts which do not fall obviously under any of the headings which follow.

Arnull: *The General Principles of EC Law and the Individual* (Leicester University Press, 1990)

Arnull: *The General Principles of EC Law and the Individual* (Leicester University Press, 1990)

Audretsch: *Supervision in European Community Law* (2nd edition 1986)

Green, Hartley & Usher: *The Legal Foundations of the Single European Market* (Oxford, 1991)

Holland: *European Community Integration* (Pinter, 1993)

Hartley: *The Foundations of European Community Law* (OUP: 2nd edition 1988)

Lodge (ed): *The European Community and the Challenge of the Future* (Pinter, 1993)

O'Keeffe & Twomey: *Legal Issues of the Maastricht Treaty* (Chancery, 1993)

Schermers: *Judicial Protection in the European Communities* (Kluwer: 4th edition 1987)

Snyder: *New Directions in European Community Law* (Weidenfeld & Nicholson, 1990)

Timmermans & Volker: *Division of Powers between the European Communities and their Member States in the field of External Relations* (Kluwer, 1981)

Toth: *The Oxford Encyclopedia of European Community Law* (Clarendon Press, 1991)

Vaughan *et al*: *Law of the European Communities* (volumes 50 and 51 of Halsbury's *Laws of England* (Butterworths)

General books

Closa: 'The Concept of Citizenship in the Treaty on European Union' [1992] *CMLRev* 1137

Lasok: 'Europe of XV: What Next?' (1995) 14 *SLR* 33

Foundations

Lasok: 'Towards a Political Union' (1992) 6 *SLR* 36

Lasok: 'Maastricht and the European Constitutionalism' (1993) 8 *SLR* 34

Ver Loren van Themaat: 'Some Preliminary Observations on the Intergovernmental Conference: The Relationship Between the Concepts of a Common Market, a Monetary Union, Political Union and Sovereignty' [1991] *CMLRev* 291.

Institutions

Bieber: 'The Settlement of Institutional Conflict on the Basis of Article 4 EEC' [1984] *CMLRev* 505

Bieber: 'Overlapping Legal Systems' [1988] *ELRev* 147

Crosby: 'The Single Market and the Rule of Law' [1991] *ELRev* 451

Curtin: 'The Constitutional Structure of the Union: A Europe of Bits and Pieces' [1993] *CMLRev* 17

da Cruz Vilaca: 'The Court of First instance of the European Communities: A significant step towards the Consolidation of the European Community as a Community Governed by the Rule of Law' [1990] *YEL* 1.

Edward: 'The Impact of the SEA on the Institutions' [1987] *CMLRev* 19

Emiliou: 'Protecting Parliamentary Prerogatives' [1993] *ELRev* 56

Everling: 'Reflections on the Structure of the European Union' [1992] *CMLRev* 1053

Hahn: 'The European Central Bank: Key to European Monetary Union or Target?' [1991] *CMLRev* 783

Harlow: 'A Community of Interests? Making the Most of European Law' [1992] *MLR* 331

Kok: 'The Court of Auditors of the European Communities: "The Other European Court in Luxembourg"' [1989] *CMLRev* 345

Lenaerts: 'Some Reflections on the Separation of Powers in the European Community' [1991] *CMLRev* 11

Weiler: 'The Community System: The Dual Character of Supranationalism' [1981] *YEL* 267

Weiler: 'The Transformation of Europe' [1991] *Yale LJ* 2403

Cass: 'The word that saves Maastricht? The principle of subsidiarity and the division of power within the European Community' [1992] *CMLRev* 1107

Subsidiarity

Cass: 'Subsidiarity: "Backing the right horse?"' [1993] *CMLRev* 241

Emiliou: 'Subsidiarity: An Effective Barrier Against "the Enterprises of Ambition"'? [1992] *CMLRev* 383

Toth: 'The Principle of Subsidiarity in the Maastricht Treaty' [1992] *CMLRev* 1079

Barents: 'The Internal Market Unlimited: Some Observations on the Legal Basis of Community Legislation' [1993] *CMLR* 85

Legislation

Bieber: 'Legislative Procedure for the Establishment of the Single Market' [1988] 25 *CMLRev* 711

Bradely: 'The European Court and the Legal Basis of Community Legislation' [1988] 13 *ELRev* 379

Emiliou: 'Implied Powers and the legal basis of Community Measures' [1993] *ELRev* 138

Geradin: 'Legal Basis of Waste Directive' [1993] *ELRev* 418

Ungerer: 'Institutional Consequences of Broadening and Deepening the Community: The Consequences for the Decision Making Process' [1993] *CMLRev* 71

Bebr: 'How Supreme is Community Law in the National Courts?' [1974] 11 *CMLRev* 3

Primacy of Community Law

Bieber: 'The Mutual Completion of Overlapping Legal Systems: The EC and National Legal Orders' [1988] 13 *ELRev* 147

Cross: 'Pre-emption of Member State Law in the European Economic Community: A Framework for Analysis' [1992] *CMLRev* 44

Docksey and Fitzpatrick: 'The Duty of National Courts to Interpret Provisions of National Law in accordance with Community Law' [1991] *Ind LJ* 113

Fitzpatrick: 'The Significance of EC Directives in UK Sex Discrimination Law' [1989] *OJLS* 336

Lasok: 'Fisherman's Rights' (1991) 4 *SLR* 26

Lemaerts: 'Fundamental Rights to be included in the Community Catalogue' [1991] 16 *ELRev* 367

Manin: 'The *Nicolo* case of the *Conseil d'Etat* French constitutional law and the Supreme Administrative Court's Acceptance of the Primacy of Community Law over Subsequent National Statute Law' [1991] *CMLRev* 499

Monaco: 'The Limits of the European Community Order' [1976] 1 *ELRev* 269

Pescatore: 'International Law and Community Law' [1970] 7 *CMLRev* 167

Warner: 'The Relationship between EEC Law and the National Laws of the Member States' [1977] *LQR* 349

Wyatt: 'New Legal Order or Old?' [1982] 7 *ELRev* 147

de Burca: 'Giving Effect to European Community Directives' [1992] 55 *MLR* 215

Direct effect and applicability

Curtin: 'The Province of Government: Delimiting the Direct Effect of Directives' [1990] 15 *ELRev* 195

Curtin: 'Directives: The Effectiveness of Judicial Protection of Individual Rights' [1990] 27 *CMLRev* 709

Easson: 'Can Directives Impose Obligations on Individuals?' [1979] 4 *ELRev* 67

Easson: 'The Direct Effect of Directives' [1979] 28 *ICLQ* 319

Grief: 'Direct Effect of Directives and Organs of the State' [1991] *ELRev* 137

Morris: 'The Direct Effect of Directives' [1989] *JBL* 233,309

Pescatore: 'The Doctrine of Direct Effect: An Infant Disease of Community Law' [1983] *ELRev* 155

Ross: 'Beyond *Francovich*' [1993] 56 *MLR* 55

Smith: 'The *Francovich* Case: State Liability and the Individuals Right to Damages' [1992] 3 *ECLR* 129

Snyder: 'The Effectiveness of European Community Law: Institutions, Processes, Tools and Techniques' [1993] *MLR* 19

Steiner: 'Coming to Terms with EEC Directives' [1990] 106 *LQR* 144

Steiner: 'From Direct Effect to *Francovich*: Shifting means of enforcement of Community Law' [1993] *ELRev* 3

Szyszczak: 'New Remedies, New Directives (*Francovich*)' [1992] 55 *MLR*

Szyszczak: 'Sovereignty, Crisis, Compliance, Confusion, Complacency?' [1990] 15 *ELRev* 480

Temple Lang: 'Community Constitutional Law: Article 5 EEC Treaty' [1990] *CMLRev* 645

Tillotson: '*Francovich*: Member State liability for damages – first steps' (1995) 1 *SLR* 35

Timmermans: 'Directives – Their Effect within the National Legal Systems' [1979] 16 *CMLRev* 533

Winter: 'Direct Applicability and Direct Effect: Two Distinct and Different Concepts in Community Law' [172] *CMLRev* 425

Wooldridge and D'Sa: 'Damages for Breach of Community Directives' [1993] *EBLR* 255

Wyatt: 'Directly Applicable Provisions of Community Law' [1975] 125 *New LJ* 458, 575, 669, 793.

Arnull: 'Does the Court of Justice have Inherent Jurisdiction?' [1990] *CMLRev* 683

Arnull: 'Challenging EC Anti-dumping Regulations: The Problem of Admissibility' [1992] *ECLR* 73

Barav: 'The Exception of Illegality in Community Law: A critical Analysis' [1974] *CMLRev* 366

Bebr: 'Judicial Remedy of Private Parties Against Normative Acts of the European Communities: The Role of the Exception to Illegality' [1966] *CMLRev* 7

Bebr: 'Community System of Legal Remedies: A Thorny Jurisprudential Development' [1990] *CMLRev* 170

Bradley [1988] *ELRev* 379

Bradley: 'Comitology and the Law: Through a Glass Darkly' [1988] *CMLRev* 693

Bradley: 'Sense and Sensibility' [1991] *ELRev* 245

Actions for Annulment

Bradley: 'The Variable Evolution of the Standing of the European Parliament in Proceedings Before the Court of Justice' [1989] *YEL* 27.

Dashwood: 'The European Parliament and Article 173 EEC: The Limits of Interpretation, in White and Smythe', Current Issues in *European and International Law* (London, 1990)

Dinnage: 'Locus Standi and Article 173' [1979] *ELRev* 15

Greaves: 'Locus Standi under Article 173 when seeking annulment of a Regulation' [1986] 11 *ELRev* 119

Greaves: 'Judicial Review of Anti-dumping cases by the European Court of Justice' [1985] *ECLR* 135

Harding: 'The Impact of Article 177 on the Review of Community Action' [1981] *YEL* 93

Rasmussen: 'Why is Article 173 Interpreted against Private Plaintiffs?' [1980] *ELRev* 112.

Toth: 'The Authority of Judgments of the European Court of Justice: Binding Force and Legal Effects' [1984] *YEL* 1

Weiler: [1989] *ELRev* 334

Direct actions against Member States

Audretsch: 'Supervision in the EEC, OECD and Benelux – A Difference of Degree, but also in Kind?' [1987] *ICLQ* 838

Barav: 'Failure of Member States to fulfil their Obligations' [1975] *CMLRev* 369

Bridge: 'Procedural Aspects of the Enforcement of EC Law through the Legal Systems of the MS' [1984] *ELRev* 28

de Burca: 'Giving Effect to European Community Directives' [1992] 55 *MLR* 215

Dashwood & White: 'Enforcement Actions under Articles 169 & 170' [1989] *ELRev* 388

Everling: 'The Member States of the European Communities before their Court of Justice' [1984] *ELRev* 215

Gray: 'Interim Measures of Protection in the ECJ' [1979] *ELRev* 80

Harcastle: 'Interim Measures in proceedings Concerning EC Law: New Departures' [1994] *EBLR* 95

Magliveras: 'Force majeure in Community Law' [1990] *ELRev* 460

Merterns de Wilmars and Verhoughstrate: 'Proceedings against Member States for failure to fulfil their obligations' [1970] *CMLRev* 385

Oliver: 'Enforcing Community Rights in English Courts' [1987] *MLR* 881

Smith: 'The *Francovitch* Case: State Liability and the Individual Right to Damages' [1992] 3 *ECLR* 129

Steiner: 'From direct effects to Francovich: shifting means of enforcement of Community Law' [1993] *ELRev* 3

Steiner: 'How to make the Action fit the Case: domestic remedies for breach of EEC law' [1987] *ELRev* 102

Szyzczak: 'New Remedies, New Directives (*Francovitch*)' [1992] *MLR*

Judicial Review and Article 177

Alexander: 'The Temporal Effects of Preliminary Rulings [1988] YEL 11 Arnull: The Scope of Article 177' [1988] *ELRev* 40

Arnull: 'National Courts and the Validity of Community Acts' [1988] *ELRev* 125

Arnull: 'The Uses and Abuses of Article 177 EEC' [1989] *MLR* 622

Arnull: 'References to the European Court' [1990] *ELRev* 375

Arnull: 'Precedent and the European Court' [1993] *CMLRev* 247

Arnull: 'The Evolution of the Court's Jurisdiction under Article 177' [1993] *ELRev* 129

Barav: 'Preliminary Rulings Procedure in EC Law' [1977] *ELRev* 3

Barav: 'Preliminary Censorship? The Judgment in *Foglia v Novello*' [1980] *ELRev* 443

Beaumont: 'European Court and jurisdiction and enforcement of judgments in both civil and commercial matters' [1990] *ICLQ* 700

Bebr: 'Preliminary Rulings – Their Authority and Temporal Effect' [1981] *CMLRev* 475

Bebr: 'The Possible Implications of *Foglia v Novello ll*' [1982] *CMLRev* 421

Bebr: 'Arbitration Tribunals and Article 177' [1985] *CMLRev* 489

Bebr: 'The Reinforcement of the Constitutional Review of Community Acts under Article 177 of the EEC Treaty' [1988] *CMLRev* 667

Dashwood & Arnull: 'English Courts and Article 177' [1984] *YEL* 255

Gray: 'Advisory Opinions and the European Court of Justice' [1983] *ELRev* 24

Kennedy: 'First Steps Towards a European Certioriari?' [1993] *ELRev* 121

Lasok: 'Use and Abuse of preliminary proceedings under Article 177 of the EEC Treaty' (1993) 10 *SLR* 34

Mortelmans: 'Art 177 Procedure and Practice' [1979] *CMLRev* 557

O'Keeffe: 'Appeals against an Order to Refer under Article 177 of the EEC Treaty' [1984] *ELRev* 87

'Oliver: Interim Measures: Some Recent Developments' [1992] *CMLRev* 7

Rasmussen: 'Between Self-Restraint and Judicial Activism: A Judicial Policy for the ECJ' [1988] *ELRev* 28

Rasmussen: 'The European Court's Acte Clair Strategy in CILFIT' [1984] *ELRev* 242

Schermers: 'The Law as it Stands on Preliminary Rulings' [1974] 1 *LIEI*

Toth: 'The Authority of Judgments of the European Court of Justice: Binding Force and Legal Effects' [1984] *YEL* 1

Watson: 'Experience and Problems in Applying Article 177 EEC' [1986] *CMLRev* 207

The Common Market

Cremona: 'The Completion of the Internal Market and the Incomplete Commercial Policy of the European Community' [1990] *ELRev* 283

Fernandez Martin & Stehmann: 'Product market integration versus regional cohesion in the Community' [1991] *ELRev* 216

McGee & Weatherill: 'The evolution of the single market - harmonisation or liberalisation' [1990] *MLR* 578

Reich: 'Competition between legal orders: a new paradigm of EC law?' [1992] *CMLRev* 861

Usher: 'The Single Market and Goods Imported From Third Countries' [1986] *YEL* 159

Vogelenzang: 'Two Aspects of Article 115' [1981] *CMLRev* 169

Gormley: *Prohibiting Restrictions On Trade Within the EC* (North Holland: 1985)

Free Movement of Goods

Oliver: *Free Movement of Goods in the EEC* (European Law Centre: 2nd edition 1988)

Arnull: 'What shall we do on Sunday?' [1991] *ELRev* 112

Chalmers: 'Free movement of goods within the European Community: an unhealthy addiction to Scotch whisky?' [1993] *ICLQ* 269

Diamond: 'Dishonourable Defences: The Use of Injunctions and the EEC Treaty: Case Study of the Shops Act 1950' [1991] *MLR* 72

Gormley: 'Actually or Potentially, Directly or Indirectly? Obstacles to the Free Movement of Goods' [1989] *YEL* 197

Kramer: 'Environmental Protection and Article 30 EEC Treaty' [1993] *CMLRev* 111

Marenco & Banks: 'Intellectual Property and the Community rules on free movement: Discrimination unearthed' [1990] *ELRev* 224

Mortelmans: 'Article 30 of the EEC Treaty and Legislation Relating to Market Circumstances: Time to Consider a New Definition?' [1991] *CMLRev* 115

Steiner: 'Drawing the Line: Uses and Abuses of Article 30 EEC' [1992] *CMLRev* 749

Usher: 'The Single Market and Goods Imported from Third Countries' [1986] *YEL* 159

White: 'In Search of Limits to Article 30 EEC Treaty' [1989] *CMLRev* 235

Free Movement of Workers	Guild: 'Falling through the net: Family reunion rights in EC Law' [1993] 3 *Lawyers' Europe* 2
	Lasok: 'Students' rights in the European Community' (1994) 12 *SLR* 46
	Spalin: 'Abortion, Speech and the European Community' [1992] *JSWFL* 17
	Steiner: 'Social Security for Migrants' [1992] *JSWFL* 17
	van Oeverbek: 'AIDS/HIV Infection and the free movement of persons within the European Economic Community' [1990] *CMLRev* 791
	Wikeley: 'Migrant Workers and Unemployment Benefit in the European Community' [1988] *JSWL* 300
Freedom of Establishment and the Right to Provide Services	Cath: 'Freedom of Establishment of Companies: A New Step Towards Completion of the Internal Market' [1986] *YEL* 247
	Eidenmuller: 'Deregulating the Market for Legal Services in the European Community: Freedom of Establishment and Freedom to Provide Services for EC Lawyers in the Federal Republic of Germany' [1990] *MLR* 604
	Foster: 'European Community Law and the Freedom of Lawyers in the United Kingdom and Germany' [1991] *ICLQ* 608
	Lasok: 'Students' rights in the European Community' (1994) 12 *SLR* 46
	Whelan & Barnet: 'Lawyers in the Market: Delivering Legal Services in Europe' [1992] *Journal of Law and Society* 49
Free movement of capital and European Monetary Union	Lasok: 'Towards an Economic and Monetary Union' (1992) 7 *SLR* 33
Common Policies	Greaves: *Transport Law of the European Community* (1991)
	Snyder: *Law of the Common Agricultural Policy* (Sweet and Maxwell, 1985)
	Usher: *Legal Aspects of Agriculture in the European Community* (1988)
	Blumenthal: 'Implementing the Common Agricultural Policy: Aspects of the Limitations on the Powers of the Member States' [1984] *NILQ* 28

Butler: The EC's Common Agricultural Policy in Lodge (ed) *The European Community and the Challenge of the Future* (Pinter: 2nd edition, 1993).

Sherlock & Harding: 'Controlling Fraud within the European Community' [1991] *ELRev* 20

Goyder: *EC Competition Law* (OUP: 2nd edition 1993)

Competition

Kerse: *EEC Antitrust Procedure* (European Law Centre: 4th edition, 1994)

Korah: *An Introductory Guide to EC Competition Law and Practice* (ESC: 5th edition 1994)

Whish: *Competition Law* (Butterworths: 3rd edition, 1993)

Baden Fuller: 'Price variations – the Distillers case and Article 85' [1979] *ICLQ* 128

van Bael: 'Heretical reflections on the basic dogma of EEC antitrust: single market integration' [1980] *RSDIC* 39

Brittan: 'The law and policy of merger control in the EEC' [1990] *ELRev* 351

Chard: 'The Economics of the application of Article 85 to selective distribution systems' [1982] *ELRev* 83

Daltrop & Ferry: 'The relationship between Articles 85 and 86: Tetra Pak' [1991] *EIPR* 31

Ehlermann: 'Managing monopolies: the role of the state in controlling market dominance in the European Community' [1993] *ECLR* 61

Faull: 'Joint ventures under the EC competition rules' [1984] *ECLR* 358

Forrester & Norall: 'The laicisation of Community law: self-help and the rule of reason: how competition law is and could be applied' [1984] *CMLRev* 11

Goh: 'Enforcing EC competition law in Member States' [1993] *ECLR* 114

Halvorsen: 'EC Merger Control: Competition Policy or Industrial Policy?' [1992] *LIEI* 49

Hoskins: 'Garden Cottage revisited: the availability of damages in the national courts for breaches of the EEC competition rules' [1992] *ECLR* 257

Joshua: 'The element of surprise' [1986] *ELRev* 3

Joshua: 'Proof in contested EEC competition cases' [1987] *ELRev* 315

Joshua: 'Information in EEC competition law procedures' [1986] *ELRev* 409

Korah: 'Concept of a Dominant position within the meaning of Article 86' [1980] *CMLRev* 395

Korah: 'The rise and fall of provisional validity' [1981] NWJ *Int'l L and Bus* 320

Korah: 'Comfort letters – reflections on the Perfume cases' [1981] *ELRev* 14

Korah: 'The judgment in Delimitis – a milestone towards a realistic assessment of the effects of an agreement – or a damp squib?' [1992] *EIPR* 167

Korah: 'Elective distribution' [1994] *ECLR* 101

Lasok: 'Assessing the economic consequences of restrictive agreements: a comment on the *Delimitis* case' [1991] *ECLR* 194

Riley: 'More radicalism please: the Notice on co-operation between national courts and the Commission in applying Articles 85 and 86 of the EEC Treaty' [1993] *ECLR* 91

Schechter: 'The Rule of Reason in European Competition Law' [1982] *LIEI* 1

Subbiotto: 'The right to deal with whom one pleases under EEC competition law' [1992] *ECLR* 234

Venit: 'The "Merger" control regulation: Europe comes of age - per Caliban's dinner' [1990] *CMLRev* 7

Venit: 'The research and development block exemption regulation' [1985] *ELRev* 151

Whish: 'The enforcement of EC competition law in the domestic courts of Member States' [1994] *ECLR* 60

Whish & Sufrin: 'Article 85 and the Rule of Reason' [1987] *YEL* 1

Winckler & Hansen: 'Collective Dominance Under the EC Merger Control Regulation' [1993] *CMLRev* 787

Barnard: 'A social policy for Europe: Politicians 1:0 Lawyers' [1992] *Int J Comp Labour Law and Industrial Relations* 15

Collins: 'Transfers of undertakings and Insolvency' [1989] *ILJ* 144

Colneric: 'The prohibition on discrimination against women under Community law' [1992] *Int J Comp Labour Law and Industrial Relations* 191

Curtin: 'Occupational Pensions Schemes and Article 119: Beyond the Fringe?' [1987] *CMLRev* 215

Curtin: 'Effective Sanctions and the Equal Treatment Directive: The *von Colson* and *Hartz* cases' [1985] *CMLRev* 505

Docksey: 'Information and consultation of Employees: The United Kingdom and the Vredeling Directive' [1986] *MLR* 281

Docksey: 'The Principle of Equality between Men and Women: A Fundamental Right Under Community Law' [1991] *ILJ* 258

Eberlie: 'The New Health and Safety Legislation of the European Community' [1990] *ILJ* 81

Fitzpatrick, 'Equality in Occupational Pensions: The New Frontiers after Barber' (1991) 54 *MLR* 271.

Hepple: 'The Implementation of the Community Charter of Fundamental Social Rights' [1990] *MLR* 643

Hepple & Byre: 'EEC Labour Law in the United Kingdom - a New Approach' [1989] *ILJ* 129

Luckhaus: 'Payment for caring: A European Solution?' [1986] *Public Law* 526

McCrudden: 'The effectiveness of European equality law: national mechanisms for enforcing gender equality in the light of European requirements' [1993] *OJLS* 320

Prechal: 'Combating Indirect Discrimination in Community Law Context' [1993] *LIEI* 81

Spicker: 'The Principle of Subsidiarity and the Social Policy of the European Community' [1991] *JESP* 3

Szyszczak: 'European Court rulings on Discrimination and Part-time work and the Burden of Proof in Equal Pay Claims' [1990] *ILJ*

Social Policy

Szyszczak: '1992 and the Working Environment' [1992] *JSWFL* 3

Vogel-Polsky: 'What future is there for a social Europe following the Strasbourg Summit?' [1990] *ILJ* 65

Watson: 'The Community Social Charter'[1991] *CMLRev* 37

Watson: 'Social Policy after Maastricht' [1993] *CMLRev* 481

Wedderburn: 'The Social Charter in Britain: Labour Law and Labour Courts?' [1991] *MLR* 1

Wedderburn: 'Companies and Employees: Common Law or Social Dimension?' [1993] *LQR* 220

Whiteford: 'Social Policy after Maastricht' [1993] *ELRev* 202

Index

Note: Article numbers refer to the
Treaty of Rome 1957

UNIVERSITY OF WOLVERHAMPTON
LIBRARY